Quantitative Risk Management Using Python

Peng Liu

Quantitative Risk Management Using Python

An Essential Guide for Managing Market, Credit, and Model Risk

Apress®

Peng Liu
Santorini
Singapore, Singapore

ISBN-13 (pbk): 979-8-8688-1529-4   ISBN-13 (electronic): 979-8-8688-1530-0
https://doi.org/10.1007/979-8-8688-1530-0

Copyright © 2025 by Peng Liu

This work is subject to copyright. All rights are reserved by the Publisher, whether the whole or part of the material is concerned, specifically the rights of translation, reprinting, reuse of illustrations, recitation, broadcasting, reproduction on microfilms or in any other physical way, and transmission or information storage and retrieval, electronic adaptation, computer software, or by similar or dissimilar methodology now known or hereafter developed.

Trademarked names, logos, and images may appear in this book. Rather than use a trademark symbol with every occurrence of a trademarked name, logo, or image we use the names, logos, and images only in an editorial fashion and to the benefit of the trademark owner, with no intention of infringement of the trademark.

The use in this publication of trade names, trademarks, service marks, and similar terms, even if they are not identified as such, is not to be taken as an expression of opinion as to whether or not they are subject to proprietary rights.

While the advice and information in this book are believed to be true and accurate at the date of publication, neither the authors nor the editors nor the publisher can accept any legal responsibility for any errors or omissions that may be made. The publisher makes no warranty, express or implied, with respect to the material contained herein.

   Managing Director, Apress Media LLC: Welmoed Spahr
   Acquisitions Editor: Celestin Suresh John
   Development Editor: James Markham
   Coordinating Editor: Gryffin Winkler

Cover image by Freepik (www.freepik.com)

Distributed to the book trade worldwide by Springer Science+Business Media New York, 1 New York Plaza, New York, NY 10004. Phone 1-800-SPRINGER, fax (201) 348-4505, e-mail orders-ny@springer-sbm.com, or visit www.springeronline.com. Apress Media, LLC is a Delaware LLC and the sole member (owner) is Springer Science + Business Media Finance Inc (SSBM Finance Inc). SSBM Finance Inc is a **Delaware** corporation.

For information on translations, please e-mail booktranslations@springernature.com; for reprint, paperback, or audio rights, please e-mail www.bookpermissions@springernature.com.

Apress titles may be purchased in bulk for academic, corporate, or promotional use. eBook versions and licenses are also available for most titles. For more information, reference our Print and eBook Bulk Sales web page at http://www.apress.com/bulk-sales.

Any source code or other supplementary material referenced by the author in this book is available to readers on GitHub (https://github.com/Apress). For more detailed information, please visit https://www.apress.com/gp/services/source-code.

If disposing of this product, please recycle the paper

This book is dedicated to my family, particularly my wife, Zheng, and my children, Jiayu, Jiaran, and Jiaxin. Jiayu comes first this time, as his older sisters already declared victory in my other books.

Contents

About the Author		xi
About the Technical Reviewer		xiii
Foreword		xv
Preface		xvii
Introduction		xix

1 Introduction to Quantitative Risk Management 1
   1.1 Understanding Different Types of Risk in Financial Markets 5
      1.1.1 Market Risk 6
      1.1.2 Credit Risk 15
      1.1.3 Liquidity Risk 17
      1.1.4 Operational Risk 17
      1.1.5 Model Risk 18
      1.1.6 Legal and Regulatory Risk 19
      1.1.7 Systemic Risk 19
      1.1.8 Environmental, Social, and Governance (ESG) Risk 20
      1.1.9 A Summary of Common Risk Types 21
   1.2 Common Financial Instruments 22
      1.2.1 Low-Risk Assets 22
      1.2.2 Moderate-Risk Assets 23
      1.2.3 High-Risk Assets 25
      1.2.4 Derivatives 26
      1.2.5 A Summary of Financial Instruments by Risk Level 27
   1.3 Summary 28

2 Fundamentals of Risk and Return in Finance 31
   2.1 Understanding Return................................... 31
   2.2 Understanding Risk 33
   2.3 Risk-Return Trade-Off.................................. 37
   2.4 Measuring Return 38
      2.4.1 Absolute Return 38
      2.4.2 Percentage Return 38
      2.4.3 Logarithmic Return 39

		2.4.4	Total Return vs. Price Return	39
		2.4.5	Annualized Returns	40
		2.4.6	Single-Period vs. Multi-Period Returns	41
	2.5	Measuring Risk		42
		2.5.1	Annualization of Risk Measures	43
		2.5.2	Difference in Volatility Calculated Using Daily vs. Monthly Data	44
	2.6	Measuring Risk-Adjusted Return		46
		2.6.1	Sharpe Ratio	46
		2.6.2	Sortino Ratio	47
		2.6.3	Treynor Ratio	47
		2.6.4	Evaluating Performance Measures in Portfolio Optimization	48
	2.7	Summary		63
3	**Managing Credit Risk**			**65**
	3.1	Expected and Unexpected Credit Loss		67
		3.1.1	Unexpected Loss	69
		3.1.2	Stress Loss	69
	3.2	Probability of Default		70
		3.2.1	Logistic Regression	71
		3.2.2	Decision Trees and Random Forests	72
		3.2.3	Other Machine Learning Classifiers	73
	3.3	Loss Given Default		73
	3.4	Exposure at Default		76
	3.5	Expected Credit Loss		78
		3.5.1	Capital Regulation Using Risk-Weighted Asset	79
	3.6	Building a PD Model		82
		3.6.1	Data Processing and Exploration	83
		3.6.2	Dealing with Outliers	84
		3.6.3	Dealing with Missing Data	86
		3.6.4	Dealing with Categorical Data	86
		3.6.5	Train-Test Split	87
		3.6.6	Developing Logistic Regression Model	88
		3.6.7	Model Evaluation	88
		3.6.8	ROC Curve	90
	3.7	Summary		93
4	**Managing Market Risk**			**95**
	4.1	Variance		96
		4.1.1	Unbiasedness in Sample Variance	97
		4.1.2	Variance in Practice	100
		4.1.3	Limitations of Variance As a Risk Measure	101
	4.2	Maximum Drawdown (Max Drawdown)		107
		4.2.1	Distinctive Features of Maximum Drawdown	108
		4.2.2	Calculating Max Drawdown	110

	4.3	Value at Risk	113
		4.3.1 Historical Simulation Approach	114
		4.3.2 Variance-Covariance (Parametric) Approach..................	115
		4.3.3 Monte Carlo Simulation	120
	4.4	Summary	122
5	**Risk Management Using Financial Derivatives**............................		125
	5.1	Hedging with Futures Contracts..	127
		5.1.1 Hedging Mechanism Using Futures	127
		5.1.2 Optimal Hedge Ratio	129
		5.1.3 Scenario Analysis at Maturity..................................	132
		5.1.4 Consideration of Basis Risk	133
		5.1.5 Implementing the Dynamic Hedging Strategy	134
	5.2	Hedging with Option Contracts	141
		5.2.1 Protective Put Strategy	142
		5.2.2 Implementing the Protective Put Strategy	147
		5.2.3 Covered Call Strategy	152
		5.2.4 Implementing the Covered Call Strategy	157
	5.3	Summary	161
6	**Static and Dynamic Hedging**		163
	6.1	Dynamic Hedging..	166
		6.1.1 Dynamic Delta Hedging Strategy	167
		6.1.2 Continuous Rebalancing and Gamma Hedging	168
		6.1.3 Dynamic Hedging in Action	170
	6.2	Static Hedging..	177
		6.2.1 Static Hedging for a Forward Contract	177
		6.2.2 Static Hedging for a European Put Option	182
		6.2.3 Static Hedging for Digital Option.............................	190
		6.2.4 Static Hedging with Constant Volatility	191
		6.2.5 Static Hedging with Changing Volatility	194
		6.2.6 Static Hedging of Digital Call Option in Action	196
	6.3	Summary	199
7	**Managing Model Risk in Finance**		201
	7.1	Model Risk Due to Data	202
		7.1.1 Data Risks in Financial Machine Learning	205
		7.1.2 Mitigation Strategies...	211
	7.2	Model Risk Due to Model Selection	214
		7.2.1 Model Bias and Approximation Error	215
		7.2.2 Mitigation Strategies...	217
	7.3	Model Risk Due to Cost Function....................................	218
		7.3.1 Mitigation Strategies...	220

	7.4	Model Risk Due to Optimization Procedure	221
		7.4.1 Estimation Error	222
		7.4.2 Mitigation Strategies	224
	7.5	Conclusion	225

References 229

Index 231

About the Author

Peng Liu is an Assistant Professor of Quantitative Finance (Practice) at Singapore Management University and an adjunct researcher at the National University of Singapore. He holds a Ph.D. in statistics from the National University of Singapore and has over ten years of working experience across the banking, technology, and hospitality industries. Peng is the author of *Bayesian Optimization* (Apress, 2023) and *Quantitative Trading Strategies Using Python* (Apress, 2023).

About the Technical Reviewer

Sonal Raj is an engineer, mathematician, data scientist, and Python evangelist from India, who has carved a niche in the financial services domain. He is a Goldman Sachs and D.E. Shaw alumnus who currently serves as Vice President and heads the Data Management and Research division for a leading high-frequency trading firm.

Sonal holds a dual master's degree in Computer Science and Business Administration and is a former research fellow of the Indian Institute of Science. His areas of research range from image processing, real-time graph computations to electronic trading algorithms. Sonal is the author of the titles *Graph Data Analytics* (BPB, 2024), *The Pythonic Way* (BPB, 2021), and *Neo4j High Performance* (Packt, 2015), among others. During his career, Sonal has been instrumental in designing low latency trading algorithms, trading strategies, market signal models, and components of electronic trading systems. He is also a community speaker and a Python and data science mentor to young minds in the field.

When not engrossed in reading fiction or playing symphonies, he spends far too much time watching rockets lift off.

He is a loving son, husband, and a custodian of his personal library.

Foreword

It is a sincere privilege to introduce *Quantitative Risk Management Using Python* by Peng Liu. Working with Peng at an international bank, I had the opportunity to witness his keen interest in risk management and his thoughtful approach to navigating complex financial challenges. In my roles as his supervisor and friend, I learned a lot from his technical insights and was quietly encouraged by his steady pursuit of excellence.

Peng's transition from the world of corporate risk management to academia is a journey marked by his passion for both understanding and teaching the intricate dynamics of financial risk. In this book, he bridges the gap between abstract risk theories and their tangible applications using Python. His ability to demystify subjects ranging from market, credit, and model risk to sophisticated hedging strategies makes this work an indispensable resource for practitioners, researchers, and students alike.

I believe readers will truly benefit from the clarity, depth, and accessible style of this book. Its thoughtful presentation of complex risk management concepts makes them both understandable and relevant to real-world challenges, offering a reliable guide for both experienced professionals and those new to the field.

Hong Kong   Matteo Crippa
April 2025

Preface

I must confess: the main reason I decided to write this book was to better understand the topics myself and hopefully teach them in a university course without sounding completely lost. When I transitioned from working as a risk management professional at an international bank to academia in 2022, I quickly realized that knowing how to manage risk is one thing; teaching it is an entirely different beast.

Over time—and especially with the rapid pace of change brought about by large language models and other breakthroughs in AI—I have come to realize that risk management is more important than ever. Not just in financial institutions, but also in everyday life. So, this book became my way of learning by doing, in the hope that it might also help others, whether you are just starting out or navigating mid-career challenges.

The chapters cover a range of topics that I believe are essential for developing a solid foundation in risk management. From the classic risk-return trade-off to the use of futures and options for hedging and eventually the weeds of static and dynamic hedging strategies, there is something for everyone here. You will also find practical ways to measure and manage market risk, a solid introduction to credit risk, and a full chapter dedicated to model risk, which is becoming increasingly relevant as machine learning gains ground in finance.

Throughout, I have tried to strike a balance between theory and practice, using Python to make the concepts more accessible and applicable. We will not hope to turn readers into quants overnight, but rather to give you the tools and intuition to approach quantitative risk management with confidence and maybe even enjoy it along the way.

I hope you find this book helpful and have fun reading and learning along the way!

Singapore, Singapore
April 2025

Peng Liu

Introduction

In an increasingly complex financial landscape, effective risk management is a critical skill for professionals navigating the dynamic world of finance. This book intends to provide a comprehensive and practical approach to understanding and applying risk management techniques using Python.

The book serves as an essential resource for finance professionals, academics, and students looking to deepen their knowledge of quantitative risk management. It bridges theoretical concepts with hands-on Python implementations, equipping readers with the tools needed to assess, mitigate, and manage financial risks effectively. Whether you are involved in investment management, banking, financial analytics, or fintech and beyond, this book offers valuable insights into the intricate mechanisms that drive market, credit, and model risk.

What You Will Learn

The book systematically introduces key aspects of financial risk management, beginning with foundational principles and advancing to sophisticated techniques for managing risk in various financial contexts. Readers will gain expertise in

- **Fundamentals of Risk and Return:** Understanding different types of financial risk, the role of diversification in portfolio management, and the trade-off between risk and return
- **Credit Risk Management:** Assessing and managing risks associated with default and counterparty credit exposure
- **Market Risk Management:** Identifying, measuring, and mitigating risks stemming from market fluctuations
- **Risk Management Using Financial Derivatives:** Exploring how derivatives such as options and futures can be leveraged to manage risk
- **Static and Dynamic Hedging Strategies:** Applying hedging techniques to minimize exposure and protect investment positions
- **Model Risk Management:** Evaluating risks in the development and deployment of machine learning models within the financial sector

Who Should Read This Book?

This book is designed for finance professionals, quantitative analysts, risk managers, students, and academics seeking a structured and practical guide to risk management using Python. Whether you are an industry practitioner looking to enhance your risk modeling skills or a student aiming to build a solid foundation in quantitative finance, this book provides the necessary knowledge and tools to navigate financial risks with confidence.

Why This Book?

- **Hands-On Python Applications:** Demonstrates real-world Python implementations across credit risk, market risk, and portfolio management
- **Comprehensive Coverage:** Covers fundamental concepts as well as advanced topics in financial risk management
- **Practical Focus:** Bridges the gap between theoretical models and their application in financial decision-making

With its blend of theory, practice, and programming, *Quantitative Risk Management Using Python* is a valuable guide for mastering financial risk management in today's evolving financial landscape.

Introduction to Quantitative Risk Management

Financial risk means potential loss in the world of finance. If you invest, risk is everywhere and sometimes is considered even more important than financial return. The flavor of financial risk ranges from day-to-day fluctuations in stock prices, also called volatility, to broader, more unpredictable shocks caused by global events. Common types of financial risk include market risk (price fluctuations), credit risk (borrower defaults), and liquidity risk (difficulty in asset liquidation). These risks are not just abstract ideas; they bring about real challenges that can impact investment portfolios, financial institutions, and even the entire financial system as a whole.

For example, a recent study by Marani et al. (2021) analyzed disease outbreaks over the past four centuries and revealed that extreme pandemics are more frequent than previously assumed. The research estimates an annual probability of approximately 2% for a pandemic with an impact similar to COVID-19, suggesting that an individual born in the year 2000 would have about a 38% chance of experiencing such an event by now. Furthermore, the study indicates that a pandemic of comparable scale could be expected within the next 59 years. Such an extreme pandemic can disrupt markets, causing volatility, liquidity shortages, and systemic failures. This unpredictability makes it essential that financial professionals have a solid understanding of risk dynamics.

Pandemics such as COVID-19 have had undeniably profound effects on our daily lives, reshaping economies, healthcare systems, and social norms, transforming practices like remote work from niche to mainstream. For instance, the S&P 500 plummeted by approximately 34% from its peak in February 2020 to its trough in March 2020 (see Figure 1-1), and the world economy decreased by 3.5% in 2020. In light of these far-reaching impacts, countries and companies are increasingly prioritizing supply chain resilience, emphasizing the importance of diversifying suppliers and establishing alternative sources to mitigate the risk of primary supply disruptions. To properly manage supply chain risk in case of another pandemic, the overall supply chain system needs to have both adaptability and redundancy, which seems to move in the opposite direction against lean management.

Figure 1-1 The S&P 500 plummeted by over 30% from its peak in February 2020 to its trough in March 2020

See Listing 1-1 used to generate Figure 1-1.

```python
import yfinance as yf
import matplotlib.pyplot as plt

# Define the ticker symbol for S&P 500 ETF
ticker = '^GSPC'

# Fetch data from January 1, 2020, to April 1, 2020
sp500 = yf.download(ticker, start='2020-01-01', end='2020-04-01')

# Plot the closing prices
plt.figure(figsize=(8, 5))
plt.plot(sp500.index, sp500['Close'], label='S&P 500', color='blue')
plt.title('S&P 500 Performance (Jan - Mar 2020)')
plt.xlabel('Date')
plt.ylabel('Closing Price (USD)')
plt.legend()
plt.grid(True)
plt.xticks(rotation=45)
plt.tight_layout()
plt.show()
```

Listing 1-1 S&P 500 price curve

But why does risk exist in the first place? Given the inherent uncertainty in the world around us, risk exists because the future is unpredictable and driven by complex interactions between human behavior, environmental changes, and

1 Introduction to Quantitative Risk Management

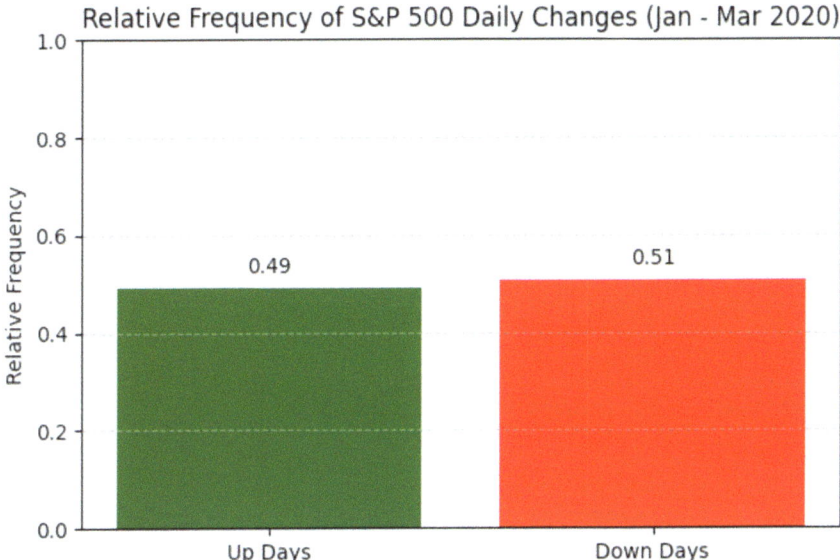

Figure 1-2 Calculating the relative frequency as the empirical probability of S&P trending up or down in this period

biological evolution. This uncertainty means that we cannot accurately forecast when or where a pandemic might occur, its severity, or its specific impacts. And, as a result, the outcome is a random event. Therefore, quantifying and managing such uncertainty and randomness is the central theme of risk management.

The most effective tool for characterizing the randomness of uncertain events is the probability distribution, which captures all possible outcomes and assigns a probability to each. For example, when predicting the likelihood of rain tomorrow, we might assign a probability of 70% to the event of rain. This implies a 30% chance that it will not rain, as the probabilities of all possible outcomes must sum to one. Referring to our previous S&P 500 daily price curve in Figure 1-1, we can calculate the relative frequency of the next day's price moving up or down by counting the occurrences of each outcome and turning the absolute count into relative frequency. These frequencies allow us to approximate the probability that the market is trending upward or downward the following day.

As illustrated in Figure 1-2, the relative frequency, which serves as an empirical probability measure, indicates a 51% likelihood that the S&P 500 closing price would decrease during the period from January to March 2020. Although it is impossible to predict with absolute certainty whether the index will rise or fall on any given day, this approach provides a quantified perspective on the most probable outcome among all possibilities.

See Listing 1-2 used to generate Figure 1-2.

```python
# Calculate daily percentage change
sp500['Daily Change'] = sp500['Close'].diff()

# Calculate relative frequency of going up or down
total_days = len(sp500['Daily Change'].dropna())
up_days = len(sp500[sp500['Daily Change'] > 0])
down_days = len(sp500[sp500['Daily Change'] < 0])

up_frequency = up_days / total_days
down_frequency = down_days / total_days

# Prepare data for the bar chart
categories = ['Up Days', 'Down Days']
frequencies = [up_frequency, down_frequency]

# Plot the bar chart
plt.figure(figsize=(6, 4))
bars = plt.bar(categories, frequencies, color=['green', 'red'])
plt.title('Relative Frequency of S&P 500 Daily Changes (Jan - Mar 2020)')
plt.ylabel('Relative Frequency')
plt.ylim(0, 1)
plt.grid(axis='y', linestyle='--', alpha=0.7)

# Add exact values as legend
for bar, freq in zip(bars, frequencies):
    plt.text(bar.get_x() + bar.get_width() / 2, bar.get_height() + 0.02,
             f"{freq:.2f}", ha='center', va='bottom', fontsize=10)

plt.tight_layout()
plt.show()
```

Listing 1-2 Calculating the relative frequency of going up or down

This book, *Quantitative Risk Management Using Python*, provides a clear and structured guide to the diverse risks that are analyzed and managed in modern financial markets. We will attempt to quantify and manage these risks from multiple perspectives, including financial data, statistical techniques, and mathematical models, ultimately supporting more informed and risk-aware decision-making. At times, effectively managing risk can be even more critical than pursuing high financial returns, especially when dealing with large-scale portfolios. Beyond conceptual and theoretical discussions, we also place a strong emphasis on practical implementation using Python, hoping that readers gain both a robust theoretical framework and the hands-on skills needed to navigate real-world challenges.

In the following sections of this chapter, we will first discover key categories of financial risk, including market, credit, and liquidity risk, and then learn common financial instruments and their use in risk management. We aim to build a good foundational understanding of the risk landscape and a practical set of quantitative tools to help you navigate the world of financial risk management with confidence.

1.1 Understanding Different Types of Risk in Financial Markets

To start, let us take a closer look at what financial markets are about and the different types of risk involved. In financial markets, retail investors, wholesale institutions, and even central governments engage in financial transactions such as buying and selling certain financial instruments, such as stocks, bonds, commodities, and derivatives. These activities promote price discovery, in that they reflect the aggregate beliefs of market participants and provide a way to approximate each instrument's "fair value" through the dynamics of supply and demand toward market equilibrium.

Although some traders seek arbitrage profits by exploiting temporary deviations from the fair value of an asset (which could be due to sudden shocks), others prioritize maximizing returns, minimizing risk, or a combination of both objectives. For example, retail investors can hope to achieve high returns by investing in long-term growth stocks, whereas large institutions often employ low-risk strategies to preserve capital with steady returns and minimal volatility. Consequently, trading activities can vary substantially based on an investor's goals, resources, and market outlook. In general, market participants have different intentions and employ varying strategies within financial markets.

These activities also come with various risks that can pose significant challenges if not properly managed. For example, **market risk** captures the potential losses due to fluctuations in market prices. Examples include a sudden drop in stock prices after the market observes a negative earnings report or a massive sell-off triggered following an announcement of a political policy (think about how the real estimate market reacts when the government introduces a new policy). If you are not prepared, market risk can lead to substantial losses in your investment portfolio since it will likely fluctuate on the downside (everyone likes upside fluctuation). Besides, there is **credit risk**, which comes into play when a borrower fails to repay the debt. This risk is particularly significant for banks and bond investors, who are often regulated to report and manage risk exposure should a default event occur. Lastly, **liquidity risk** says that an investor might not be able to buy or sell an asset quickly as they hope, or even if it is possible, such a fast trade comes with a significant price change (think about selling a property at a fairly low price when in urgent need of cash), potentially leading to losses or missed opportunities.

Beyond these, there are other risks, such as **operational risk**, which deals with failures in internal processes or systems in companies; **legal risk**, which involves potential losses from lawsuits or changes in regulations; **systemic risk**, which is the risk of a collapse in the entire financial system; and **model risk**, which presents the potential loss due to misspecification of the model assumption or incorrect model estimation. The challenges of managing these risks are further compounded by the volatile nature of financial markets. For example, a predictive model trained and deployed today may not be as valid two months later due to changes in market conditions. In this section, we will introduce these various types of risk and explore how they can impact financial assets.

Consider an investment firm that operates both in the corporate bond market and in the stock market, where volatility in the price of the shares introduces market risk. One morning, the firm discovers that a major bond issuer has defaulted on its debt, exposing the institution to considerable credit risk: there is now a real threat that they may not fully recover their investment. At the same time, the firm faces unexpected withdrawal requests from clients, which require them to sell real estate assets rapidly at a substantial discount. This action demonstrates liquidity risk, as the firm must quickly convert assets into cash at the expense of their market value. Meanwhile, the firm's forecasting algorithm, which is based on a black-box model, does not account for sudden changes in market dynamics, thus resulting in greater potential losses than anticipated; this issue exemplifies the model risk.

In response to these challenges, regulators introduce new measures (reminiscent of post-2008 financial reforms), placing greater compliance demands on the firm and amplifying its legal risk. In addition, a technical glitch on a critical trading day completely halts order executions, illustrating just how impactful operational risk can be when internal systems fail. Finally, the firm's global reach makes it susceptible to external shocks: a significant geopolitical event, such as an armed conflict, triggers a worldwide sell-off that jeopardizes the stability of the entire financial system, presenting significant systemic risk.

Let us look at each specific type of financial risk in detail.

1.1.1 Market Risk

Market risk is arguably the most common form of risk faced by individual investors in financial markets. It involves potential losses arising from unforeseen fluctuations in asset prices, which can affect everything from stocks and bonds to foreign exchange rates and commodities such as oil and gold. Various factors, including economic news, political events, natural disasters, and changes in investor sentiment, can trigger these price swings. Moreover, because price discovery is an ongoing process, supply and demand constantly shape asset values, making any apparent market equilibrium only temporary.

We can classify market risk according to the underlying market of the financial instrument, such as equity, interest rate, currency, or commodity markets. Let us examine these distinct risks in more detail.

Equity risk refers to the potential for changes in stock prices to affect the value of your investments. When you hold shares in a company, you effectively share in its successes and setbacks. For example, if a company underperforms and releases a poor earnings report, its stock price can drop, causing losses for shareholders. Equity risk also includes broader market fluctuations: a sudden economic downturn can spark a widespread sell-off, impacting virtually all stocks. Because stock prices are inherently unpredictable, owning equities carries the possibility of a decline in value (assuming you hold a long position). Of course, various protective measures, such as purchasing a put option, can help limit losses, and we will explore these hedging techniques later in the book.

Interest rate risk refers to the uncertainty in potential changes in the interest rate, which can have a pronounced effect on the value of fixed-income securities such as bonds. As an example, imagine that you own a bond that pays an annual coupon at 2%. If interest rates on the market later increase to 3%, newly issued bonds will likely offer that higher rate. Consequently, investors will be less willing to pay the full price for a bond yielding only 2%, causing its market value to drop. This inverse relationship between bond prices and interest rates stems from the fact that the fixed coupon of a bond becomes more (or less) attractive depending on the prevailing interest rate environment.

Currency risk, also known as **foreign exchange (or forex) risk**, arises whenever you invest in assets denominated in a currency other than your home currency. For example, suppose that you are a US-based investor who purchases shares of a European company. Now, you are exposed to two types of risk: equity risk, as introduced before, and currency risk, which comes from a depreciation of the euro against the dollar. Such depreciation would lead to a lower investment return when you convert your investment back to dollars. Conversely, if the euro appreciates against the dollar, your returns would increase accordingly. Currency risk is especially important for multinational companies and international portfolio managers with investment portfolio across multiple countries.

Commodity risk involves fluctuating prices of raw materials, such as those of oil, gold, and agricultural products. These prices can be highly volatile due to supply-demand imbalances in the market, policy instability, or natural disasters around the world. These price shocks can affect both producers on the supply side and consumers on the demand side. For example, when political conflicts disrupt oil production in the Middle East, oil prices can rapidly rise, affecting not only energy companies but also associated industries dependent on oil. Again, investors and firms exposed to commodities often adopt hedging strategies (such as purchasing futures and options) to protect themselves against sudden price swings.

Market risk is an essential consideration in almost every type of financial investment. It arises because prices in financial markets are perpetually changing, driven by a complex blend of economic indicators, political developments, changing investor sentiment, and unforeseen global events. Although it is impossible to completely eliminate market risk—given that no one can fully control these external influences—we can still employ several strategies to mitigate and manage its effects.

One of the most widely used approaches to managing market risk is **diversification**, which involves spreading investments across different asset classes, sectors, or geographic regions. As Harry Markowitz famously observed, "Diversification is the only free lunch in Finance." By avoiding "putting all your eggs in one basket," the underperformance of one asset can be balanced by the outperformance of another, thereby reducing overall portfolio volatility. When equity markets become volatile, holding bonds or commodities can often help stabilize the portfolio. As an example,

Figure 1-3 Comparing the wealth curve of three strategies in 2024

let us maintain a balanced 50/50 portfolio of equities (SPY) and bonds (AGG) in the year of 2024. We adopt an equal-weightage strategy with monthly rebalancing so that the risk profile of the portfolio remains relatively stable even if one asset class outperforms the other over a given month. This is the central idea of diversification: rather than relying exclusively on volatile equities or conservative bonds, the portfolio spreads its exposure, thereby lowering overall volatility compared to a single-asset strategy.

As shown in Figure 1-3, the monthly rebalanced portfolio of 50/50 shows a significantly smoother return path than the 100% buy-and-hold strategy (SPY), with an annualized volatility of approximately 7.27% compared to SPY 12.58%. Although this balanced approach does not match the upside potential of SPY, it provides a middle ground that delivers a higher return than bonds alone (AGG) but far less volatile than stocks. The result illustrates a key benefit of diversification: by combining two relatively uncorrelated assets and periodically rebalancing, the portfolio avoids the extreme fluctuations of equities while still capturing a portion of stock market gains.

See Listing 1-3 used to generate Figure 1-3.

```
import yfinance as yf
import pandas as pd
import numpy as np
import matplotlib.pyplot as plt

# ---------------------------------------------------------------
# 1. Download Historical Data
# ---------------------------------------------------------------
```

1.1 Understanding Different Types of Risk in Financial Markets

```python
tickers = ["SPY", "AGG"]
data = yf.download(tickers, start="2024-01-01", end="2025-01-01")
    ["Adj Close"]

# Drop any rows with missing values for simplicity
data.dropna(inplace=True)

# If the index has time zone info, remove it:
if data.index.tz is not None:
    data.index = data.index.tz_localize(None)

# Calculate daily returns
daily_returns = data.pct_change().dropna()

# ------------------------------------------------------------------
# 2. Define Monthly Rebalance Dates
# ------------------------------------------------------------------
# We'll use the last calendar day of each month, but then we'll
# map that to the nearest *actual* trading date via asof().
# This ensures we don't hit missing index errors.

calendar_month_ends = pd.date_range(
    start=daily_returns.index[0],
    end=daily_returns.index[-1],
    freq='M'
)

# Convert these month-ends to actual trading days (or the most
    recent trading day before them):
monthly_rebalance_dates = []
for date in calendar_month_ends:
    # .asof(date) gives the last valid index on or before 'date'
    # If no valid date is found, it returns NaT, so we skip it
    trading_date = daily_returns.index.asof(date)
    if pd.notnull(trading_date):
        monthly_rebalance_dates.append(trading_date)

monthly_rebalance_dates = pd.DatetimeIndex(
    monthly_rebalance_dates)

# ------------------------------------------------------------------
# 3. Simulate Monthly Rebalancing
# ------------------------------------------------------------------
initial_capital = 100_000.0
target_weights = np.array([0.5, 0.5])   # 50% in SPY, 50% in AGG

# Series to hold portfolio values for plotting
portfolio_values = pd.Series(dtype=float)

# Initialize positions on the first rebalance date
start_date = monthly_rebalance_dates[0]
spy_price = data.loc[start_date, "SPY"]
agg_price = data.loc[start_date, "AGG"]
```

```python
spy_shares = (initial_capital * target_weights[0]) / spy_price
agg_shares = (initial_capital * target_weights[1]) / agg_price

# Record the initial portfolio value
portfolio_values.loc[start_date] = spy_shares * spy_price +
    agg_shares * agg_price

# Go through each subsequent monthly period
for i in range(len(monthly_rebalance_dates) - 1):
    period_start = monthly_rebalance_dates[i]
    period_end = monthly_rebalance_dates[i + 1]

    # Get all trading days in [period_start, period_end]
    period_days = daily_returns.loc[period_start:period_end].
    index

    # Track day-to-day value within the month
    for day in period_days:
        # Update the portfolio value based on unchanged share
        counts
        spy_price = data.loc[day, "SPY"]
        agg_price = data.loc[day, "AGG"]
        daily_value = spy_shares * spy_price + agg_shares *
        agg_price
        portfolio_values.loc[day] = daily_value

    # At period_end, we rebalance to 50/50 (unless period_end is
    the final date)
    if i < len(monthly_rebalance_dates) - 1:
        # Use .asof() again for the final day price if necessary
        final_day_price_spy = data["SPY"].asof(period_end)
        final_day_price_agg = data["AGG"].asof(period_end)

        final_value = spy_shares * final_day_price_spy +
        agg_shares * final_day_price_agg

        # Re-allocate to 50/50
        spy_shares = (final_value * target_weights[0]) /
        final_day_price_spy
        agg_shares = (final_value * target_weights[1]) /
        final_day_price_agg

# ----------------------------------------------------------------
# 4. Calculate Portfolio Returns and Cumulative Returns
# ----------------------------------------------------------------
portfolio_returns = portfolio_values.pct_change().fillna(0)
cumulative_portfolio = (1 + portfolio_returns).cumprod() - 1

# ----------------------------------------------------------------
# 5. Compare to SPY and AGG Buy-and-Hold (No Rebalancing)
# ----------------------------------------------------------------
cumulative_spy = (1 + daily_returns["SPY"]).cumprod() - 1
```

1.1 Understanding Different Types of Risk in Financial Markets

```python
cumulative_agg = (1 + daily_returns["AGG"]).cumprod() - 1

# Align indices for plotting (in case of any missing dates at the
    ends)
cumulative_portfolio = cumulative_portfolio.reindex(daily_returns
    .index, method='ffill')

# ----------------------------------------------------------------
# 6. Calculate Annualized Volatility
# ----------------------------------------------------------------
trading_days_per_year = 252
# The daily std. dev. of the portfolio returns * sqrt(252)
vol_portfolio = portfolio_returns.std() * np.sqrt(
    trading_days_per_year)
vol_spy = daily_returns["SPY"].std() * np.sqrt(
    trading_days_per_year)
vol_agg = daily_returns["AGG"].std() * np.sqrt(
    trading_days_per_year)

print("Annualized Volatility:")
print(f"Monthly Rebalanced 50/50 Portfolio: {vol_portfolio:.2%}")
print(f"SPY (Equities) Buy & Hold:          {vol_spy:.2%}")
print(f"AGG (Bonds) Buy & Hold:             {vol_agg:.2%}")

# ----------------------------------------------------------------
# 7. Plot the Cumulative Returns
# ----------------------------------------------------------------
plt.figure(figsize=(10, 6))
plt.plot(cumulative_portfolio, label='Monthly Rebalanced 50/50',
    linewidth=2)
plt.plot(cumulative_spy, label='SPY (Equities) Buy & Hold',
    linestyle='--')
plt.plot(cumulative_agg, label='AGG (Bonds) Buy & Hold',
    linestyle=':')
plt.title("Cumulative Returns: Monthly Rebalanced 50/50 vs. SPY &
    AGG")
plt.xlabel("Date")
plt.ylabel("Cumulative Return")
plt.legend()
plt.grid(True)
plt.show()
```

Listing 1-3 Comparing the wealth curve of three strategies in 2024

As shown in Figure 1-4, applying the same equal-weight strategy in 2020, when the COVID-19 pandemic initially emerged, resulted in smaller drawdowns than a purely equity-focused approach, illustrating how spreading exposure across asset classes can mitigate losses under adverse conditions. Observing the annualized volatilities, the monthly rebalanced 50/50 portfolio has a volatility of about 18.08%, substantially lower than the 33.45% registered by an all-equity (SPY) portfolio. In contrast, the all-bond (AGG) allocation remains the least volatile at 8.37%. Notably, diversification is especially beneficial during market downturns.

Note that in real-world settings, such rebalancing is often done at intervals (e.g., monthly or quarterly) to manage both market risk and transaction costs. We have seen that this combination of assets leads to reduced portfolio swings. Although returns on a balanced portfolio may be somewhat lower in booming equity markets (as shown in Figure 1-3), the reward comes during downturns, when the bond component tends to cushion losses (see Figure 1-4). We can continue to add even more asset classes (commodities, international equities, alternative investments, etc.) so as to further diversify the market risk. However, we must be aware that diversification only reduces unsystematic risk specific to a company or industry, not eliminate systematic risk that affects the entire market.

Another approach to managing market risk is hedging, which involves taking off-setting positions in different financial instruments to limit potential losses. Hedging often involves the use of derivatives, such as options, futures, and swaps. For example, an investor with a substantial equity portfolio might purchase put options that could generate profit (when exercised) if the underlying stocks decline, thereby cushioning against losses. Likewise, currency forwards or futures can lock in the transaction price in advance and help mitigate exchange rate fluctuations in international investments. However, these hedging activities often come with costs, such as premiums for options. Thus, a comprehensive risk management strategy needs to consider these additional transaction costs as well, as they could also diminish potential upside gains.

Beyond diversification and hedging, we can also employ a variety of other strategies to manage market risk. For example, we can perform tactical asset allocation to adjust portfolio exposures periodically in response to evolving market

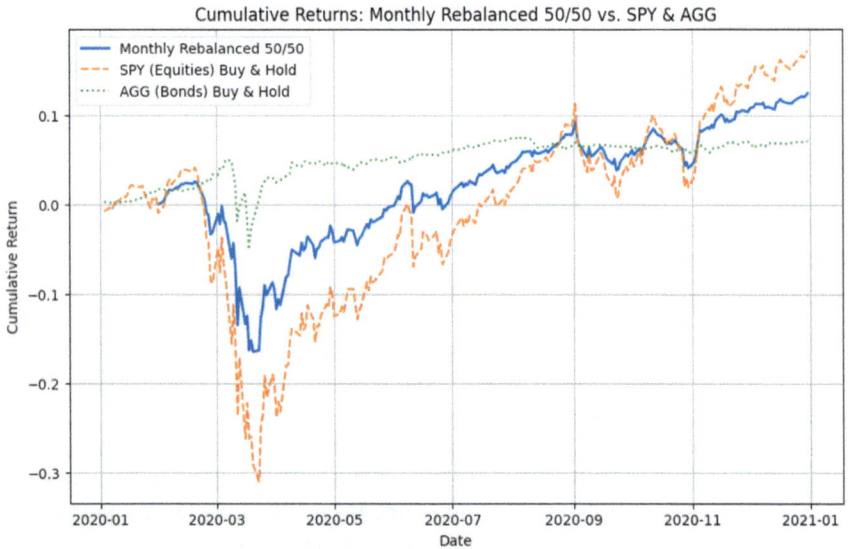

Figure 1-4 Comparing the wealth curve of three strategies in 2020

conditions. We have seen this in the previous equal weightage strategy, but such periodic rebalancing may also be done to cater to investor's specific risk-reward preference. Some investors also implement stop-loss orders, which automatically liquidate positions once they fall below a predetermined price, thereby preventing small losses from spiraling into large ones. As another example, risk parity strategies allocate capital based on the risk contribution of each asset rather than traditional fixed percentage allocations, aiming to balance volatility between different asset classes.

Managing market risk begins with recognizing the uncertainty inherent in market prices and adopting strategies to mitigate or even minimize potential losses. Because higher returns typically come with higher risk, reducing volatility often involves sacrificing some portion of potential gains, but this trade-off can prove to be well worth it if it prevents significant drawdowns during market downturns. In addition, effective risk management calls for a proactive approach: rather than simply reacting to sudden changes in market conditions, proactive risk management recommends that we continuously monitor trends and recalibrate portfolios (such as monthly rebalancing) as needed to maintain an acceptable risk-return balance.

We now provide a mathematical view on why mixing stocks and bonds in a portfolio typically reduces overall risk. Assume that the correlation between stock and bond is less than 1. In our two-asset portfolio setup, let R_S be the random variable for stock returns, and R_B be the random variable for bond returns. We form a portfolio P by allocating a fraction w to the stock index (such as SPY) and $(1-w)$ to the bond index (such as AGG). Then the total portfolio return R_P can be expressed as

$$R_P = w\,R_S + (1-w)\,R_B.$$

Similarly, the portfolio variance can be expressed as

$$\sigma_P^2 = \mathrm{Var}(R_P) = \mathrm{Var}\bigl(w\,R_S + (1-w)\,R_B\bigr).$$

By standard properties of variance, we have

$$\sigma_P^2 = w^2\,\mathrm{Var}(R_S) + (1-w)^2\,\mathrm{Var}(R_B) + 2\,w\,(1-w)\,\mathrm{Cov}(R_S, R_B).$$

Now denote

$$\sigma_S^2 = \mathrm{Var}(R_S), \quad \sigma_B^2 = \mathrm{Var}(R_B), \quad \rho_{S,B} = \mathrm{Corr}(R_S, R_B).$$

Then $\mathrm{Cov}(R_S, R_B) = \rho_{S,B}\,\sigma_S\,\sigma_B$.

Therefore, we have

$$\sigma_P^2 = w^2\,\sigma_S^2 + (1-w)^2\,\sigma_B^2 + 2\,w\,(1-w)\,\rho_{S,B}\,\sigma_S\,\sigma_B.$$

Since $\rho_{S,B} < 1$ (it is very unlikely that bonds move in perfect sync with stocks), the product $\rho_{S,B}\,\sigma_S\,\sigma_B$ is less than $\sigma_S\,\sigma_B$. Hence, the cross-term

$$2\,w\,(1-w)\,\rho_{S,B}\,\sigma_S\,\sigma_B$$

is smaller than the corresponding term if stocks and bonds perfectly moved together ($\rho_{S,B} = 1$). This implies that

$$\sigma_P^2 < w^2\,\sigma_S^2 + (1-w)^2\,\sigma_B^2 + 2\,w\,(1-w)\,\sigma_S\,\sigma_B$$

(where we have used the fact that $\rho_{S,B} < 1$)

Simplifying, we have

$$\sigma_P < w\,\sigma_S + (1-w)\,\sigma_B$$

This means that the standard deviation of the portfolio is strictly lower than the weighted sum of the individual standard deviations when the correlation is less than 1. Therefore, as long as the returns of stocks and bonds are not perfectly positively correlated ($\rho_{S,B} \neq 1$), the combined variance is reduced compared to owning only stocks or only bonds, in any weight allocation. This lower variance (or volatility) is precisely the mathematical reason why diversifying between stocks and bonds helps reduce risk in a portfolio.

Now that we have shown that diversification helps reduce total portfolio risk, the next question is to what extent we can reduce the risk. That is, how do we allocate the weights across these two assets so as to achieve the minimal risk of our portfolio? To answer this question, we need to derive the global minimum-variance (GMV) portfolio weights for our two-asset model, assuming that there are no constraints such as short-sale bans or leverage limits.

Recall the definition of portfolio variance that we would like to minimize:

$$\sigma_P^2 = w^2\,\sigma_S^2 + (1-w)^2\,\sigma_B^2 + 2\,w(1-w)\,\rho_{S,B}\,\sigma_S\,\sigma_B.$$

Since this is a quadratic function of w, we can take the derivative $\frac{d}{dw}\sigma_P^2$ and set it to zero to obtain the closed-form optimality condition:

$$\frac{d\sigma_P^2}{dw} = 2w\,\sigma_S^2 - 2(1-w)\,\sigma_B^2 + 2\,\rho_{S,B}\,\sigma_S\,\sigma_B\left[1 - 2w\right] = 0.$$

After a bit of algebra, we can solve for w^*:

$$w^* = \frac{\sigma_B^2 - \rho_{S,B}\,\sigma_S\,\sigma_B}{\sigma_S^2 + \sigma_B^2 - 2\,\rho_{S,B}\,\sigma_S\,\sigma_B}.$$

This is the weight of the stock index (SPY) that produces the minimum variance in the two-asset framework. Consequently, the weight for the bond index (AGG) is

$$1 - w^* = 1 - \frac{\sigma_B^2 - \rho_{S,B}\, \sigma_S\, \sigma_B}{\sigma_S^2 + \sigma_B^2 - 2\rho_{S,B}\, \sigma_S\, \sigma_B}.$$

Of course, when our goal is to maximize the portfolio return (recall that $R_P = w\, R_S + (1-w)\, R_B$), we can simply invest all our budget in the higher-return asset, which is the stock index.

Now, let us look at credit risk in the following section.

1.1.2 Credit Risk

Credit risk evaluates the ability of a borrower, also known as a counterparty, to repay the principal and the interest agreed on in a loan. Typical lenders include banks, specialized lending firms, and bond investors, all of whom expect to recoup their invested principal plus any associated interest. However, there is no guarantee of repayment; borrowers may default on part or all of their debt. Thus, credit risk captures the possibility that a borrower or counterparty will fail to meet the obligations stipulated by a loan or debt agreement. In the following section, we will explore several common types of credit risk, including default risk, credit spread risk, and downgrade risk.

Default risk is often viewed as the most common type of credit risk, which captures both the probability that a borrower will fail to repay a loan and the potential loss incurred if such a default occurs. In the worst case, lenders or bondholders could face a complete loss of their principal. To manage this risk, financial institutions typically employ three interrelated models: the probability of default (evaluating the likelihood that the borrower will default), the loss given default (estimating how much might be lost when default occurs), and the exposure at default (estimating the total amount at risk at the time of default). When taken together, these models provide an overall expected credit loss calculation, indicating how much a lender might expect to lose should the borrower eventually fail to meet the debt obligations. Banks and financial institutions commonly use this framework to set credit limits, price loans, and maintain sufficient capital reserves.

Credit spread risk arises when the creditworthiness of a borrower deteriorates, even if this change does not result in a real default. The primary mechanism at work is the "credit spread," defined as the yield differential between a risk-free bond (such as a US Treasury) and a bond exposed to credit risk. If investors suddenly perceive a company to be more likely to default, perhaps due to unfavorable financial news, adverse market conditions, or other negative signals, they will demand a higher yield to compensate for the increased uncertainty. Because coupon payments and face value of a bond are generally fixed, the only way for yield to increase is for the market price of the bond to drop accordingly. Consequently, bondholders can incur losses based solely on a market-driven reassessment of the borrower's credit profile, regardless of any actual default.

Downgrade risk refers to the possibility that a borrower's credit rating may be lowered by agencies such as Moody's or Standard & Poor's, signaling increased credit risk. A recent example is Intel's removal from the Dow Jones Industrial Average on November 8, 2024, after a 25-year tenure, reflecting its declining market position and financial performance. Such downgrades typically lead to a decrease in the value of the issuer's securities. For bondholders, a downgrade results in a higher yield premium, causing the bond market price to fall. Consequently, if an investor holds a bond from a downgraded entity, the bond's market value diminishes, leading to a potential loss upon sale. This underscores the importance of monitoring credit ratings, as they directly influence bond valuations and investment returns.

As an example, suppose that an investor holds a corporate bond from a company with a face value of $1,000, a fixed annual coupon of 5% ($50 per year), a current yield to maturity (YTM) of 6%, and a risk-free yield of 3%. Following a credit rating downgrade from A to BBB due to deteriorating financials, the market now demands an 8% yield to compensate for the increased perceived risk. Although there is no immediate expectation of default, the bond will continue to pay its fixed coupon. To align with the market's demand for a higher yield, the price of the bond must decrease, since its fixed coupon and face value remain unchanged. This price decline, driven by the increase in the credit spread, reflects the risk of credit spread rather than an actual default loss, since the downgrade impacts the market value of the bond rather than its cash flow reliability.

The probability of default is one of the most commonly monitored risks in financial risk management, as it reflects the likelihood that a company will not meet its obligations. As a quick exercise, consider a firm with a 2% chance of default in the first year and a 3% chance in the second year, conditional on surviving the first year. To determine the overall probability of default at the end of Year 2 in a single step, note that the firm can default immediately in the first year with probability 0.02. Alternatively, if it survives the first year (which happens with probability 0.98), then it faces a 0.03 chance of default in the second year. Consequently, the total probability of default by the end of Year 2 is

$$0.02 + (0.98 \times 0.03) = 0.02 + 0.0294 = 0.0494 = 4.94\%.$$

As an extension to the credit risk framework, the credit migration matrix is a widely used tool to characterize the transition probabilities among different states. In particular, it systematically captures the probabilities of transitioning between different credit ratings over a given time period. This transition probability provides us with a measure of the likelihood of upgrades, downgrades, and defaults among different credit grades. For example, we can adopt a frequency-based approach to estimate these transition probabilities using historical data at different time periods, thus describing the evolving credit quality of borrowers. This matrix also measures intermediate changes in creditworthiness that can lead to changes in credit spreads, offering deeper insights into potential credit deterioration paths.

Next, we look at the liquidity risk.

1.1.3 Liquidity Risk

Liquidity risk measures the ease with which an asset can be bought or sold without causing a significant impact on its price. Highly traded assets, such as popular stocks, are typically very liquid because of consistent supply and demand throughout trading hours. This allows transactions to occur seamlessly, either at the prevailing market price via a market order or at a preset price using a limit order. In contrast, assets such as real estate can be highly illiquid, particularly when the property is in a less desirable location or condition. Selling such assets often requires drastically lowering the price to attract buyers. In markets with limited participants, this lack of liquidity can force sellers to accept prices below the intrinsic value of an asset or force buyers to pay more than the asset is worth. This highlights the challenges and potential costs associated with trading in less liquid markets.

There are two primary types of liquidity risk: asset liquidity risk and funding liquidity risk. Asset liquidity risk arises when an asset cannot be sold at the desired price due to a lack of willing buyers. In such cases, the seller faces two options: wait for a buyer willing to pay the desired price or reduce the asking price to attract more buyers. This risk highlights the challenges of selling less liquid assets promptly without incurring a loss. In contrast, funding liquidity risk refers to the inability to meet short-term financial obligations, such as covering day-to-day operational costs or making scheduled debt payments such as housing mortgages. Addressing this risk requires maintaining sufficient cash flow to meet these consistent and periodic commitments, ensuring that operations and debt servicing remain uninterrupted. Both types of liquidity risk underscore the importance of liquidity management in financial decision-making.

1.1.4 Operational Risk

Operational risk refers to internal factors that can disrupt an organization's day-to-day functions, compared to external forces such as market fluctuations or macroeconomic events. These disruptions often come from breakdowns in internal processes, hardware or software systems, and human activities, either inadvertent or deliberate. For example, a sudden power outage can stop trading floors or payment processing unless backup generators are in place, and a rogue trader may bypass internal oversight, incurring substantial unauthorized losses. Even seemingly minor errors, such as incorrect data entry or flawed calculations, can entail material, financial, or reputational damage. To mitigate these risks, firms commonly implement robust internal controls, formalized procedures, and carefully designed system redundancies. Automation can also reduce human error, while comprehensive guidelines ensure that staff are well-informed about best practices and compliance requirements. By recognizing potential vulnerabilities within operations and proactively countering them, an organization can better protect itself against disruptions that might otherwise lead to significant losses.

1.1.5 Model Risk

Model risk arises when the mathematical models used to guide financial decision-making, whether highly transparent or so-called "black-box" models, differ significantly from actual market behavior. As the adage goes, "All models are wrong, but some are useful." In practice, the usefulness of a model in modern settings, particularly when employing deep learning or other advanced neural network architectures, hinges on three interlinked elements: the quality and representativeness of the underlying data, the choice of model architecture, and the available computational resources.

With respect to data, financial markets directly shape the information inputs that feed into these models. Predictive accuracy is highly dependent on having current and comprehensive data, capturing the genuine statistical signals needed for reliable forecasting. Outdated data may not reflect future phenomena, incomplete data could fail to capture critical aspects of the market, and flawed or misspecified data would inevitably lead to incorrect outputs or instability in model predictions. Ensuring representativeness in time, for example, by carefully selecting historical data that match as closely as possible the conditions likely to prevail in the future, is just as vital as preserving an appropriate signal-to-noise ratio.

The model assumptions also require close scrutiny. These assumptions, in effect, define how the chosen architecture transforms the data into the final predictions. Deep neural networks, for instance, impose relatively few explicit assumptions on functional form and can approximate highly complex relationships in the data. However, they often face the risk of overfitting, where a model that excels in historical or training data may not be able to generalize when faced with new information. In contrast, simpler models, such as linear regression, are built on stronger structural assumptions, usually linearity in relationships, and thus run the risk of underfitting. Balancing these trade-offs to obtain robust, generalizable models is a delicate but essential part of the model design process.

Model validation and ongoing monitoring further mitigate the risk of relying on a model that may have become outdated or simply failed to account for emerging realities. Once a model has been developed, often using historical data, it lacks immediate awareness of real-time events in the external environment. Consequently, a model might still issue optimistic forecasts for a company that, in reality, has suffered sudden reputational damage and may soon face a decline in share price. Regular re-evaluation, combined with updated data feeds, stress testing, and comparative benchmarks, can help detect such discrepancies before they lead to potential financial losses.

In a later chapter of the book, we will take a deeper look at model risk in finance, emphasizing the importance of robust validation techniques and dynamic adaptation. Next, we turn to legal and regulatory risks.

1.1.6 Legal and Regulatory Risk

Legal and regulatory risk refers to the prospect of financial or reputational damage resulting from changes in laws, regulations, or government directives. Such changes often require businesses to adapt their operational procedures and risk management strategies rapidly. For example, in the banking sector, dedicated teams are not uncommon, whose primary role is to interpret and implement policies issued by regulatory authorities, including the Prudential Regulation Authority (PRA) in the United Kingdom and the Monetary Authority of Singapore (MAS) in Singapore, to ensure continuous compliance.

One prominent example is the Basel regulatory framework, which governs the capital adequacy requirements for banks. This framework has undergone multiple refinements, including Basel I, Basel II, Basel III, and beyond, to keep up with ever-changing market dynamics and financial innovations. A similarly influential standard is the International Financial Reporting Standard 9 (IFRS 9), which imposes nuanced requirements to estimate expected losses across various portfolios. Noncompliance with these obligations can lead to severe penalties, including substantial fines and potential reputational setbacks for the institutions involved. These realities illustrate why proactive measures, including rigorous monitoring of legal and regulatory developments and strong internal controls, are vital to mitigating legal and regulatory risk in modern financial institutions.

1.1.7 Systemic Risk

Systemic risk refers to a major threat that endangers the entire financial system, often originating with the failure of a single institution or market and then triggering a broader chain reaction. Regulators and policymakers focus on systemic risk precisely because it reaches beyond isolated firms and markets, carrying the potential to ignite a full-blown financial crisis and produce severe economic downturns. One well-known example occurred in the late 1990s, when the hedge fund Long-Term Capital Management (LTCM) experienced severe distress. To avoid widespread repercussions, the Federal Reserve convened an emergency meeting with major banks in an effort to engineer a rescue plan. Such interventions aim to restore confidence because if market sentiment collapses, even a localized disruption could escalate into a global crisis.

When an entity is considered "too big to fail," government agencies often intervene—potentially using taxpayer funds—to conduct a bailout. However, this assistance is not guaranteed, as the sovereign debt itself can default under extreme conditions. A major driver of systemic risk is the high degree of interconnectivity among financial institutions. Banks, insurance companies, and other financial entities often hold each other's debt or rely on similar funding channels; consequently, the failure of a key player can have a ripple effect. The collapse of Lehman Brothers in 2008, for example, led to a huge impact on the global financial system due to the firm's extensive network of loans, derivatives, and credit arrangements. These interdependencies indicate how quickly a localized problem can spread, posing a systemic threat that demands careful monitoring, robust regulation, and coordinated policy responses.

1.1.8 Environmental, Social, and Governance (ESG) Risk

ESG risk involves understanding the potential financial impact of environmental, social, and governance factors on investments. In recent years, ESG risk has become an important topic of financial analysis as investors and companies recognize their importance in managing real risks that can affect long-term performance. ESG provides different perspectives that allow us to assess how well a company is prepared to face the challenges of the modern world, from climate change to social responsibility to ethical leadership. Let's break down what ESG risk encompasses and discuss why it is becoming a big deal in the investing world.

Environmental risk contains a wide spectrum of concerns, including climate change, depletion of natural resources, waste management, and pollution. Businesses that rely heavily on fossil fuels or do not mitigate their environmental impact can face substantial legal, financial, and reputational challenges. Heightened regulatory measures, such as those designed to reduce carbon emissions, can significantly increase operational costs for companies not prepared to adapt. In parallel, organizations linked to environmental harm or ecological disasters risk losing public trust and enduring long-term damage to their brand. These realities underscore why investors and stakeholders increasingly focus on the environmental footprint of a company when evaluating its overall viability.

Social risk focuses on how companies manage relationships with employees, suppliers, customers, and the broader communities where they operate. Issues such as labor standards, diversity and inclusion, human rights, and consumer protection have become central to ensuring sustainability and fostering stakeholder confidence. As an example, an unfavorable review from a former employee on Glassdoor can put a bad look on the public image of an organization, potentially deterring both prospective talent and investors. In today's interconnected economy, companies demonstrating proactive and responsible social practices are often more resilient, with a stronger capacity to avoid costly controversies.

Governance risk, meanwhile, refers to the internal policies, leadership structures, and oversight mechanisms that guide corporate decision-making. It involves factors such as board diversity, executive compensation schemes, shareholder rights, and transparency in financial disclosures. Many companies, for example, strive to ensure that their boards meet certain benchmarks in terms of gender, professional background, or other diversity measures, recognizing that broader representation often correlates with more balanced and effective leadership. By maintaining high standards in environmental, social, and governance (ESG) practices, organizations can not only mitigate risk but also strengthen their reputations and long-term competitiveness.

Table 1-1 Overview of risks in financial markets

Type of Risk	Description
Market Risk	Risk of losses due to changes in market prices of financial instruments like stocks, bonds, foreign exchange rates, and commodities. Influenced by economic news, political events, natural disasters, and investor sentiment. Includes equity risk, interest rate risk, currency risk, and commodity risk.
Credit Risk	Risk that a borrower will not repay a loan or fulfill financial obligations. Key for banks, lenders, and bond investors. Includes default risk, credit spread risk, and downgrade risk.
Liquidity Risk	Risk that an investor cannot buy or sell an asset quickly without significantly impacting its price. Includes asset liquidity risk (lack of buyers or sellers) and funding liquidity risk (inability to access funds).
Operational Risk	Risk of loss due to failures in internal processes, systems, people, or external events. Examples are process failures, system outages, human errors, and natural disasters.
Model Risk	Risk arising from inaccuracies in the mathematical models used for financial decision-making. Can result from wrong assumptions, poor-quality data, or errors in implementation.
Legal and Regulatory Risk	Risk of financial loss due to changes in laws, regulations, or government policies. Includes regulatory changes, compliance costs, and potential legal actions.
Systemic Risk	Risk of a breakdown in the entire financial system, often triggered by the failure of a major institution. Can cause a chain reaction or contagion effect, leading to a global crisis.
ESG Risk	Risk related to environmental, social, and governance factors affecting investments. Includes environmental risks (e.g., climate change), social risks (e.g., labor practices), and governance risks (e.g., corporate policies).

1.1.9 A Summary of Common Risk Types

Table 1-1 provides a high-level overview of the various types of financial risk prevalent in financial markets. Each type of risk, be it market, credit, liquidity, operational, model, legal and regulatory, systemic, or ESG, presents unique challenges and requires specific strategies for effective management. By recognizing the characteristics and implications of each risk type, we can make more informed decisions, adapt to changing conditions, and better protect our assets against potential financial disruptions.

In the final section, we explore commonly used financial products and their varying risk profiles. These instruments serve as fundamental risk management tools in modern financial markets, enabling many practitioners to hedge, diversify, and control the myriad of uncertainties inherent in investment and lending activities in the financial markets.

1.2 Common Financial Instruments

Having explored the various types of financial risks, we now look at the common financial instruments as tools used to navigate these risks in the financial markets. These tools include stocks, bonds, derivatives, and more, which are often used by investors and institutions to build and manage portfolios. Not all financial instruments are created equal when it comes to risk, so we will also rank them in terms of their riskiness to help you better understand where they fit within a broader investment strategy.

For example, bonds are generally considered less risky than stocks. Bonds are debt products that generally offer an interest payment (called a coupon), which may be fixed or floating, over a set period, and return the principal at maturity. They are typically less volatile, making them a safer choice for more conservative investors. However, while stocks offer the potential for higher returns, they come with greater volatility and risk. Then, there are other instruments like derivatives, which can be used to hedge risks or, conversely, to take on additional risk (called leverage) in pursuit of higher returns. Understanding the risk profile of each instrument is crucial because it helps us determine how best to incorporate them into the investment strategy based on the specific risk tolerance and investment objective.

In this section, we will attempt to group common financial instruments by the typical risk levels, ranging from low-risk options that offer more stability to high-risk choices that come with the potential for higher returns, but also greater volatility. We start with low-risk assets.

1.2.1 Low-Risk Assets

Low-risk assets are generally known for their stability and are less prone to significant price swings compared to higher-risk investments. They are the bedrock of conservative investment strategies, appealing primarily to those who prioritize capital preservation and steady income over pursuing higher returns. These are assets that are used to protect the principal amount invested since they provide a relatively predictable, albeit modest, return. Although they may not deliver spectacular gains, such reliability makes them attractive, especially in uncertain or volatile market conditions. Let us take a closer look at some common low-risk assets and their risk-return characteristics.

- **Cash and Cash Equivalents**: These are considered the safest assets around. Cash equivalents include instruments such as money market funds, Treasury bills, and savings accounts. The primary appeal of these assets is that the principal is almost always guaranteed, which means you are highly unlikely to lose money. However, this safety comes at a cost—they offer very low returns, often barely keeping up with inflation. For example, a savings account might provide a return of 1–2% per year, which is minimal but stable. These are ideal for risk-averse investors who prioritize liquidity, which means they can easily access their money as needed, without worrying about market fluctuations. They're also a great option for those who need to park their funds temporarily while deciding on more strategic and longer-term investments.

- **Government Bonds**: Government bonds, especially those issued by stable governments, such as US Treasury bonds, are another popular low-risk asset. They are considered low-risk because they are backed by the government's ability to tax its citizens and print money if needed. This means that government bonds are highly unlikely to default, although such defaults have happened before. A notable example is the 2012 Greek debt crisis, when Greece restructured its sovereign bonds under severe economic pressure. Government bonds provide regular interest payments, known as coupons, which can offer a reliable income stream to investors. They are less volatile than stocks, meaning that their prices do not fluctuate as much in response to market news or economic data. However, the trade-off is that the returns are typically lower than the riskier assets. For example, a ten-year US Treasury bond could yield around 2–3% annually, which is better than cash but still relatively modest. These are a good option for conservative investors or retirees who want to ensure a steady income without taking on much risk.
- **Investment-Grade Corporate Bonds**: These are bonds issued by companies with strong credit ratings, such as those rated BBB or higher by agencies like Standard & Poor's or Moody's. Although they are slightly riskier than government bonds (due to the small probability of default), they are still considered relatively low risk. To account for such default risk, the returns, or yields, on investment-grade corporate bonds are typically higher than those on government bonds, offering a bit more income for a bit more risk. For example, an investment-grade corporate bond might yield 3–5% per year, which is attractive to investors looking for a balance between risk and return. These bonds are suitable for those who want a higher yield than government bonds without taking too much risk in high-yield or junk bonds.

In summary, low-risk assets offer safety and stability. They're perfect for investors who want to protect their principal and enjoy a predictable income stream without worrying about market turbulence. Although the returns on these assets are lower than most higher-risk investments, the trade-off is still safety and stability, especially in times of economic uncertainty or for those nearing retirement who need to safeguard their savings.

1.2.2 Moderate-Risk Assets

Moderate-risk assets seek a sweet spot between risk and return. These assets are good investment vehicles for investors who are looking to take on a bit more risk, but are not yet ready to dive into high-risk investments. They offer a nice balance, providing the potential for higher returns than low-risk assets while still maintaining a reasonable level of stability. Let us take a closer look at some common types of moderate-risk assets.

- **Dividend-Paying Stocks**: Dividend-paying stocks represent shares of listed companies that provide dividends to shareholders. These stocks are considered moderately risky because they provide a dual benefit: the potential for both capital appreciation (as the stock price increases) and a steady income stream through dividends (should this be provided). Companies that pay dividends are usually more mature and have stable cash flows, and issuing such dividends also has a promoting effect, thus leading to lower volatility in their stock prices compared to those of high-growth companies. However, a certain level of risk is involved. If the market goes down or the company's financial status worsens, the stock price will drop, and the dividend payout may be reduced or even avoided. Despite these risks, these dividends remain an important consideration for investors seeking long-term growth and short-term income, particularly during periods of market uncertainty.
- **Real Estate Investment Trusts (REITs)**: REITs allow investors to participate in the real estate market without having to purchase and own properties directly. The purchase is made through a company that owns and operates the real estate to generate rental income. These real estate properties could include multiple types, including office buildings, shopping malls, or apartments. Investors then enjoy a percentage of the rental income based on the total ownership of shares. Like stocks, real estate property could increase in value, along with dividend payout, which amounts to a steady stream of income. REITs are subject to market risk that causes housing prices to move downward, as well as interest rate risk that influences property value given rising interest rates.
- **High-Yield Bonds (Junk Bonds)**: High-yield bonds, often referred to as junk bonds, are issued by relatively risky companies with lower credit ratings. These companies are considered more likely to default on their debt than creditworthy companies, so bond yields are set higher to attract investors to take up the additional risk. This means that if the issuing company fails to meet its debt obligations, bondholders could lose part or all of their investment. The higher return of high-yield bonds thus comes from the risk premium taken by bond investors. In addition, these bonds also offer diversification benefits, as their returns are often less correlated with traditional stocks and (low-yield) bonds.

In summary, moderate-risk assets provide a middle ground for those who prefer more than just the safety of low-risk options but aren't quite ready to dive into high-risk territory. These assets combine the potential for higher returns with a level of stability that can help cushion against market volatility.

1.2.3 High-Risk Assets

High-risk assets carry the potential for substantial returns, but also bear the equivalent possibility of significant losses. These assets are geared toward investors who exhibit higher risk tolerance, seek notable portfolio growth, and are comfortable with the increased volatility that may ensue. In other words, the prices of high-risk assets can deliver considerable rewards but also fluctuate dramatically in response to market conditions, economic factors, or even company-specific news. Let us now look at several common categories of such high-risk assets.

Stocks (equities) issued by smaller companies or startups are commonly regarded as high-risk assets due to their increased volatility. Unlike dividend-paying stocks that can provide a steady income stream and often exhibit more moderate price fluctuations, shares of newly established or smaller-scale businesses face increased uncertainty. Their limited size makes them more susceptible to market dynamics, sometimes resulting in rapid price movements. Although this volatility can yield substantial returns in a bullish environment, it also creates the possibility of significant losses if the market declines or the company fails to meet performance expectations. To mitigate this elevated risk, investors often diversify their portfolios, for instance, by holding stocks from multiple sectors or asset classes.

Cryptocurrencies, such as Bitcoin and Ethereum, are among the most volatile assets in modern financial markets. Their rapid price fluctuations can generate sizable returns, yet this potential is also accompanied by a similarly high degree of risk. Prices are influenced by a multitude of factors, including market sentiment, technological innovation, regulatory developments, and broader macroeconomic conditions. In contrast to traditional assets, cryptocurrencies typically lack intrinsic value and government backing, which further amplifies their risk profile. In addition, ongoing regulatory uncertainties and the susceptibility of digital exchanges or wallets to security breaches add additional complexity to their investment landscape. Consequently, while cryptocurrencies can yield impressive gains, we must also recognize potential significant losses and exercise due diligence before allocating capital to this emerging asset class.

- **Commodities**, such as oil, gold, silver, and various agricultural products, can be highly speculative investments due to their wide exposure to factors such as geopolitical events (for instance, unrest in oil-producing regions), weather patterns (which affect crop yields), and global economic cycles (shaping industrial demand for metals). These factors can result in sudden and substantial price movements, leading to increased risk for investors. At the same time, commodities may offer valuable diversification benefits and provide a hedge against inflation, since they often appreciate in price during periods of rising inflation.

- **Private equity and venture capital** involve the acquisition of stakes in privately held companies, often startups or businesses in the early stages of development.

Although such investments can generate substantial returns, often exceeding those in public equity markets, this potential is also accompanied by increased risks. A venture may also face liquidity risk because private shares cannot be readily bought or sold on the open market. Those investing in private equity or venture often need to wait several years for the company to go public or be acquired, which typically brings a significant amount of return. Furthermore, the lack of regular financial disclosures and the high failure rate among early-stage companies amplify the risk profile. However, for those equipped to bear these uncertainties, private equity and venture capital can offer a capital boost for high-growth sectors. This requires a long-term investment horizon and the patience to tolerate elevated levels of volatility.

In general, high-risk assets can provide significant growth opportunities, but also require a careful approach to risk management.

Next, we look at another class of risky assets, called derivatives.

1.2.4 Derivatives

Derivatives are a different breed of financial instruments. Unlike traditional investments in which you own an asset directly, derivatives are contracts that derive their value from the performance of something else, such as a stock, bond, commodity, or even an interest rate. This indirect relationship gives derivatives their unique versatility: they can be used to hedge against risk, speculate on future price movements, or even take advantage of arbitrage opportunities when markets experience temporary frictions. Let us look at some common types of derivatives:

- **Options** serve as financial contracts that give the right, but not the obligation, to buy or sell an underlying asset at a predetermined strike price on or before a specified expiration date. This structure (assuming a call option) gives us a unique advantage in that we can reap the benefit of unlimited upside potential, along with limited downside risk, without committing to its full purchase or sale. Options can also be used for hedging purposes, which can mitigate downside risk and protect against adverse price movements. When used for speculative purposes, they can offer outsized returns relative to the initial premium (paid to purchase the option). However, options exhibit a varied risk profile. On the one hand, option buyers face limited risk, which is capped at the premium paid for the contract. However, option writers (sellers) may incur substantial losses if the market moves against them since their potential liability can far exceed the premium received. This combination of versatility and asymmetrical risk makes options a powerful but potentially dangerous tool.
- **Futures and Forwards** are derivative contracts that obligate one to buy or sell an underlying asset at a predetermined price on a specified future date. Futures are standardized instruments traded on regulated exchanges, which enjoy a high level of liquidity and transparency, while forwards are privately negotiated over-

the-counter (OTC) contracts that offer more customization, but lack sufficient oversight and market visibility. Hedgers such as farmers and oil producers are frequent users of futures and forwards as they are interested in locking the future prices to be transacted. After locking the prices, these farmers and producers are no longer subject to unfavorable market fluctuations, although they also give up opportunities for the upside volatility and resulting return. Similarly, speculators would bet on price movements for profit. Being derivative contracts, they provide a leverage effect, meaning even a small change in the price of the underlying asset could lead to substantial gains or losses.

- **Swaps** are derivative contracts that allow two parties to exchange specified cash flows or assets, often to manage or transfer risk. The most commonly encountered variants are interest rate swaps, wherein one party exchanges a fixed interest rate for a floating interest rate (or vice versa), and currency swaps, through which counterparties swap principal and interest payments denominated in different currencies. A typical use case involves converting a floating rate loan to a fixed rate obligation, thereby stabilizing payments and insulating the borrower from interest rate fluctuations. However, participating in a swap introduces counterparty risk, as each party depends on the other's capacity to meet ongoing payment obligations. If the counterparty's creditworthiness deteriorates, or if the counterparty defaults, the non-defaulting party can face financial losses and find itself without the anticipated hedge.

Derivatives represent a category of highly adaptable instruments that can be used to achieve various objectives, including hedging strategies and speculative positions. Although subsequent chapters will illustrate specific hedging examples, it is equally important to recognize the substantial losses that can arise from the improper or excessive use of these products. Furthermore, derivatives do not simply align with conventional low-, medium-, or high-risk classifications, given their structural complexities and the diverse ways in which they can be utilized. Consequently, it is more appropriate to treat them as a separate asset category in any comprehensive risk assessment.

1.2.5 A Summary of Financial Instruments by Risk Level

Table 1-2 categorizes different financial instruments by their typical risk levels, providing a unified overview of the spectrum of investment options available in financial markets. Low-risk assets, such as cash equivalents, government bonds, and investment-grade corporate bonds, are ideal for investors who prioritize stability and capital preservation. Moderate-risk assets, such as dividend-paying stocks, REITs, and high-yield bonds, offer a balanced approach, providing the potential for higher returns while maintaining a reasonable level of risk. On the other hand, high-risk assets, including stocks of smaller companies, cryptocurrencies, commodities, and private equity, cater to investors with a higher risk appetite, offering the possibility of significant returns but with greater volatility. Finally, derivatives are a unique class

Table 1-2 Classification of financial instruments by risk level

Risk level	Asset type	Examples
Low-Risk Assets	Stability and predictable income; ideal for conservative investors.	Cash Equivalents (e.g., savings accounts, money market funds), Government Bonds, Investment-Grade Corporate Bonds
Moderate-Risk Assets	Balance of risk and return, with moderate volatility.	Dividend-Paying Stocks, REITs, High-Yield Bonds
High-Risk Assets	High returns and high volatility; suited for high-risk tolerance.	Stocks (e.g., smaller companies or startups), Cryptocurrencies, Commodities (e.g., oil, gold), Private Equity, Venture Capital
Derivatives	Instruments that derive value from underlying assets; used for hedging or speculation.	Options, Futures, Forwards, Swaps

of instruments that can range from low to high risk depending on their usage; they are highly versatile tools that are used for both hedging and speculative strategies.

1.3 Summary

This chapter introduced the multifaceted nature of financial risk by examining how unexpected events, ranging from daily market fluctuations to historic pandemics, can severely impact investment portfolios and the broader financial system. We introduced standard categories of risk, including market, credit, liquidity, operational, model, legal and regulatory, systemic, and ESG considerations, each highlighting distinct challenges. Through real-world examples, such as the 2020 market sell-off and the ongoing focus on climate-driven regulations, we saw how these risk dimensions can manifest abruptly, underscoring the need for robust risk assessment and mitigation strategies.

We then explored how probability distributions serve as indispensable tools in capturing the randomness of market-driven outcomes, offering quantitative insights into the likelihood of favorable and adverse scenarios. Building on this probabilistic foundation, we demonstrated practical risk management techniques such as diversification, hedging, and tactical asset allocation. By presenting a balanced 50/50 equity-bond portfolio vs. a purely equity-oriented investment, we illustrated how mixing uncorrelated assets can reduce volatility and drawdowns, particularly during periods of market turbulence.

Finally, we surveyed an array of financial instruments and classified them by typical risk levels, from low-risk government bonds and investment-grade securities to moderate-risk assets such as dividend-paying stocks and REITs, all the way up to high-risk ventures such as early-stage equities and cryptocurrencies. Derivatives, which function as contracts derived from underlying assets, were also discussed for their dual capacity to hedge against unwanted risk or amplify speculative positions. Together, these discussions serve as a gateway to the quantitative methods and analytical frameworks detailed in the following chapters.

Fundamentals of Risk and Return in Finance

The world of finance revolves around two fundamental concepts: risk and return. When we invest, the goal is often to maximize return, minimize risk, or reach an optimal trade-off between the two. However, a higher level of risk often accompanies higher potential returns, and these two quantities are often positively correlated. For example, the previous chapter introduced low-risk and high-risk products, which also correspond to (relatively stable) low-return and (likely volatile) high-return assets. This risk manifests itself in the uncertainty of the investment outcome, meaning that we are not certain about whether the investment will be profitable or not, and, if profitable, how much. Thus, a risk-averse investor tends to prefer low-risk products that deliver more or less guaranteed returns.

Understanding how risk and return are intertwined is crucial for making informed investment decisions. The trade-off is simple: to aim for higher returns, we need to face higher risk. This additional risk that investors take on is what generates the "risk premium," an additional layer of return that compensates for the burden of this uncertainty. In essence, risk-seeking investors are not just gambling for higher rewards; they're earning a premium for venturing into more volatile territories. This concept is similar to starting a business; if it is successful, the return could be tremendous, and the corresponding risk of losing market competition or not gaining the right market share is also high. Grasping this risk-return dynamic is therefore at the heart of constructing and managing a successful investment portfolio.

2.1 Understanding Return

So what is the return of a financial asset? Return is the financial reward we receive for putting our money to work in the financial market instead of not investing at all (even saving in the bank gives us fixed interest). Return measures how much our investment has grown or decreased over some period of time. That is, we only need to use the price of our current portfolio P_t to subtract the previous price P_{t-1} and obtain the difference $P_t - P_{t-1}$. To avoid the impact of the unit, we often convert this difference in a relative term, giving $\frac{P_t - P_{t-1}}{P_{t-1}}$, which represents how much percentage change the portfolio experiences from period $t - 1$ to t. This is to facilitate the comparison across different assets and time periods.

Returns can come from a variety of sources, depending on the specific type of instrument invested. In practice, all components are included in the calculation of the return. For example, if our portfolio is a stock that pays dividends D_t in the time period t, then our previous return calculation will be $\frac{P_t - P_{t-1} + D_t}{P_{t-1}}$. Common sources of return include

- **Capital Appreciation:** This is the increase in the value of the asset itself, such as a stock price rising over time.
- **Dividends:** Dividends are cash payments made to shareholders, typically distributed from a company's profits.
- **Interest Payments:** Bonds and other fixed-income securities generate returns through regular interest payments (coupon payment).

These are three common streams of income: capital gains, dividends, and interest. However, we can also define custom derivative products with desired payoff structures to satisfy investor needs with either return maximization or risk minimization.

In addition, it is a common practice to annualize returns, which means converting the original calculated returns from the previous period (which could be daily, monthly, or quarterly) into a standardized annual basis. This gives a clearer picture of how an investment performs on a yearly basis and makes it easier to compare different investment opportunities, regardless of their time frames. However, converting to an annual basis is not a straightforward process, such as multiplying a quantity by 12 to convert the figure from monthly to yearly. In finance, money invested in the financial market (such as saving in a bank) gives interest, and different ways to calculate the interest could make a notable difference, due to the process of compounding.

For example, if a stock return is 2% in a single month, the annualized return would not simply be 12 times that monthly return. Due to the effect of compounding, the annualized return would be slightly higher, capturing the cumulative impact of returns reinvested over time. This practice of annualization provides a consistent and accurate measure of the performance of an investment over different periods.

Note that there are also different ways to report this return. For example, we can use the absolute return to measure the total amount of money gained or lost or the percentage return to represent the gain or loss as a proportion of the initial investment. We can use cumulative return to generate the wealth curve and indicate the total wealth across each period of the investment horizon or use a single-period return to report the individual percentage return in each period. Additionally, we can use risk-adjusted return to consider the risk taken to achieve the return or use the ratio of the two (return divided by risk) to give the return per unit risk (similar to the idea of Sharpe ratio introduced later in this chapter).

2.2 Understanding Risk

Now, let us flip to the other side of the coin: risk. While return represents the financial reward of an investment, risk is the uncertainty surrounding how much of that return we will actually receive (if it is indeed a positive return). In finance, risk is most often associated with volatility, which measures the fluctuations in an investment's value over time. The greater the volatility, the more the value can swing from day to day, week to week, or year to year, indicating a higher level of uncertainty or risk. When drawn on the graph, a high-volatility asset would look more wiggly than a low-volatility one.

So far, we have used volatility as a measure of risk. However, such volatility means both upside and downside volatility. While everyone loves the upside jump (assuming that you have the asset), we are generally more interested in (and concerned with) the downside. In addition, we have learned that the risk itself can take many forms, such as market risk, credit risk, liquidity risk, and operational risk (see Chapter 1). These different types of risk do not exist in isolation. Often, a single investment may be subject to multiple risks simultaneously, each influencing the overall risk profile in complex ways (which are determined by their correlation). Although volatility provides a lens for understanding some of the risks, it is only part of the bigger picture in assessing and mitigating the uncertainty that comes with investing.

Let us look at one simulated example to compare the wealth curve of stable vs. volatile stocks and analyze how varying volatility levels can affect an investor's wealth trajectory over the course of a year. We first assign different drift (average return) and volatility parameters to two stocks—one labeled "stable" and the other "volatile"—to see how daily random fluctuations accumulate into different wealth paths. The stable stock shows less severe price changes but similarly limited upside potential, whereas the volatile stock experiences more dramatic gains or losses day by day. As seen in Figure 2-1, although both stocks begin with the same initial investment and share an identical average daily return, increased volatility in the second stock can lead to substantial divergence in their final outcomes, making its wealth curve more extreme compared to the first stock.

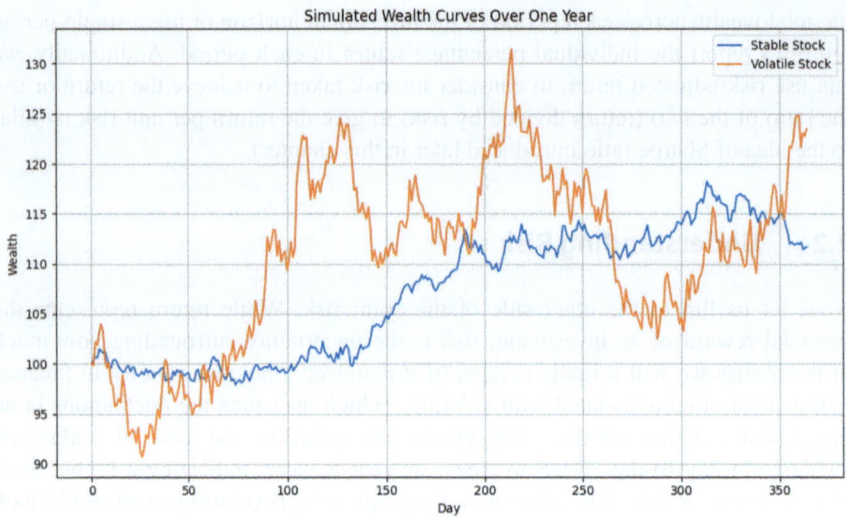

Figure 2-1 Comparing the wealth curve of stable and volatile stocks over one year

See Listing 2-1 used to generate Figure 2-1.

```
import numpy as np
import matplotlib.pyplot as plt

# Number of days in a simulated year
num_days = 365

# Simulation parameters
initial_wealth = 100.0    # starting wealth for both stocks

# Stable Stock parameters
stable_daily_drift = 0.0005     # e.g., 0.05% mean daily return
stable_daily_vol = 0.005        # e.g., 0.5% standard deviation

# Volatile Stock parameters
volatile_daily_drift = 0.0005   # same drift for easier comparison
volatile_daily_vol = 0.015      # e.g., 1.5% standard deviation

# Arrays to hold wealth values over the simulation
stable_wealth = np.zeros(num_days)
volatile_wealth = np.zeros(num_days)

# Initialize
stable_wealth[0] = initial_wealth
volatile_wealth[0] = initial_wealth

# Seed for reproducibility; remove or change if desired
np.random.seed(42)

# Simulation loop for each day
```

2.2 Understanding Risk

```
for i in range(1, num_days):
    # Random daily return for the stable stock
    stable_shock = np.random.normal(stable_daily_drift,
    stable_daily_vol)
    stable_wealth[i] = stable_wealth[i-1] * (1 + stable_shock)

    # Random daily return for the volatile stock
    volatile_shock = np.random.normal(volatile_daily_drift,
    volatile_daily_vol)
    volatile_wealth[i] = volatile_wealth[i-1] * (1 +
    volatile_shock)

# Create a day index for plotting
days = np.arange(num_days)

# Plot both wealth curves
plt.figure(figsize=(10, 6))
plt.plot(days, stable_wealth, label='Stable Stock')
plt.plot(days, volatile_wealth, label='Volatile Stock')
plt.title('Simulated Wealth Curves Over One Year')
plt.xlabel('Day')
plt.ylabel('Wealth')
plt.legend()
plt.grid(True)
plt.tight_layout()
plt.show()
```

Listing 2-1 S&P 500 price curve

Note that the parameters used in this simulation constitute two Gaussian (also called normal) distributions. Each normal distribution is specified with two parameters, mean (also called drift) and variance, which roughly correspond to the asset return and volatility. In this simulation, we used the same mean but different variances for the two distributions. Figure 2-2 shows the Probability Density Function (PDF) of stable and volatile stocks in terms of their daily returns. A PDF specifies the different outcomes and the corresponding probabilities. Clearly, the volatile stock shows wider coverage and, therefore, a higher degree of uncertainty.

Listing 2-2 is used to generate the graph. In general, we would observe that a higher standard deviation σ leads to a wider range of possible outcomes in the end, even if the mean parameter μ remains the same. In addition, the PDF with higher volatility is flatter and wider, indicating a higher uncertainty in day-to-day returns.

```
import numpy as np
import matplotlib.pyplot as plt
from scipy.stats import norm

# Parameters for Stable Stock
stable_mean = 0.0005    # 0.05% mean daily return
stable_vol = 0.005      # 0.5% std. dev.

# Parameters for Volatile Stock
volatile_mean = 0.0005  # same mean for direct comparison
```

```
volatile_vol = 0.015      # 1.5% std. dev.

# Range of possible daily returns for plotting PDF
x = np.linspace(-0.05, 0.05, 1000)

# Calculate the PDF values
stable_pdf = norm.pdf(x, loc=stable_mean, scale=stable_vol)
volatile_pdf = norm.pdf(x, loc=volatile_mean, scale=volatile_vol)

# Plot
plt.figure(figsize=(8, 5))
plt.plot(x, stable_pdf, label='Stable Stock PDF')
plt.plot(x, volatile_pdf, label='Volatile Stock PDF')
plt.title('PDF of Stable vs. Volatile Stock Daily Returns')
plt.xlabel('Daily Return')
plt.ylabel('Probability Density')
plt.legend()
plt.grid(True)
plt.tight_layout()
plt.show()
```

Listing 2-2 Comparing PDFs of stable and volatile stocks

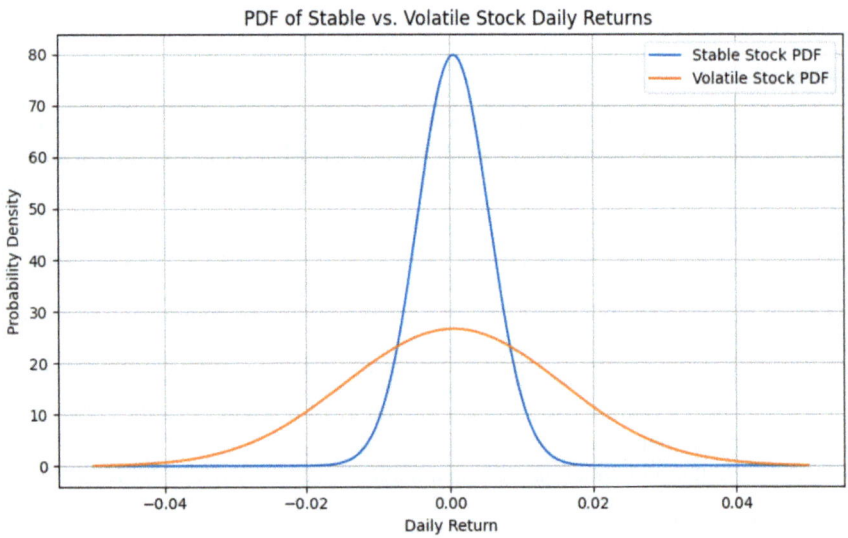

Figure 2-2 Probability density function of stable vs. volatile stock daily returns

2.3 Risk-Return Trade-Off

We have learned that higher potential returns come with higher risks. This relationship is known as the risk-return trade-off. This means that it is very difficult to find a financial product with a higher return and a lower risk in the market. Even if there is, it could be a temporary promotion. This trade-off is often visualized in the mean-variance space of a portfolio, where the mean corresponds to the expected return and the variance (or, equivalently, standard deviation) represents the risk. Picture a two-dimensional plot, with risk on the horizontal axis and return on the vertical axis. The financial instruments we have discussed so far, with different levels of risk, will fill in the graph from the lower left to the upper right, signifying the generally monotone relationship between risk and return.

In this mean-variance graph, the upper-right quadrant contains high-risk and high-return assets, such as stocks, commodities, and derivatives. These investments can offer attractive returns, but come with significant volatility and the potential for loss. The lower-left quadrant contains stable and low-return assets, such as bonds, savings accounts, and other fixed-income securities. These assets tend to provide more stability and lower returns, appealing to risk-averse investors. Also, see Figure 2-3 for an illustration.

This trade-off is the fundamental theme in modern portfolio management, pioneered by Markowitz (1952), who proposed that a diversified portfolio seeks to optimize the balance between risk and return. This balance mixes assets from

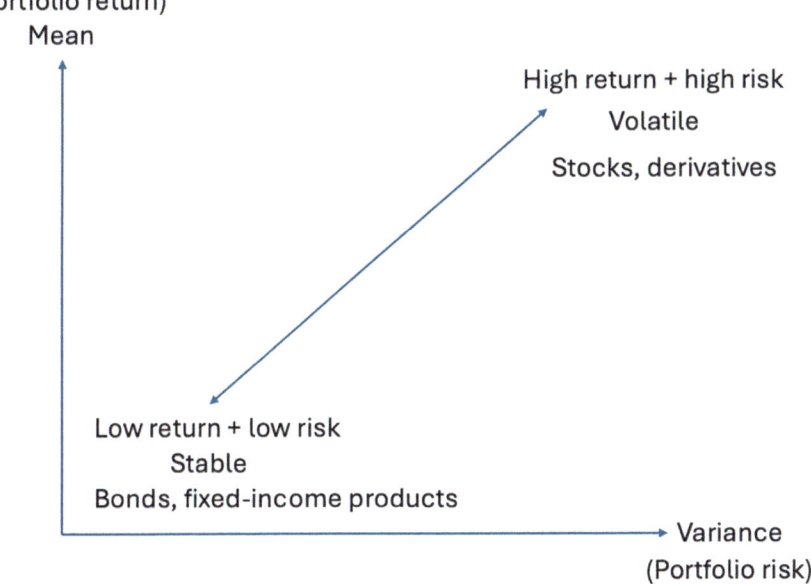

Figure 2-3 Mean-variance space of risk-return trade-off

different parts of the mean-variance space to match the investor's risk tolerance and return objectives. Let us take a closer and more quantitative look at how to measure risk and return.

2.4 Measuring Return

Return is a key measure of financial performance in financial markets. It quantifies how much the asset has appreciated or depreciated over a specific period of time. It also provides a standardized way to assess financial growth in various asset classes. In the following section, we break down the concept of return and explore different ways in which it can be measured and interpreted.

As briefly introduced earlier, return can take several forms, including absolute return and percentage return. We also have logarithmic return, total return, price return, annualized return, single-period return, and multi-period return.

2.4.1 Absolute Return

As the most straightforward form of return, absolute return is the total profit or loss of an investment. For example, if we invested $1,000 and ended up with $1,200, the absolute return is simply $200. Although the calculation is intuitive, the absolute return does not provide a good context about the base, in that a $200 gain will not be so attractive for a total investment of $10,000 (which corresponds to a 2% return).

2.4.2 Percentage Return

To create a level playing field for comparing investments, we can convert absolute returns into a percentage term of the initial investment via the following formula:

$$\text{Percentage Return} = \frac{\text{Terminal Value} - \text{Initial Value}}{\text{Initial Value}}$$

Denoting the percentage return of period $t-1$ to t as R_t and the asset prices in the period t as S_t, we have the following:

$$R_t = \frac{S_t - S_{t-1}}{S_{t-1}} = \frac{S_t}{S_{t-1}} - 1$$

For example, if the investment grows from $1,000 to $1,200, the percentage return is

$$\frac{1200 - 1000}{1000} = 20\%$$

2.4 Measuring Return

This allows us to compare returns across investments of different sizes and time frames. We may also refer to this percentage return as the simple return.

2.4.3 Logarithmic Return

Logarithmic return, or log return (also known as continuously compounded return), offers an alternative to simple percentage returns, especially when analyzing longer-term investments or volatile assets:

$$\text{Log Return} = \ln\left(\frac{\text{Terminal Value}}{\text{Initial Value}}\right)$$

Log returns are additive over time, which simplifies calculations for returns that involve multiple periods. To see this, let us define the single-period log return at time period t as

$$r_t = \ln\left(\frac{S_t}{S_{t-1}}\right)$$

and for multiple periods, the cumulative log return is

$$r_{\text{total}} = \ln\left(\frac{S_n}{S_0}\right)$$

Using the property of logarithms, we have the following:

$$r_{\text{total}} = \ln\left(\frac{S_n}{S_{n-1}} \cdot \frac{S_{n-1}}{S_{n-2}} \cdots \frac{S_2}{S_1} \cdot \frac{S_1}{S_0}\right)$$

which simplifies to

$$r_{\text{total}} = r_1 + r_2 + \cdots + r_n$$

Hence, log returns are additive over time, while simple returns require compounding. We can convert the cumulative log return back to a simple return via the following:

$$R_{\text{total}} = e^{r_{\text{total}}} - 1$$

2.4.4 Total Return vs. Price Return

The price return measures only the change in the price of an asset, while the total return incorporates both price changes and any cash flows, like dividends or interest, received during the holding period. By comparison of the two, the total return is a more comprehensive measure of performance, as it includes all components of investment income.

For a stock that pays dividends, the total return would be

$$\text{Total Return} = \frac{\text{Terminal Value} + \text{Dividends Received} - \text{Initial Value}}{\text{Initial Value}}$$

2.4.5 Annualized Returns

One practical challenge when comparing different investments is the different holding periods. For example, comparing the return on a stock held for three months to the return on a bond held for a full year would be difficult without holding them on the same investment horizon. To make returns comparable, we often convert them to an annualized return, which shows the equivalent yearly return as if the investment had grown at a steady rate for a full year.

To annualize a single-period return, we typically employ compounding, the principle that each period's earnings are reinvested to generate additional returns in subsequent periods. At the start, the initial principal is multiplied by $(1 + R)$ to include both the original amount and the gain for that period. If multiple periods follow, this multiplication is repeated each time, so after n periods, the total growth factor becomes $(1 + R)^n$, which gives an exponential growth.

We can use the following formula to calculate the annualized return for an investment period that is within one year:

$$\text{Annualized Return} = (1 + \text{Single Period Return})^{\text{Number of Periods per Year}} - 1$$

For example, if the monthly return is 1%, the annualized return would be $(1 + 0.01)^{12} - 1 = 12.68\%$. The difference from simply multiplying 1% by 12 is due to the effect of compounding.

When an investment is held over multiple years, we use the geometric mean to find the average annual return and compound it to obtain the final value:

$$\text{Annualized Return} = \left(\frac{\text{Terminal Value}}{\text{Initial Value}}\right)^{\frac{1}{\text{Number of Years}}} - 1$$

For example, if an investment grows from $1,000 to $2,000 over five years, the annualized return is

$$\left(\frac{2000}{1000}\right)^{\frac{1}{5}} - 1 = 14.87\%$$

2.4 Measuring Return

Now, if the return is calculated using a frequency that is different than yearly (such as monthly return) and lasts more than a year, we can still convert it into years by adjusting the exponent to account for the total number of years covered by the investment:

$$\text{Annualized Return} = \left(\frac{\text{Terminal Value}}{\text{Initial Value}}\right)^{\frac{12}{\text{Number of Months}}} - 1$$

For example, if an investment grew from \$1,000 to \$1,500 over 18 months, we can calculate the annualized return as $\left(\frac{1500}{1000}\right)^{\frac{12}{18}} - 1 = 1.5^{\frac{2}{3}} - 1 \approx 0.287$ or 28.7%.

2.4.6 Single-Period vs. Multi-Period Returns

When an investment covers more than one period, we need to account for how returns compound as time passes. Compounding does not mean we add up single-period returns; instead, since interest earned in the interim periods can also be revested, the net return from compounding will be slightly higher than the additive approach. That is, when returns compound, the return for each period is based on the value generated in the previous periods. This compounding determines the real growth (or decline) of an investment over multiple periods.

To calculate the multi-period return, we resort to the 1 + R formatted return, which is in contrast to the simple return R. Thus, to calculate the terminal return R_{0T} (in a simple return format), we can use

$$R_{0T} = (1 + R_{01})(1 + R_{12}) \cdots (1 + R_{T-1,T}) - 1$$

In this formula, we multiply all the single-period 1 + R formatted returns for each period, which essentially captures how returns build on each other. We then subtract 1 at the end to bring the result back into a simple return format.

Let's look at an example in which an investment experiences the following returns over three months: +5%, −2%, and +3%. To calculate the multi-period return, we multiply the individual period returns $R_{03} = (1 + 0.05) \times (1 - 0.02) \times (1 + 0.03) - 1 = 0.05954$ or 5.95%.

There is another quicker way to get the same result, which is using the terminal price and the initial price alone. Specifically, the cumulative return over multiple periods can also be calculated as

$$R_{0T} = \frac{S_T}{S_0} - 1$$

where S_0 is the initial price of the asset, and S_T is the price in the final period T. In the previous example, if we know the initial price and the final price, we can simply calculate $R_{03} = \frac{S_T}{S_0} - 1$. Both approaches give the same result, but compounding makes the step-by-step growth more visible.

2.5 Measuring Risk

So far, we have been discussing the risk of an asset and how it correlates with return. The risk is due to randomness in the outcome (terminal price of the asset), and thus uncertainty in the final result gives the risk. Generally, a more uncertain outcome corresponds to a higher risk, which means that the terminal return could be very high or low. This level of uncertainty is also known as the volatility of the asset. The higher the volatility, the more ups and downs we will see in the asset price curve.

To understand and quantify volatility in a more concrete way, we often use two core measures: variance and standard deviation. These are fundamental to how we measure risk in finance. Assume that we have the simple return R_i on an asset over multiple periods, where $i = 1, 2, \ldots, T$. The mean return can be calculated as

$$R_P = \frac{\sum_{i=1}^{T} R_i}{T}$$

This mean return R_P gives us a sense of where the asset's returns generally sit, on average, over time. In practice, the returns fluctuate, sometimes above and sometimes below. Thus, we need to capture such deviations from the mean and get a sense of its volatility as an indicator of risk.

The first step to quantifying risk is to measure how much each return deviates from the mean. For each single-period return R_i, the deviation from the mean is $R_i - R_P$. Now, deviations can be positive (if a return is above the mean) or negative (if it is below), and simply summing them up could potentially cancel out the ups and downs. To avoid such a cancellation, we often square each deviation to make all the deviations positive.

$$\sigma_P^2 = \frac{\sum_{i=1}^{T} (R_i - R_P)^2}{T}$$

This gives us the variance σ_P^2, which says how spread out the returns are around the mean. The larger this number, the more the returns are deviating, and hence the riskier the asset. However, the unit of variance is the square of the returns, which makes it hard to interpret directly, so we could take an additional step to square-root the variance to obtain the standard deviation.

Specifically, to bring variance back to the same scale as the original returns, we can take the square root:

$$\sigma_P = \sqrt{\frac{\sum_{i=1}^{T} (R_i - R_P)^2}{T}}$$

2.5 Measuring Risk

This square root of the variance is known as the standard deviation, which is often just called volatility. Now we are back to the same units as the returns themselves, making it easier to understand and compare. Volatility essentially tells us how much we could expect the asset return to deviate from its average. The higher the volatility, the more erratic the asset's return, and thus the greater the risk involved. Therefore, volatility can be considered the standardized version of the spread of asset returns.

Note that squaring each deviation is more convenient mathematically than taking the absolute value of each single-period return. Squaring preserves the sign but makes all terms positive, just like taking the absolute value, but it also allows us to use powerful tools from calculus and algebra. For example, when minimizing or maximizing functions (such as variance), the squared deviations are differentiable, whereas absolute value functions are not smooth (they have a "kink" at zero), which makes mathematical analysis more difficult.

By squaring the deviations, we penalize larger deviations more heavily than smaller ones. This makes variance (and hence standard deviation) particularly sensitive to extreme values or outliers. In finance, large deviations from the mean are often of greater concern (i.e., higher risk), so squaring helps capture this idea that bigger deviations should have a disproportionately bigger impact on our risk measure.

In addition, many financial models assume that returns are normally distributed, which fits well with the properties of variance. The normal distribution has a natural relationship with variance and standard deviation, allowing us to easily calculate probabilities and make predictions about return behavior. The use of variance is aligned with these statistical properties, making it a natural fit for risk measurement in contexts where the normal distribution is a good approximation.

2.5.1 Annualization of Risk Measures

Variance and standard deviation give us a gauge of the level of risk for a particular asset. For example, if we look at two assets with the same average return but different volatilities, the one with the higher volatility is considered riskier because its returns deviate more widely from the mean. However, as with asset returns, when assessing the risk of an investment, it's important to compare assets on the same time scale. Risk metrics such as volatility also need to be annualized to make them comparable across different time periods.

The goal of annualizing volatility is thus to estimate what the risk of an asset would be on an annual basis, based on historically observed returns that last either shorter or longer than a full year. To do this, we can use the following formula:

$$\sigma_{P,T} = \sqrt{T} \cdot \sigma_P$$

where $\sigma_{P,T}$ is the annualized volatility, σ_P is the single-period volatility (daily, monthly, or quarterly), and T is the number of periods in a year (252 for trading days, 12 for months, or 4 for quarters). The key insight here is that volatility scales with the square root of time. This means that we can estimate the volatility for a full year simply by multiplying the square root of the number of periods in a year.

Notice that as the time period T increases, the annualized volatility $\sigma_{P,T}$ grows at a decreasing rate due to the square root operation. This means that doubling the number of periods does not double the annualized volatility; it only increases it by a factor of $\sqrt{2}$.

Correspondingly, the annualized variance $\sigma_{P,T}^2$ grows linearly with time:

$$\sigma_{P,T}^2 = T \cdot \sigma_P^2$$

Although volatility increases with $\sqrt{T}$, variance increases directly with T. This linear relationship with variance makes it straightforward to aggregate risk over multiple periods.

As an example, suppose that the standard deviation (volatility) of a stock's daily returns is 0.1%. To annualize this daily volatility, we can use the following formula:

$$\sigma_{P,T} = 0.001 \cdot \sqrt{252} \approx 0.0159 \text{ or } 1.59\%$$

This means that the annualized volatility would be around 1.59%, assuming 252 trading days in a year.

2.5.2 Difference in Volatility Calculated Using Daily vs. Monthly Data

When calculating stock volatility, the frequency of data (daily vs. monthly) significantly impacts the outcome. For example, daily volatility captures short-term fluctuations in the stock price. This means that it reflects all minor market movements, such as those caused by day-to-day news, investor sentiment, and market microstructure noise. Daily volatility is more sensitive to sudden spikes or drops in the stock price, providing a more granular view of risk. On the other hand, monthly volatility smooths out the day-to-day fluctuations by averaging them over the month. It primarily captures broader trends in the stock price rather than the small movements seen in daily data, which are already smoothed out when aggregating at a monthly level. Monthly volatility is, therefore, less reactive to short-term noise and is influenced by longer-term forces such as economic cycles or company fundamentals. Therefore, in general, daily volatility is higher than monthly volatility because it encompasses the fine details of price movements, while monthly volatility averages out these short-term variations.

Also, when it comes to compounding risk, different data granularity will lead to different results. When calculating volatility using daily returns, we get a compounded picture of risk because we are summing up many individual daily movements (up to 252 trading days in a year). Multiplying by $\sqrt{252}$ further amplifies the impact of these frequent price changes at a yearly level. However,

2.5 Measuring Risk

when using monthly returns, we have only 12 data points in a year. These monthly returns already aggregate the effects of the daily movements within each month. Thus, the annualization multiplier is $\sqrt{12}$, which is much smaller, reflecting less compounding of risk over the same period. Therefore, the volatility derived from daily data will tend to be higher because it captures the compounded effect of frequent price changes, whereas monthly data smooth out this noise.

Daily volatility also offers a more immediate reflection of market conditions. It is sensitive to short-term market shocks like corporate earnings announcements, geopolitical events, or unexpected macroeconomic data releases. This makes daily volatility a good measure for traders who are concerned with short-term risk and potential rapid market movement. It offers a more real-time gauge of risk. On the other hand, monthly volatility provides a more stable view of the risk of a stock, as it does not react as quickly to short-term market shocks. It is more appropriate for long-term investors who are less concerned with daily noise and more focused on general market trends and the company's fundamentals. Choosing which type of volatility to use thus depends on the investment horizon and frequency.

From a statistical estimation perspective, the more data points we have, the more reliable the statistical measures (such as mean and standard deviation) are likely to be. With daily data, we typically have 252 observations per year, compared to just 12 with monthly data. This larger sample size reduces the estimation errors, which leads to a more precise calculation of volatility. More data points mean that estimates are less sensitive to outliers or random noise. With monthly data, a single large return can significantly skew the volatility measure, while daily data spread such impacts across multiple observations.

For example, higher-frequency data often improve the modeling and forecasting of volatility. Many financial models, like GARCH (Generalized Autoregressive Conditional Heteroskedasticity), benefit from high-frequency data to predict volatility more accurately. With more data points, the model can better capture patterns, correlations, and the persistence of volatility over time, leading to more accurate risk forecasts.

It also allows for more effective detection of market anomalies. For example, in volatility clustering, periods of high volatility often follow each other. Daily data allows for the detection of such clusters quickly, while monthly data might obscure these patterns. In mean reversion or momentum, certain stocks exhibit short-term momentum or mean reversion, where prices either continue to move in the same direction or revert to a historical mean. These patterns are more easily detected and taken into account using daily data.

In summary, while monthly data provide a smoother, more aggregated view of stock volatility suitable for long-term trends, daily data offer more granularity, accuracy, and timeliness. This granularity allows better risk management and improved forecasting and is particularly valuable for those who need a real-time assessment of market risks or engage in short-term trading strategies. Therefore, higher-frequency data are generally preferred for calculating volatility and managing financial risks effectively.

2.6 Measuring Risk-Adjusted Return

Now that we have covered both asset return and risk, how can we combine them to obtain a unified view? This combination means merging the risk and return into a single number, which will make it easier to compare different assets on a risk-adjusted basis. In the following, we introduce three of the most widely used metrics: the Sharpe ratio, the Sortino ratio, and the Treynor ratio.

2.6.1 Sharpe Ratio

The Sharpe ratio is one of the most popular risk-adjusted performance metrics and is proposed by Sharpe (1966). It measures how much excess return an asset (or, more generally, a portfolio, if it is a single asset) generates per unit of risk taken. It is defined as

$$\text{Sharpe Ratio} = \frac{R_P - R_f}{\sigma_P}$$

where R_P denotes the average return of the portfolio, R_f is the risk-free rate (such as the return on a Treasury bond), and σ_P is the volatility of the portfolio returns.

The Sharpe ratio essentially tells us how much return is being earned per unit of risk. A higher Sharpe ratio indicates a better risk-adjusted return, suggesting that the investment is generating more return for each unit of risk taken. A Sharpe ratio above one is often considered acceptable or decent, while a Sharpe ratio above two is often deemed excellent. A negative return could also lead to a negative Sharpe ratio.

Let us look at an example of calculating the Sharpe ratio. Consider a portfolio with an annualized return of 5% and an annualized volatility of 20%, and another portfolio with an annualized return of 10% and an annualized volatility of 50%. Given a risk-free rate of 3%, the Sharpe ratios would be calculated as $\frac{0.05-0.03}{0.20} = 0.10$ and $\frac{0.10-0.03}{0.50} = 0.14$, respectively. Here, the second portfolio has a higher Sharpe ratio, making it more attractive on a risk-adjusted basis, even though it has a higher absolute volatility.

However, there is no differentiation between the upside risk and the downside risk in the overall volatility term in the Sharpe ratio. Since most of us are risk averse (taking $100 dollars away from us inflects more aversion than the joy brought by giving us $100), most would prefer to minimize the downside risk more. This leads to the following risk-adjusted return that focuses only on the risk below the target return.

2.6.2 Sortino Ratio

The Sortino ratio is a refinement of the Sharpe ratio that focuses only on downside risk (negative deviations from a target return), rather than overall volatility. This treatment allows us to focus only on the downside risk rather than the upside volatility. The Sortino ratio is defined as

$$\text{Sortino Ratio} = \frac{R_P - R_f}{\sigma_D}$$

where σ_D is the downside deviation (standard deviation of negative returns).

By focusing on returns that fall below a specified threshold (often the risk-free rate), the Sortino ratio does not penalize a portfolio for its upside volatility (positive returns). Thus, a higher Sortino ratio indicates that an investment generates higher returns per unit of downside risk. This means that either the excess return is high or the downside volatility is low. Therefore, the Sortino ratio is especially valuable for investors who are primarily concerned with avoiding losses, such as risk-averse individuals or those near retirement.

2.6.3 Treynor Ratio

The Treynor ratio is another measure of risk-adjusted return, similar to the Sharpe ratio but focusing on the systematic risk (market risk) instead of the total risk. As mentioned earlier, systematic risk is a major type of financial risk and impacts all assets in the market. Based on the Capital Asset Pricing Model (CAPM), it is measured by the beta of a portfolio β_M, which represents its sensitivity to the overall market. It is defined as

$$\text{Treynor Ratio} = \frac{R_P - R_f}{\beta_M}$$

Based on CAPM, β_M is defined as

$$\beta_M = \frac{\text{Cov}(R_P, R_M)}{\text{Var}(R_M)}$$

where the covariance term $\text{Cov}(R_P, R_M)$ measures the strength of comovement between the returns of the portfolio and the overall market. A high positive covariance indicates that portfolio returns generally move in the same direction as the market. $\text{Var}(R_M)$ measures the variance of the market returns.

The Treynor ratio essentially measures how much excess return is generated per unit of market risk. Unlike the Sharpe ratio, which uses total volatility σ_P in the denominator, the Treynor ratio considers only the portion of risk that cannot be diversified (since the market factor is a systematic risk). A higher Treynor ratio

Table 2-1 Comparison of Sharpe, Sortino, and Treynor ratios

Metric	Definition	When to Use
Sharpe ratio	$\dfrac{R_P - R_f}{\sigma_P}$	Use when you want to assess overall risk-adjusted performance, accounting for all sources of risk (both systematic and idiosyncratic).
Sortino ratio	$\dfrac{R_P - R_f}{\sigma_D}$	Use when you are more concerned with downside risk and want to avoid penalizing upside volatility. Ideal for conservative or risk-averse investors.
Treynor ratio	$\dfrac{R_P - R_f}{\beta_M}$	Use when focusing on the market (systematic) risk of a well-diversified portfolio, and you wish to assess performance relative to that systematic risk only.

implies a better risk-adjusted performance, relative to the market risk undertaken. Since it uses β_M, it is particularly relevant when evaluating portfolios against a benchmark index (e.g., the S&P 500). It is useful for comparing well-diversified portfolios.

Table 2-1 provides a summary of the different measures of risk-adjusted return and specific situations on when to use them.

The next section explores the use of these different performance measures in a portfolio optimization context.

2.6.4 Evaluating Performance Measures in Portfolio Optimization

In this section, we will assess these performance metrics in the context of different portfolio selection strategies, each set to optimize a particular performance metric. We will focus on three major US stocks as risky assets and apply various optimization strategies to maximize returns, minimize risk, and optimize risk-adjusted returns. This exercise allows us to better appreciate the roles of different performance metrics in optimization management.

2.6.4.1 Data Preparation

As shown in Listing 2-3, we start by importing the necessary libraries and downloading the necessary financial data for three major US stocks: Apple Inc. (AAPL), Microsoft Corporation (MSFT), and Amazon.com, Inc. (AMZN). We will also use the S&P 500 Index (SPY) as our market benchmark to calculate the Treynor ratio. For all assets, we retrieve five years of daily adjusted closing prices between 2019 and 2024. We also calculate daily and annualized returns and risk measures for the stocks. Note that the first row contains NaN values because there is no previous day to compare. Thus, we remove the first row using the dropna() function.

```
import numpy as np
import pandas as pd
import yfinance as yf
import matplotlib.pyplot as plt
from scipy.optimize import minimize

```

2.6 Measuring Risk-Adjusted Return

```python
# Define the tickers
tickers = ['AAPL', 'MSFT', 'AMZN', 'SPY']

# Fetch data from Yahoo Finance
data = yf.download(tickers, start='2019-01-01', end='2024-01-01')
    ['Adj Close']

# Calculate daily returns
returns = data.pct_change().dropna()
```
Listing 2-3 Downloading asset data

As shown in Listing 2-4, to make our metrics comparable on a yearly basis, we will annualize the daily returns and risk measures. For simplicity, we will multiply the average daily return by 252 to convert to an annualized scale (and similarly for annualized volatility), assuming independence and stationarity of returns. Note that such arithmetic scaling does not take into account the effect of compounding, and the geometric mean is often used when dealing with real-world financial returns.

```python
# Define the number of trading days in a year
trading_days = 252

# Calculate annualized mean returns
annual_returns = returns.mean() * trading_days

# Calculate annualized volatility (standard deviation)
annual_volatility = returns.std() * np.sqrt(trading_days)

# Display the annualized returns and volatility
print("Annualized Returns:\n", annual_returns)
print("\nAnnualized Volatility:\n", annual_volatility)

# Output
Annualized Returns:
 Ticker
AAPL    0.378031
AMZN    0.198360
MSFT    0.320295
SPY     0.167224
dtype: float64

Annualized Volatility:
 Ticker
AAPL    0.322345
AMZN    0.352214
MSFT    0.304909
SPY     0.209957
dtype: float64
```
Listing 2-4 Downloading asset data

2.6.4.2 Defining the Portfolios
We'll evaluate five different portfolios based on the following criteria:

- Maximizing Portfolio Return
- Minimizing Portfolio Risk
- Maximizing Sharpe Ratio
- Maximizing Sortino Ratio
- Maximizing Treynor Ratio

We assume a risk-free rate of 3% when calculating the Sharpe ratio and the Sortino ratio.

In addition, to calculate the Treynor ratio, we also need the beta of each stock relative to the market (S&P 500 in this case). As discussed, beta measures the volatility of a stock relative to the market portfolio. See Listing 2-5 for detailed processing.

```
risk_free_rate = 0.03

# Calculate covariance matrix
cov_matrix = returns.cov() * trading_days

# Calculate market variance
market_variance = returns['SPY'].var() * trading_days

# Calculate beta for each stock
betas = cov_matrix.loc[['AAPL', 'AMZN', 'MSFT'], 'SPY'] / 
    market_variance

print("Betas:\n", betas)

# Output
Betas:
 Ticker
AAPL    1.235198
AMZN    1.087888
MSFT    1.197498
Name: SPY, dtype: float64
```

Listing 2-5 Calculating asset betas

Note that in the code above, we have used the *.var()* function to calculate the sample variance, which assumes a default setting of *ddof=1* in the input arguments. Given limited data, it is more often to calculate sample variance as a better (consistent) approximation to the theoretical population variance, if we were to be able to access all the data available.

As shown in Listing 2-6, for all portfolios, we also enforce the following common constraints:

- **Fully Invested:** The sum of all portfolio weights is equal to 1. This is also referred to as the budget constraint, in that all available capital should be allocated among the assets in the portfolio and should not be kept in the pocket.
- **No Short Selling:** All weights are between 0 and 1. This is often an optional constraint to reflect the fact that, in some markets such as China, shorting is not allowed.

2.6 Measuring Risk-Adjusted Return

```python
# Number of assets
num_assets = len(tickers) - 1

# Initial guess for weights
init_guess = num_assets * [1. / num_assets]

# Bounds for weights: no short selling
bounds = tuple((0, 1) for _ in range(num_assets))

# Constraint: sum of weights is 1
constraints = ({'type': 'eq', 'fun': lambda x: np.sum(x) - 1})
```

Listing 2-6 Defining portfolio constraints

We will also define different objective functions for each portfolio optimization criterion. For the first portfolio that aims at maximizing return, we can convert it to a minimization problem (a common practice in optimization) by minimizing the negative of the portfolio's expected return.

```python
def portfolio_return(weights, mean_returns):
    return np.dot(weights, mean_returns)

def neg_portfolio_return(weights, mean_returns):
    return -portfolio_return(weights, mean_returns)
```

Listing 2-7 Defining optimization objective for portfolio 1

For the second portfolio, our aim is to minimize the portfolio's variance.

```python
def portfolio_variance(weights, cov_matrix):
    return np.dot(weights.T, np.dot(cov_matrix, weights))
```

Listing 2-8 Defining optimization objective for portfolio 2

For the third portfolio that aims at maximizing the portfolio Sharpe ratio, we define a function that calculates the portfolio excess return over the risk-free interest rate (the numerator of the Sharpe ratio) and the portfolio volatility (the denominator of Sharpe ratio).

```python
def sharpe_ratio(weights, mean_returns, cov_matrix,
    risk_free_rate):
    p_return = portfolio_return(weights, mean_returns)
    p_variance = portfolio_variance(weights, cov_matrix)
    p_volatility = np.sqrt(p_variance)
    return (p_return - risk_free_rate) / p_volatility

def neg_sharpe_ratio(weights, mean_returns, cov_matrix,
    risk_free_rate):
    return -sharpe_ratio(weights, mean_returns, cov_matrix,
    risk_free_rate)
```

Listing 2-9 Defining optimization objective for portfolio 3

The fourth portfolio aims to maximize the Sortino ratio, which focuses on downside risk instead of total volatility. Note that the target return can be set to the risk-free rate or any desired threshold.

```python
def sortino_ratio(weights, returns, risk_free_rate, target_return
    =0):
    portfolio_returns = returns[['AAPL', 'MSFT', 'AMZN']].dot(
    weights)
    downside = portfolio_returns[portfolio_returns <
    target_return]
    expected_return = portfolio_returns.mean() * trading_days
    downside_deviation = np.sqrt((np.square(downside -
    target_return)).mean()) * np.sqrt(trading_days)
    return (expected_return - risk_free_rate) /
    downside_deviation

def neg_sortino_ratio(weights, returns, risk_free_rate,
    target_return=0):
    return -sortino_ratio(weights, returns, risk_free_rate,
    target_return)
```

Listing 2-10 Defining optimization objective for portfolio 4

Finally, the last portfolio aims at maximizing the Treynor ratio, which measures excess return per unit of systematic risk (the beta).

```python
def treynor_ratio(weights, mean_returns, betas, risk_free_rate):
    p_return = portfolio_return(weights, mean_returns)
    p_beta = np.dot(weights, betas)
    return (p_return - risk_free_rate) / p_beta

def neg_treynor_ratio(weights, mean_returns, betas,
    risk_free_rate):
    return -treynor_ratio(weights, mean_returns, betas,
    risk_free_rate)
```

Listing 2-11 Defining optimization objective for portfolio 5

2.6.4.3 Optimizing the Portfolios

Now that we've defined our objective functions and constraints, let us perform the optimizations for each portfolio, starting with the first portfolio that maximizes return.

```python
# Optimize Portfolio 1: Maximizing Return
def optimize_max_return(mean_returns, constraints, bounds,
    init_guess):
    result = minimize(neg_portfolio_return, init_guess, args=(
    mean_returns,),
                      method='SLSQP', bounds=bounds, constraints=
    constraints)
    return result

result_max_return = optimize_max_return(annual_returns[['AAPL', '
    AMZN', 'MSFT']], constraints, bounds, init_guess)

print("Portfolio 1: Maximizing Return")
print("Weights:", result_max_return.x)
```

2.6 Measuring Risk-Adjusted Return

```
print("Expected Annual Return:", portfolio_return(
    result_max_return.x, annual_returns[['AAPL', 'AMZN', 'MSFT'
    ]]))
print("Annual Volatility:", np.sqrt(portfolio_variance(
    result_max_return.x, cov_matrix.loc[['AAPL', 'AMZN', 'MSFT'],
    ['AAPL', 'AMZN', 'MSFT']])))
print("\n")

# Output
Portfolio 1: Maximizing Return
Weights: [1.00000000e+00 6.31439345e-16 0.00000000e+00]
Expected Annual Return: 0.37803071152250534
Annual Volatility: 0.3223453947637612
```

Listing 2-12 Optimizing portfolio 1

The optimal allocation result is not surprising. Since Apple has the highest annualized return, the maximum return portfolio will allocate all weight to this asset.

Now, let us turn to portfolio 2 that minimizes risk.

```
# Optimize Portfolio 2: Minimizing Risk
def optimize_min_risk(cov_matrix, constraints, bounds, init_guess
    ):
    result = minimize(portfolio_variance, init_guess, args=(
    cov_matrix,),
                      method='SLSQP', bounds=bounds, constraints=
    constraints)
    return result

result_min_risk = optimize_min_risk(cov_matrix.loc[['AAPL', 'AMZN
    ', 'MSFT'], ['AAPL', 'AMZN', 'MSFT']], constraints, bounds,
    init_guess)

print("Portfolio 2: Minimizing Risk")
print("Weights:", result_min_risk.x)
print("Expected Annual Return:", portfolio_return(result_min_risk
    .x, annual_returns[['AAPL', 'AMZN', 'MSFT']]))
print("Annual Volatility:", np.sqrt(portfolio_variance(
    result_min_risk.x, cov_matrix.loc[['AAPL', 'AMZN', 'MSFT'], [
    'AAPL', 'AMZN', 'MSFT']])))
print("\n")

# Output
Portfolio 2: Minimizing Risk
Weights: [0.3180772 0.2094853 0.4724375]
Expected Annual Return: 0.313115822392309
Annual Volatility: 0.288101952001344
```

Listing 2-13 Optimizing portfolio 2

Now, each individual weight allocation is closer to each other, with MSFT getting close to half of the total allocation, possibly due to the lowest volatility out of the three stocks.

As shown in Listing 2-14, now we turn to portfolio 3 that maximizes the Sharpe ratio.

```python
# Optimize Portfolio 3: Maximizing Sharpe Ratio
def optimize_max_sharpe(mean_returns, cov_matrix, risk_free_rate,
    constraints, bounds, init_guess):
    result = minimize(neg_sharpe_ratio, init_guess, args=(
    mean_returns, cov_matrix, risk_free_rate),
                      method='SLSQP', bounds=bounds, constraints=
    constraints)
    return result

result_max_sharpe = optimize_max_sharpe(annual_returns[['AAPL', '
    AMZN', 'MSFT']],
                                        cov_matrix.loc[['AAPL', '
    AMZN', 'MSFT'], ['AAPL', 'AMZN', 'MSFT']],
                                        risk_free_rate,
    constraints, bounds, init_guess)

print("Portfolio 3: Maximizing Sharpe Ratio")
print("Weights:", result_max_sharpe.x)
print("Expected Annual Return:", portfolio_return(
    result_max_sharpe.x, annual_returns[['AAPL', 'AMZN', 'MSFT'
    ]]))
print("Annual Volatility:", np.sqrt(portfolio_variance(
    result_max_sharpe.x, cov_matrix.loc[['AAPL', 'AMZN', 'MSFT'],
    ['AAPL', 'AMZN', 'MSFT']])))
print("Sharpe Ratio:", sharpe_ratio(result_max_sharpe.x,
    annual_returns[['AAPL', 'AMZN', 'MSFT']],
                                     cov_matrix.loc[['AAPL', 'AMZN'
    , 'MSFT'], ['AAPL', 'AMZN', 'MSFT']], risk_free_rate))
print("\n")

# Output
Portfolio 3: Maximizing Sharpe Ratio
Weights: [7.17495581e-01 5.81132364e-17 2.82504419e-01]
Expected Annual Return: 0.3617201069615052
Annual Volatility: 0.3018898876667841
Sharpe Ratio: 1.0988115883088032
```

Listing 2-14 Optimizing portfolio 3

Indeed, the third portfolio gives the highest Sharpe ratio out of the three portfolios analyzed so far (whose Sharpe ratios are 1.079 for the first portfolio and 0.982 for the second portfolio).

Now we turn to portfolio 4 that maximizes the Sortino ratio. We also set the target return to zero in Listing 2-15.

```python
# Optimize Portfolio 4: Maximizing Sortino Ratio
def optimize_max_sortino(weights, returns, risk_free_rate,
    constraints, bounds, init_guess, target_return=0):
    return minimize(neg_sortino_ratio, init_guess, args=(returns,
     risk_free_rate, target_return),
                    method='SLSQP', bounds=bounds, constraints=
    constraints)
```

2.6 Measuring Risk-Adjusted Return

```python
result_max_sortino = optimize_max_sortino(init_guess, returns,
    risk_free_rate, constraints, bounds, init_guess)

# Extract weights from optimization result
weights_sortino = result_max_sortino.x

# Calculate expected return and downside deviation
expected_return_sortino = portfolio_return(weights_sortino,
    annual_returns[['AAPL', 'AMZN', 'MSFT']])
portfolio_returns_sortino = returns[['AAPL', 'MSFT', 'AMZN']].dot
    (weights_sortino)
downside_sortino = portfolio_returns_sortino[
    portfolio_returns_sortino < 0]
downside_deviation_sortino = np.sqrt((np.square(downside_sortino)
    ).mean()) * np.sqrt(trading_days)
sortino = (expected_return_sortino - risk_free_rate) /
    downside_deviation_sortino

print("Portfolio 4: Maximizing Sortino Ratio")
print("Weights:", weights_sortino)
print("Expected Annual Return:", expected_return_sortino)
print("Downside Deviation:", downside_deviation_sortino)
print("Sortino Ratio:", sortino)
print("\n")

# Output
Portfolio 4: Maximizing Sortino Ratio
Weights: [7.51230682e-01 2.48769318e-01 4.48859699e-18]
Expected Annual Return: 0.3333341715302924
Downside Deviation: 0.30636490028556385
Sortino Ratio: 0.9901074543707634
```

Listing 2-15 Optimizing portfolio 4

Finally, we optimize the fifth portfolio by maximizing the Treynor ratio as shown in Listing 2-16.

```python
# Optimize Portfolio 5: Maximizing Treynor Ratio
def optimize_max_treynor(mean_returns, betas, risk_free_rate,
    constraints, bounds, init_guess):
    result = minimize(neg_treynor_ratio, init_guess, args=(
    mean_returns, betas, risk_free_rate),
                      method='SLSQP', bounds=bounds, constraints=
    constraints)
    return result

result_max_treynor = optimize_max_treynor(annual_returns[['AAPL',
    'AMZN', 'MSFT']],
                                          betas[['AAPL', 'AMZN', '
    MSFT']],
                                          risk_free_rate,
    constraints, bounds, init_guess)

print("Portfolio 5: Maximizing Treynor Ratio")
print("Weights:", result_max_treynor.x)
```

```python
print("Expected Annual Return:", portfolio_return(
    result_max_treynor.x, annual_returns[['AAPL', 'AMZN', 'MSFT'
    ]]))
print("Beta:", np.dot(result_max_treynor.x, betas[['AAPL', 'AMZN'
    , 'MSFT']]))
print("Treynor Ratio:", treynor_ratio(result_max_treynor.x,
    annual_returns[['AAPL', 'AMZN', 'MSFT']], betas[['AAPL', '
    AMZN', 'MSFT']], risk_free_rate))
print("\n")

# Output
Portfolio 5: Maximizing Treynor Ratio
Weights: [1.00000000e+00 0.00000000e+00 3.88578059e-16]
Expected Annual Return: 0.3780307115225055
Beta: 1.2351976772098658
Treynor Ratio: 0.2817611447494436
```

Listing 2-16 Optimizing portfolio 5

Let us summarize the optimized portfolios' weights, expected returns, volatility, and risk-adjusted ratios.

```python
################################################################
# Additional code snippet for generating the final summary table
################################################################

# 1) Helper to compute the same Sortino ratio
#    but directly from daily returns (annually scaled).
def compute_annual_sortino_ratio(weights, daily_returns, rf=0.03,
    target_return=0.0):
    """
    Computes the annualized Sortino ratio for a given portfolio (
    weights) and daily returns.
    The logic here mirrors the approach in 'sortino_ratio()', but
     uses daily returns
    and scales to annual figures, ensuring consistency with your
    optimization code.
    """
    # 1) Construct daily portfolio returns from the chosen assets
    pf_daily_returns = daily_returns[['AAPL', 'MSFT', 'AMZN']].
    dot(weights)

    # 2) Annualized portfolio return = mean(daily) * 252
    pf_annual_return = pf_daily_returns.mean() * 252

    # 3) Extract returns below the target threshold
    negative_returns = pf_daily_returns[pf_daily_returns <
    target_return]
    if len(negative_returns) == 0:
        # Means no negative returns at all -> "infinite" Sortino
        return np.nan

    # 4) Annualize the downside deviation
```

2.6 Measuring Risk-Adjusted Return

```python
    #       (mean of squared deviations) -> multiply by #days ->
    sqrt
    downside_var = np.mean((negative_returns - target_return)**2)
    downside_dev_annual = np.sqrt(downside_var * 252)
    if downside_dev_annual == 0:
        return float('inf')

    # 5) Compute the actual Sortino ratio
    sortino_ratio_val = (pf_annual_return - rf) /
    downside_dev_annual
    return sortino_ratio_val

# 2) Define the summary table as a dictionary with performance
  metrics for each portfolio
portfolios = {
    'Max Return': {
        'Weights': result_max_return.x,
        'Return': portfolio_return(result_max_return.x,
    annual_returns[['AAPL', 'AMZN', 'MSFT']]),
        'Volatility': np.sqrt(portfolio_variance(
    result_max_return.x, cov_matrix.loc[['AAPL', 'AMZN', 'MSFT'],
    ['AAPL', 'AMZN', 'MSFT']])),
        'Beta': np.dot(result_max_return.x, betas[['AAPL', 'AMZN'
    , 'MSFT']].values.flatten()),
        'Downside Deviation': downside_deviation_sortino,  #
    Replace with actual downside deviation calc
        'Sharpe Ratio': (portfolio_return(result_max_return.x,
    annual_returns[['AAPL', 'AMZN', 'MSFT']]) - risk_free_rate) /
     np.sqrt(portfolio_variance(result_max_return.x, cov_matrix.
    loc[['AAPL', 'AMZN', 'MSFT'], ['AAPL', 'AMZN', 'MSFT']])),
        'Sortino Ratio': (portfolio_return(result_max_return.x,
    annual_returns[['AAPL', 'AMZN', 'MSFT']]) - risk_free_rate) /
     downside_deviation_sortino,  # Replace with actual
    calculation
        'Treynor Ratio': treynor_ratio(result_max_return.x,
    annual_returns[['AAPL', 'AMZN', 'MSFT']], betas[['AAPL', '
    AMZN', 'MSFT']].values.flatten(), risk_free_rate)
    },
    'Min Risk': {
        'Weights': result_min_risk.x,
        'Return': portfolio_return(result_min_risk.x,
    annual_returns[['AAPL', 'AMZN', 'MSFT']]),
        'Volatility': np.sqrt(portfolio_variance(result_min_risk.
    x, cov_matrix.loc[['AAPL', 'AMZN', 'MSFT'], ['AAPL', 'AMZN',
    'MSFT']])),
        'Beta': np.dot(result_min_risk.x, betas[['AAPL', 'AMZN',
    'MSFT']].values.flatten()),
        'Downside Deviation': downside_deviation_sortino,  #
    Replace with actual downside deviation calc
        'Sharpe Ratio': (portfolio_return(result_min_risk.x,
    annual_returns[['AAPL', 'AMZN', 'MSFT']]) - risk_free_rate) /
     np.sqrt(portfolio_variance(result_min_risk.x, cov_matrix.loc
    [['AAPL', 'AMZN', 'MSFT'], ['AAPL', 'AMZN', 'MSFT']])),
```

```python
        'Sortino Ratio': (portfolio_return(result_min_risk.x,
annual_returns[['AAPL', 'AMZN', 'MSFT']]) - risk_free_rate) /
 downside_deviation_sortino,  # Replace with actual
calculation
        'Treynor Ratio': treynor_ratio(result_min_risk.x,
annual_returns[['AAPL', 'AMZN', 'MSFT']], betas[['AAPL', '
AMZN', 'MSFT']].values.flatten(), risk_free_rate)
    },
    'Max Sharpe': {
        'Weights': result_max_sharpe.x,
        'Return': portfolio_return(result_max_sharpe.x,
annual_returns[['AAPL', 'AMZN', 'MSFT']]),
        'Volatility': np.sqrt(portfolio_variance(
result_max_sharpe.x, cov_matrix.loc[['AAPL', 'AMZN', 'MSFT'],
 ['AAPL', 'AMZN', 'MSFT']])),
        'Beta': np.dot(result_max_sharpe.x, betas[['AAPL', 'AMZN'
, 'MSFT']].values.flatten()),
        'Downside Deviation': downside_deviation_sortino,  #
Replace with actual downside deviation calc
        'Sharpe Ratio': sharpe_ratio(result_max_sharpe.x,
annual_returns[['AAPL', 'AMZN', 'MSFT']],
                                    cov_matrix.loc[['AAPL', '
AMZN', 'MSFT'], ['AAPL', 'AMZN', 'MSFT']], risk_free_rate),
        'Sortino Ratio': (portfolio_return(result_max_sharpe.x,
annual_returns[['AAPL', 'AMZN', 'MSFT']]) - risk_free_rate) /
 downside_deviation_sortino,  # Replace with actual
calculation
        'Treynor Ratio': treynor_ratio(result_max_sharpe.x,
annual_returns[['AAPL', 'AMZN', 'MSFT']], betas[['AAPL', '
AMZN', 'MSFT']].values.flatten(), risk_free_rate)
    },
    'Max Sortino': {
        'Weights': weights_sortino,
        'Return': expected_return_sortino,
        'Downside Deviation': downside_deviation_sortino,
        'Sortino Ratio': sortino
    },
    'Max Treynor': {
        'Weights': result_max_treynor.x,
        'Return': portfolio_return(result_max_treynor.x,
annual_returns[['AAPL', 'AMZN', 'MSFT']]),
        'Beta': np.dot(result_max_treynor.x, betas[['AAPL', 'AMZN
', 'MSFT']].values.flatten()),
        'Treynor Ratio': treynor_ratio(result_max_treynor.x,
annual_returns[['AAPL', 'AMZN', 'MSFT']], betas[['AAPL', '
AMZN', 'MSFT']].values.flatten(), risk_free_rate)
    }
}

# 3) Populate missing metrics for each portfolio in the summary
for pf in portfolios:
    w = portfolios[pf]['Weights']
    p_ret = portfolios[pf]['Return']
```

2.6 Measuring Risk-Adjusted Return

```python
    # -- If needed, compute portfolio volatility
    if 'Volatility' not in portfolios[pf]:
        portfolios[pf]['Volatility'] = np.sqrt(
            portfolio_variance(
                w,
                cov_matrix.loc[['AAPL','AMZN','MSFT'], ['AAPL','AMZN','MSFT']]
            )
        )

    # -- Compute Sharpe Ratio (if you want it in the summary)
    if portfolios[pf]['Volatility'] != 0:
        portfolios[pf]['Sharpe Ratio'] = (
            (p_ret - risk_free_rate) / portfolios[pf]['Volatility']
        )
    else:
        portfolios[pf]['Sharpe Ratio'] = np.nan

    # -- Compute the annualized Sortino Ratio (using the new helper)
    sortino_val = compute_annual_sortino_ratio(
        w,              # weights
        returns,        # daily returns DataFrame
        rf=risk_free_rate,
        target_return=0.0   # or set to risk_free_rate if you prefer
    )
    portfolios[pf]['Sortino Ratio'] = sortino_val

    # -- Optionally store the raw Downside Deviation if you'd like
    #    (just for the summary display)
    pf_daily_returns = returns[['AAPL','MSFT','AMZN']].dot(w)
    negative_rets = pf_daily_returns[pf_daily_returns < 0]
    if len(negative_rets) == 0:
        dd_annual = 0.0
    else:
        dd_annual = np.sqrt(np.mean((negative_rets - 0.0)**2) * 252)
    portfolios[pf]['Downside Deviation'] = dd_annual

    # -- Compute Treynor Ratio if Beta is known
    if 'Beta' in portfolios[pf]:
        b = portfolios[pf]['Beta']
        if b != 0:
            portfolios[pf]['Treynor Ratio'] = (p_ret - risk_free_rate) / b
        else:
            portfolios[pf]['Treynor Ratio'] = np.nan
    else:
        portfolios[pf]['Treynor Ratio'] = np.nan
```

```
# 4) Convert the dictionary to a DataFrame and format
summary = pd.DataFrame(portfolios).T

# Round & format columns
summary['Weights'] = summary['Weights'].apply(lambda arr: [round(
    x, 2) for x in arr])
summary['Return'] = summary['Return'].round(4)
summary['Volatility'] = pd.to_numeric(summary.get('Volatility',
    pd.Series()), errors='coerce').round(4)
summary['Beta'] = pd.to_numeric(summary.get('Beta', pd.Series()),
    errors='coerce').round(4)
summary['Downside Deviation'] = pd.to_numeric(summary.get('
    Downside Deviation', pd.Series()), errors='coerce').round(4)
summary['Sharpe Ratio'] = pd.to_numeric(summary.get('Sharpe Ratio
    ', pd.Series()), errors='coerce').round(4)
summary['Sortino Ratio'] = pd.to_numeric(summary.get('Sortino
    Ratio', pd.Series()), errors='coerce').round(4)
summary['Treynor Ratio'] = pd.to_numeric(summary.get('Treynor
    Ratio', pd.Series()), errors='coerce').round(4)

pd.set_option('display.max_columns', None)
pd.set_option('display.width', 1000)

# Finally, display the summary table
summary
```

Listing 2-17 Analyzing portfolio results

Running the code generates Figure 2-4. The result suggests that the Max Return portfolio and the Max Treynor ratio portfolio achieve the highest return, but also have high volatility and market sensitivity, leading to moderate Sharpe and Treynor ratios. The Min Risk portfolio is more diversified with the lowest volatility, but has lower returns and risk-adjusted performance, making it suitable for conservative investors. The Max Sharpe portfolio balances return and risk efficiently, achieving a high Sharpe ratio and suggesting an optimal risk-adjusted return. The Max Sortino portfolio, with its emphasis on downside risk, yields a maximum Sortino ratio and moderate return. Finally, the Max Treynor portfolio, identical to Max Return in weights, offers a strong Treynor ratio, excelling in return per unit of market risk.

	Weights	Return	Volatility	Beta	Downside Deviation	Sharpe Ratio	Sortino Ratio	Treynor Ratio
Max Return	[1.0, 0.0, 0.0]	0.378031	0.3223	1.2352	0.3210	1.0797	1.0842	0.2818
Min Risk	[0.32, 0.21, 0.47]	0.313116	0.2881	1.1865	0.3059	0.9827	0.8207	0.2386
Max Sharpe	[0.72, 0.0, 0.28]	0.36172	0.3019	1.2245	0.3057	1.0988	0.9725	0.2709
Max Sortino	[0.75, 0.25, 0.0]	0.333334	0.3043	NaN	0.3064	0.9969	1.0891	NaN
Max Treynor	[1.0, 0.0, 0.0]	0.378031	0.3223	1.2352	0.3213	1.0797	1.0832	0.2818

Figure 2-4 Summary results of each portfolio

2.6 Measuring Risk-Adjusted Return

Finally, let us visualize the efficient frontier in the mean-variance space and plot our optimized portfolios. As shown in Listing 2-18, we generate 5,000 random portfolios (random set of weights) to visualize the efficient frontier, using a scatter plot to represent the trade-off between risk (volatility) and return. We also highlight the five optimized portfolios with different markers and colors.

```python
# Function to calculate portfolio performance
def portfolio_performance(weights, mean_returns, cov_matrix):
    returns = np.dot(weights, mean_returns)
    volatility = np.sqrt(np.dot(weights.T, np.dot(cov_matrix,
        weights)))
    return returns, volatility

# Generate random portfolios
num_portfolios = 5000
results = np.zeros((3, num_portfolios))
weight_records = []

for i in range(num_portfolios):
    weights = np.random.dirichlet(np.ones(num_assets), size=1)[0]
    weight_records.append(weights)
    portfolio_ret, portfolio_vol = portfolio_performance(weights,
         annual_returns[['AAPL', 'AMZN', 'MSFT']], cov_matrix.loc[['
        AAPL', 'AMZN', 'MSFT'], ['AAPL', 'AMZN', 'MSFT']])
    results[0,i] = portfolio_vol
    results[1,i] = portfolio_ret
    results[2,i] = (portfolio_ret - risk_free_rate) /
        portfolio_vol

# Convert results to DataFrame
results_df = pd.DataFrame(results.T, columns=['Volatility', '
    Return', 'Sharpe Ratio'])

# Plot the efficient frontier
plt.figure(figsize=(10, 7))
plt.scatter(results_df.Volatility, results_df.Return, c=
    results_df['Sharpe Ratio'], cmap='viridis', alpha=0.5)
plt.colorbar(label='Sharpe Ratio')
plt.xlabel('Annualized Volatility')
plt.ylabel('Annualized Return')
plt.title('Efficient Frontier')

# Plot optimized portfolios
portfolios_to_plot = {
    'Max Return': result_max_return.x,
    'Min Risk': result_min_risk.x,
    'Max Sharpe': result_max_sharpe.x,
    'Max Sortino': weights_sortino,
    'Max Treynor': result_max_treynor.x
}

colors = ['r', 'b', 'g', 'c', 'm']
```

```
41  for (name, weights), color in zip(portfolios_to_plot.items(),
        colors):
42      p_ret, p_vol = portfolio_performance(weights, annual_returns
        [['AAPL', 'AMZN', 'MSFT']], cov_matrix.loc[['AAPL', 'AMZN', '
        MSFT'], ['AAPL', 'AMZN', 'MSFT']])
43      plt.scatter(p_vol, p_ret, marker='*', color=color, s=200,
        label=name)
44
45  plt.legend()
46  plt.show()
```

Listing 2-18 Optimizing portfolio 4

Running the code generates Figure 2-5, where all portfolios with the Max Sortino portfolio are on the efficient frontier, by definition. Each point on the graph is a portfolio, and those lying along the upper boundary are called efficient, in the sense that they have the highest return for a given risk or the lowest risk for a given return. Portfolios whose return lies below risk-free rate are considered inferior and thus not optimal; thus, the actual efficient frontier is only cut to the top half.

In addition, we also observe how optimal asset weights shift in response to changes in key inputs such as expected returns, risk (volatility), and correlations. Correctly estimating these parameters thus greatly impacts the quality of the resulting solutions (portfolio weights), and it is important to perform such a

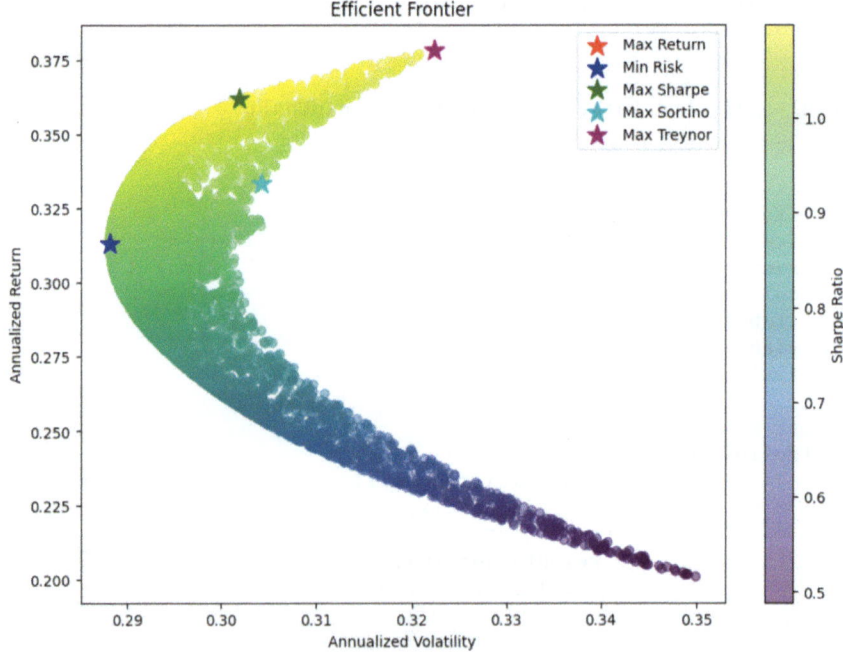

Figure 2-5 Efficient frontier with the five portfolios

sensitivity analysis on the impact of model misspecification. Such an analysis helps identify which assets are most sensitive to estimation errors, in the sense that a small change in the estimated parameter leads to a large change in the corresponding allocation weight.

2.7 Summary

In this chapter, we reviewed different approaches in the definition and calculation of risk and return, two fundamental concepts in finance, and illustrated their use in constructing and managing portfolios effectively. Returns can arise from capital appreciation, dividends, and interest and are often annualized to standardize performance across time frames. Risk comes from the uncertainty of returns and can be quantified using performance metrics such as variance (or standard deviation) or other downside risk measures (we will cover more on this in a later chapter). The risk-return trade-off highlights that higher potential returns generally require accepting greater risk.

Measuring returns involves various forms, including absolute return, percentage return, and logarithmic return. The performance of investments is often evaluated on a risk-adjusted basis, using metrics such as the Sharpe ratio, which evaluates return per unit of total volatility; the Sortino ratio, which focuses only on downside risk; and the Treynor ratio, which assesses excess return per unit of market (systematic) risk. These metrics enable investors to compare the effectiveness with which different portfolios manage risk in pursuit of returns.

Portfolio optimization strategies can vary, focusing on maximizing return, minimizing risk, or maximizing risk-adjusted returns based on the above metrics. For instance, the Max Return portfolio aims for the highest return but carries higher volatility, while the Min Risk portfolio seeks to minimize volatility at the expense of some return. The Max Sharpe portfolio balances risk and return efficiently, delivering the best risk-adjusted return when accounting for total volatility. The Max Sortino portfolio is designed to minimize downside risk, while the Max Treynor portfolio optimizes returns relative to market risk. Understanding these metrics and optimization strategies helps to build portfolios that are aligned with specific risk tolerance and return objectives.

Managing Credit Risk 3

Credit risk is a primary source of concern for institutions engaged in the lending business. When the borrower does not honor the contractual obligation to pay back the interest or the principal, the lending institution will suffer financial loss. Thus, proper management of credit risk plays an important role in sustainable financial operations and stability in the lending industry, including banks and other financial institutions. It is also a primary concern for regulatory authorities. For example, during the 2008 financial crisis, the underestimation of credit risk in subprime mortgage lending was a major contributing factor. Consequently, many modern regulatory frameworks have been proposed and are still being revised to actively detect vulnerabilities before they escalate into crises.

Credit risk refers to the potential that a borrower (also referred to as a debtor) will fail to fulfill their obligation to repay the loan or satisfy other contractual debt terms (such as paying back interest), thus resulting in a financial loss for the lender (also called the creditor). This risk materializes when the borrower defaults by not making timely payments of principal or interest, such as paying back credit card spending or home mortgage. Credit card lending typically involves a higher credit risk because it is unsecured, which means that there is no collateral to support the loan. Thus, credit card issuers typically face challenges in recovering the borrowed amount when the borrower defaults.

However, home ownership loans generally present a lower credit risk because they are secured by the property being financed. In case the borrower defaults, the lender can recover some or all of their losses through the foreclosure process, where the property is seized and sold at the prevailing market price. Despite differences in risk levels, properly and accurately assessing a borrower's creditworthiness is an important first-stage screening task. Such an assessment often comes with two decision outcomes: a binary output that indicates whether the credit card (or home loan application) is approved or not and a continuous output that indicates the credit line (or home loan amount) that limits the maximum amount to be borrowed.

Such an assessment process often involves developing credit scoring models (also called scorecards), setting appropriate interest rates for the loan based on risk levels, or asking for additional support from collateral or guarantees to reduce the lender's exposure to potential losses. This risk-based pricing principle also applies to asset financing for firms that seek loans from banks.

Credit risk management is also a key consideration for the broader financial system. For example, the 2008 global financial crisis was the result of poor credit risk management that led to significant financial loss. Why did it occur? It turned out that many financial institutions were lending money to risky borrowers with a high probability of default, particularly through subprime mortgages (a type of home loan offered to individuals who have low credit scores or limited credit history). These unmanaged credit exposures then accumulated in the banking sector and other financial entities until they reached a financial meltdown. As borrowers defaulted on their loans, a cascade of losses was triggered, resulting in a global financial crisis. Thus, proper credit risk management for the entire financial system is crucial to ensure financial robustness and stability.

The credit risk management life cycle encompasses the end-to-end process of identifying, assessing, and managing the risk of borrower default. It begins with the origination, where the borrower's creditworthiness is evaluated (typically by a scorecard) and the loan is structured. After approval and disbursement, the credit exposure enters the monitoring phase, where the performance, financial health, and external risk factors of obligors are assessed on a regular basis, mostly yearly or even shorter. If signs of stress appear, mitigation strategies, such as restructuring or additional collateral, are used to reduce potential losses. In the event of default, a recovery process would be triggered, which aims to maximize asset realization and minimize credit exposure (more on this later). Throughout the life cycle, regular portfolio-level review and reporting would be performed to ensure that credit risk exposure remains aligned with the institution's appetite and regulatory requirements. See Figure 3-1 for an illustration of the full credit management life cycle.

Figure 3-1 Illustrating the full credit management life cycle. The last two components are drawn with dashed line since not all loans are going to default

This chapter introduces common quantitative measures for credit risk management, focusing on the fundamental components that underpin this field, including probability of default (PD), loss given default (LGD), and exposure at default (EAD). We will also explore how these elements converge to form the expected credit loss (ECL), a critical metric for gauging anticipated losses. Finally, we will implement a PD model that is used to predict the PD of individual obligors.

3.1 Expected and Unexpected Credit Loss

The expected credit loss, or ECL, refers to the anticipated financial loss that a lender (such as a bank or specialized lending institution) may incur due to a borrower's failure to meet their financial obligations, such as paying back the principal or interest. Unlike traditional loss estimation methods that predominantly rely on historical default data, ECL adopts a forward-looking perspective to predict future likely outcomes and sets the expected loss accordingly. It uses both historical performance and predictive indicators to forecast potential future losses, where both statistical and machine learning tools can be used. When future potential losses are forecast, with some degree of accuracy, institutions can take proactive measures to mitigate these risks, such as only selecting borrowers with low ECL. These forecasts can help optimize credit portfolios and thus improve overall financial stability. Furthermore, ECL plays a pivotal role in regulatory compliance frameworks, notably under International Financial Reporting Standards (IFRS 9) and the Current Expected Credit Loss (CECL) model in the United States, which mandate the recognition of expected losses over the entire life of a financial instrument. Similar regulations in Singapore are also in place and set by the Monetary Authority of Singapore.

ECL is systematically calculated by integrating three fundamental components: PD, LGD, and EAD. Each component captures a distinct facet of credit risk and is connected by the following equation:

$$ECL = PD \times LGD \times EAD$$

This equation characterizes the interaction between the likelihood of default, the severity of the loss on default, and the magnitude of exposure, providing a detailed view of the anticipated losses under normal economic conditions. The expected loss is the product of the probability of a loss event (default), the expected loss per event (LGD), and the size of the exposure at the time of the event (EAD). This multiplicative relationship ensures that the impact of each component is reflected proportionately in the overall expected loss. For example, even if the PD is low, a high LGD or EAD can result in a significant ECL. In practice, PD is often subject to greater scrutiny in financial institutions, as it serves as the initial gatekeeper for identifying and filtering potential high-quality customers.

Let us look at an example of how to calculate the ECL. To calculate the lifetime ECL for a two-year term loan under the assumptions of IFRS 9, consider a loan with a principal (EAD) of $500,000, an LGD of 50%, annual marginal PDs of 3% for the first year and 5% for the second year, and a constant discount rate of 5%.

First, note that the maximum possible loss in any default scenario is

$$\$500,000 \times 50\% = \$250,000.$$

In year 1, the probability of default is 3%, giving an undiscounted expected loss of

$$\$250,000 \times 0.03 = \$7,500.$$

For year 2, we incorporate survival from year 1 (97% survival) and then apply the 5% marginal PD, leading to a year 2 unconditional default probability of

$$0.97 \times 0.05 = 0.0485,$$

which yields an undiscounted expected loss of

$$\$250,000 \times 0.0485 = \$12,125.$$

Next, we discount these amounts to the present. The year 1 expected loss is discounted by one year at 5%, giving

$$\frac{\$7,500}{1.05} \approx \$7,142.86,$$

and the year 2 expected loss is discounted for two years, giving

$$\frac{\$12,125}{(1.05)^2} \approx \$10,999.55.$$

Summing these discounted figures leads to a total lifetime ECL of approximately

$$\$7,142.86 + \$10,999.55 = \$18,142.41.$$

Although the ECL measures expected losses under normal circumstances, many financial institutions also consider unforeseen and extreme loss scenarios to ensure complete risk management. This is where unexpected loss (UL) and stress loss (SL) come into play, extending the ECL framework to consider a broader spectrum of potential credit risks. Extending ECL to cover both UL and SL also helps us assess the variability and extreme quantities of credit risk, ensuring that financial institutions are prepared not only for routine credit events but also for unforeseen and severe adverse conditions.

3.1.1 Unexpected Loss

Unexpected loss (UL) measures potential losses that exceed expected loss, reflecting the extent of tail risk across the entire distribution of credit exposures. It is mainly used to quantify and assess the capital reserves necessary to cover losses from unexpected adverse events that are beyond the usual circumstances, such as rare disasters like COVID-19, along with the ensuing economic downturns and market turbulence. These infrequent but potentially disastrous events could lead to considerable financial losses.

We can calculate UL using the Value at Risk (VaR) at a certain confidence level (α):

$$\text{UL} = \text{VaR}_\alpha - \text{ECL}$$

where VaR_α denotes the loss level that is exceeded with a probability of $1 - \alpha$. For example, at a confidence level 99%, $\text{VaR}_{0.99}$ represents the loss that is not expected to be exceeded in cases 99%, thus capturing the extreme tail threshold of the loss distribution (while ignoring those outside 99%). For example, assume that VaR at the 99% confidence level is \$15,000 and ECL is \$10,000. The UL is then calculated as $\text{UL} = 15{,}000 - 10{,}000 = \$5{,}000$. This means that there is an additional \$5,000 excess loss beyond the ECL value at the 99% confidence level. Thus, the bank (or financial institution) needs to prepare additional capital reserves to cover such extreme events.

Note that we can also use alternative downside risk measures, such as Conditional Value at Risk (CVaR), to calculate the unexpected loss. We will discuss different ways of VaR calculation and its shortcomings compared to CVaR in a later chapter.

3.1.2 Stress Loss

Stress loss (SL) refers to losses in stress scenarios, which are typically simulated adverse conditions to assess their impact on credit portfolios. This is a periodic exercise in banks and financial institutions when developing credit scoring models, as these models need to be able to withstand significant economic shocks without compromising their financial stability.

Stress testing involves simulating adverse conditions to assess their impact on credit portfolios, ensuring that financial institutions can withstand significant economic shocks without compromising their financial stability. SL is crucial for strategic planning and regulatory compliance, as it provides insight into the resilience of credit portfolios under extreme but plausible conditions.

Specifically, stress testing involves adjusting key credit risk parameters, such as PD, LGD, and EAD, based on predefined or preidentified adverse scenarios.

The resulting SL can be quantified by recalculating the ECL under these stressed conditions:

$$SL = \text{Stress PD} \times \text{Stress LGD} \times \text{Stress EAD}$$

Consider a recession scenario where economic conditions deteriorate significantly, leading to an increase in PD by 100% from 2% to 4% and an increase in LGD by 50% from 60% to 90%. Using an EAD of $1,100,000 (which is an absolute amount that represents the loss instead of probability), the stressed loss is

$$SL = 0.04 \times 0.90 \times 1,100,000 = 39,600$$

This represents a substantial increase (tripled) in the baseline EL of $13,200, highlighting the potential impact of adverse economic conditions on credit losses. The multiplicative nature of the ECL formula implies that the influence of each component is captured proportionately, providing a comprehensive measure of expected losses. In essence, it accounts for the frequency (PD) and severity (LGD) of potential credit losses and adjusts for the size of exposures (EAD).

In general, the ECL framework, through its integration of PD, LGD, and EAD, offers a good foundation for estimating credit risk. However, this also means that we need to obtain proper prediction for PD, LGD, and EAD to obtain a good estimate of ECL. For PD, we often develop statistical and econometric models to estimate the probability of default. There could be multiple considerations going into the estimation, such as sparsity (the model should not admit too many input features) and direction of travel (certain features should only have positive or negative signs in the corresponding coefficient), etc. Additional data, such as borrower-specific profile or transactional data, as well as macroeconomic indicators, are available to refine risk assessments.

On the other hand, LGD is influenced by collateral quality and recovery processes, which require quantitative asset valuations and qualitative legal recovery pathways. To evaluate EAD, we also need to have a good understanding of common credit utilization patterns and the potential for future loss.

We will dive into these three components of the ECL calculation in the following sections.

3.2 Probability of Default

Probability of default (PD) quantifies the likelihood that a borrower will fail to meet their financial obligations within a specified time horizon, typically using a one-year horizon, and could be extended to multiple years using conditional probabilities. PD serves as a critical indicator of the creditworthiness of a borrower. A PD model captures both the characteristics of the individual borrower and the broader economic conditions as its predictors. For example, individual profile factors of the borrower could cover aspects related to financial health and credit history, while

3.2 Probability of Default

broader factors include industry stability, GDP growth, unemployment rates, or other macroeconomic variables.

Additional restrictions on the direction of travel for these factors may also come into play. For example, during an economic downturn, the PD of borrowers can increase due to reduced income streams and increased financial stress, both reflected in the relevant variables. In this case, we would expect the PD to be negatively correlated with the income stream variable (higher income is associated with lower PD), and the resulting coefficient for the income stream must be negative. Similarly, if we expect the obligor PD to decrease if China's GDP increases, then we would expect the China GDP variable to be negatively correlated with PD and the corresponding coefficient to be a negative sign.

PD can be empirically calculated as the percentage between the number of defaults out of the total number of loans:

$$PD = \frac{\text{Number of Defaults}}{\text{Total Number of Loans}}$$

This empirical estimation provides a basic measure of the probability of default based on historical data. For example, consider a financial institution that has issued 10,000 loans in the past year. Of these, 200 loans have been terminated due to flagged defaults. The PD is then calculated as

$$PD = \frac{200}{10,000} = 0.02 \text{ or } 2\%$$

This implies that, based on historical data, there is a 2% probability that any given loan will default within the year. However, the past does not represent future performance; thus, practical PD estimation often uses more sophisticated models that incorporate various borrower-specific and macroeconomic variables, as discussed earlier. These advanced models aim to enhance the predictive accuracy by capturing complex, nonlinear relationships and interactions between predictors. In the following sections, we introduce some of the common methodologies used in PD estimation.

3.2.1 Logistic Regression

Logistic regression is a widely used statistical method for binary classification problems, making it suitable for modeling default events (default vs. non-default). The logistic regression model estimates the probability that a borrower i will default based on a total of k explanatory variables $\{X_j\}_{j=1}^{k}$.

$$PD_i = \frac{1}{1 + e^{-(\beta_0 + \beta_1 X_{1i} + \beta_2 X_{2i} + \cdots + \beta_k X_{ki})}}$$

where PD_i is the probability of default for the borrower i. $X_{1i}, X_{2i}, \ldots, X_{ki}$ are the explanatory (also called independent) variables of the borrower i (such as individual credit score, income, debt-to-income ratio, or other macroeconomic variables). $\beta_0, \beta_1, \ldots, \beta_k$ are the coefficients to be estimated from the data, so that the estimated PD is close to the true label (either 1 or 0). The logistic function is designed to ensure that the estimated PD is between 0 and 1, thus providing a probabilistic interpretation (i.e., how likely the underlying obligor will default). The coefficients β_j represent the log-odds change in PD for a one-unit change in the corresponding predictor X_j, which corresponds to a similar marginal interpretation in linear regression.

For example, suppose that we have a logistic regression model with two predictors: third-party credit score X_1 and debt-to-income ratio X_2, with intercept β_0 and coefficients β_1 β_2, respectively. The logistic regression model assumes the following form:

$$\text{PD}_i = \frac{1}{1 + e^{-(\beta_0 + \beta_1 X_{1i} + \beta_2 X_{2i})}}$$

Let us assume that the estimated coefficients are $\beta_0 = -1$, $\beta_1 = -0.5$, and $\beta_2 = 2$. For a borrower with a credit score of 75 and a debt-to-income ratio of 20, the PD is calculated as

$$\text{PD} = \frac{1}{1 + e^{-(-1 - 0.5 \times 75 + 2 \times 20)}} \approx 0.818$$

This relatively high PD of 81.8% indicates that this borrower has a high risk of default.

3.2.2 Decision Trees and Random Forests

Decision trees and ensemble methods such as random forests belong to the non-parametric family of models, which can be more powerful in making accurate predictions of PD. The power lies in the approximation capability that can learn complex interactions and nonlinearities automatically, without the need for explicit specification of model form.

A decision tree learns a decision rule by recursively partitioning the feature space based on a particular measure of marginal utility to classify the borrowers into default or non-default classes. Each split aims to maximize the separation between classes, as measured by the level of impurity in the resulting node, often using criteria like Gini impurity or information gain.

A random forest is an enhanced tree model that aggregates multiple decision trees, each trained on a bootstrap sample of the data and a random subset of features. The randomness of both samples and features significantly improves the model's learning capability and generalization performance. The final PD estimate is obtained by averaging the predictions of individual trees, thus reducing variance and improving robustness.

These models can automatically handle high-dimensional data (where the number of features exceeds the number of observations) and interactions between variables (multicollinearity is a major issue in linear models), providing flexible and accurate PD estimates due to their ability to capture nonlinear relationships. However, compared to simpler models like logistic regression, they typically require larger datasets and computational resources.

3.2.3 Other Machine Learning Classifiers

Advanced machine learning classifiers, such as support vector machines (SVM), gradient boosting machines (GBM), and neural networks, can further enhance PD estimation by leveraging their ability to learn highly complex and possibly nonlinear patterns in the data.

SVM works by constructing hyperplanes in high-dimensional feature spaces to separate default and non-default borrowers. These hyperplanes are learned classifiers to best classify the observations with maximum margin in between supporting hyperplanes, subject to a pre-specified tolerance threshold. It also uses a kernel function to capture nonlinear decision boundaries.

GBMs work by learning an ensemble of weak learners (which are simple decision trees) in a sequential manner, where each subsequent tree is learned to minimize the errors of the previous ones. This iterative process turns out to be particularly effective in minimizing training error.

Neural networks consist of interconnected layers of nodes that digest input features through weight sum and nonlinear transformations. Such information extraction and nonlinear activation enable the modeling of highly complex relationships between predictors and PD. In particular, we can design very powerful and complex neural networks to learn arbitrary PD functions.

These classifiers excel at capturing intricate dependencies and interactions within the data and often outperform traditional statistical models in predictive accuracy. However, complex models often have many hyperparameters, and tuning a good set of hyperparameters could be quite time-consuming. In addition, regularization techniques are often applied to avoid overfitting during the training process.

3.3 Loss Given Default

Loss given default (LGD) represents the proportion (a ratio) of the exposure (an amount) that a lender is likely to lose due to a default event. Unlike PD, which measures the likelihood that a default occurs, LGD quantifies the severity of the loss (in terms of the percentage loss out of total exposure) once a default event has occurred. PD tells us how likely defaults may occur, while LGD measures the potential magnitude of losses associated with those defaults.

The level of LGD provides valuable insight into the potential severity of the losses. For example, a high LGD indicates a relatively significant loss, often associated with illiquid collateral that is difficult to recover. In contrast, a low LGD suggests a smaller loss, which may reflect high liquidity in the underlying collateral. Loans backed by easily recoverable and liquid collateral typically exhibit lower LGD values, whereas loans with illiquid and hard-to-recover collateral are more likely to result in higher LGD. For example, loans secured by tangible assets, such as real estate, typically exhibit lower LGDs compared to unsecured loans such as credit cards, as lenders can liquidate these collaterals to offset losses. The legal system that enforces efficient debt recovery also tends to lead to a lower LGD.

LGD is defined as

$$\text{LGD} = 1 - \text{Recovery Rate}$$

where the recovery rate denotes the percentage of the total exposure that can be recovered if the default event occurs. As an alternative definition, if a lender provides a loan with an outstanding exposure (unpaid total sum) of E and recovers a total amount of R after the default event, the LGD can be expressed as

$$\text{LGD} = \frac{E - R}{E} = 1 - \frac{R}{E}$$

Thus, LGD depends on two quantities: the outstanding exposure E and the recovery amount R. Since E cannot be changed if a default event occurs, LGD essentially depends on R, which also relates to the lender's ability to recover the full or partial outstanding exposure as efficiently as possible. In general, high-quality collateral and efficient recovery mechanisms lead to a high R and a low LGD, improving the resilience of the lender against defaults. In contrast, poor collateral quality or inefficient recovery processes result in low R and high LGD, thus increasing the likelihood of further loss.

There are multiple methods that can be used to estimate LGD. We outline a few commonly used methodologies here:

- **Using Historical Recovery:** This approach involves analyzing historical default data and calculating average recovery rates for similar asset classes, loan types, and economic conditions. In other words, this approach assumes average past performance as a prediction for future LGD prediction. As an example, suppose that a lender reviews ten defaulted loans for the past three years and finds that, on average, only 40% of the outstanding amounts were recovered. Then the estimated LGD is $1 - 0.40 = 0.60$, meaning a 60% loss is expected in the event of default.
- **Using Collateral Valuation:** For secured loans, the quality and liquidity of collateral are critical determinants as they represent the recoverable amount R in the definition of LGD. Valuation models are developed to assess the current market value of collateral assets, considering factors such as depreciation, market

3.3 Loss Given Default

volatility, and liquidation costs. This is different from the previous approach that focuses on estimating the LGD alone; instead, we focus on the collateral assets and try to predict their future value, which is further assumed to be recoverable should a default event happen. For example, imagine a secured loan of $100,000 backed by collateral currently valued at $90,000. This means that we will be able to recover at most 90% of the total risk exposure. If liquidating the collateral (such as selling the property collateral) requires 10% of the collateral value (i.e., $9,000) as an additional cost, the recoverable amount becomes $90,000 − $9,000 = $81,000. Thus, our estimate of LGD is $\frac{100,000-81,000}{100,000} = 0.19$.

- **Using Expert Judgment and Heuristics:** When historical data is sparse, insufficient, or unreliable, expert judgment often plays a crucial role in supplementing LGD estimation. Subject matter experts leverage their domain knowledge and experience to provide informed LGD estimates, which are particularly valuable when data is inadequate to train a reliable model. In addition, experts can refine their estimates by incorporating insights into current and evolving economic conditions, as well as prevailing market sentiment, ensuring that the predictions remain relevant and contextually accurate. For example, in cases with limited historical data, an expert might assess that, given current economic conditions, similar loans will have an expected recovery rate of 50%, which translates to an implied LGD of $1 - 0.50 = 0.50$, or 50%.
- **Using Statistical Models:** Statistical models, including linear regression and logistic regression, can be used to predict LGD based on various predictor variables such as borrower demographics, loan attributes, collateral information, and macroeconomic indicators. These models are trained to minimize the discrepancy between predicted and actual losses by optimizing the parameters based on historical data. These models, once properly developed, can potentially capture the underlying pattern in the data and make reliable predictions on LGD. In this regard, ensuring the proper training data and modeling assumption is the key to building a reliable model. As an example, consider a linear regression model that estimates LGD as $\widehat{\text{LGD}} = 0.20 + 0.5 \times (\text{LTV} - 0.60)$, where LTV is the loan-to-value ratio expressed as a decimal. For a loan with an LTV of 0.80, the predicted LGD is $0.20 + 0.5 \times (0.80 - 0.60) = 0.30$, or 30%.
- **Using Machine Learning Models:** Advanced machine learning algorithms, such as random forests and neural networks, offer more complex and powerful models for LGD estimation. These techniques can capture complex nonlinear relationships and interactions between predictors. However, it is important to prevent these complex approximators from overfitting the data, which corresponds to good training set performance but poor out-of-sample performance. In addition, the choice of predictors and the modeling approach significantly influence the accuracy and reliability of LGD estimates. Suppose a random forest model, trained on historical loan and borrower data, predicts an LGD of 15% for a new loan of $100,000. This implies an expected loss of $0.15 \times 100,000 = \$15,000$.

It is also important to note the interaction between LGD and other components of credit risk, such as PD and EAD. For example, a high PD coupled with a high LGD signifies a particularly risky exposure, as this means that the borrower is likely to default, and if such a default happens, most of the exposure will not be recoverable. Thus, such a type of obligor requires more stringent risk mitigation measures and higher capital reserves. In contrast, a high EAD (meaning a large amount of exposure at risk) with a low LGD (meaning that the majority of the exposure can be recovered, likely due to high-quality and liquid collateral) might require careful monitoring of exposure levels to manage potential losses effectively.

3.4 Exposure at Default

Exposure at default (EAD) represents the total value to which a lender is exposed when the borrower defaults (note that the definition of default may vary in different financial institutions). Unlike PD and LGD, which quantify the probability of default and the severity of potential loss, respectively, EAD quantifies the magnitude of exposure that is at risk, thus being an absolute amount instead of a percentage. Accurately estimating EAD is a key component not only for calculating ECL but also for determining the necessary capital reserves required to absorb potential losses.

To obtain EAD, we need to consider both the outstanding principal and accrued interest on a loan, as well as any additional exposures, such as undrawn credit lines or commitments that may be utilized by the borrower before defaulting. Thus, the exact value of EAD is inherently dynamic and may fluctuate in time, similar to both PD and LGD. All three components are, therefore, point-in-time estimates.

EAD is calculated by summing the current outstanding balance of a loan with the expected utilization of any undrawn credit facilities:

$$\text{EAD}_t = E_t + \theta U_t$$

where the outstanding balance E_t denotes the current principal and the interest accrued on the loan at time t. The undrawn credit line U_t represents the portion of a revolving credit facility that remains unused by the borrower at time t. The credit conversion factor (CCF) θ_t is the time-dependent CCF reflecting the expected utilization at time t. It is a factor that estimates the proportion of the undrawn credit line that will be used at the time of default. This equation captures the total exposure at default by accounting for both the utilized and potential future drawdowns on credit facilities. The CCF θ is typically determined based on historical utilization rates and can vary depending on the type of credit facility, borrower characteristics, and prevailing economic conditions.

EAD can be estimated using the following approaches:

- **Using a Standardized Approach Based on Regulations:** Under regulatory frameworks such as Basel II and Basel III, the standardized approach prescribes

fixed CCFs for different types of credit facilities. For example, an undrawn portion of a commercial loan might have a CCF of 50%, implying that 50% of the undrawn amount is expected to be used at default.
- **Using Behavioral Models:** Behavioral models can be trained to estimate EAD by forecasting the future utilization of undrawn credit lines based on borrower-specific behavior and macroeconomic indicators. Similar to PD and LGD estimation, these models often employ statistical models such as time series analysis to predict utilization patterns.
- **Using Machine Learning Models:** Machine learning algorithms, including random forests, XGBoost, and neural networks, are increasingly utilized to model EAD due to their good learning capacity without the need for feature engineering. These models can also incorporate a wide range of features, such as borrower demographics, credit history, loan characteristics, and macroeconomic variables, to enhance predictive accuracy.

As an example, consider the following scenario with an outstanding balance E of \$1,000,000, an undrawn credit line U of \$200,000, and a credit conversion factor θ of 50%. The EAD can be calculated as

$$\text{EAD} = 1{,}000{,}000 + (200{,}000 \times 0.50) = 1{,}100{,}000$$

which indicates that the total exposure at default is \$1,100,000, comprising the outstanding balance of \$1,000,000 and an additional \$100,000 expected from the undrawn credit line.

For a portfolio with multiple undrawn credit lines, each with different CCFs based on borrower profiles and economic scenarios, the corresponding EAD for the entire portfolio ($\text{EAD}_{\text{portfolio}}$) can be aggregated as

$$\text{EAD}_{\text{portfolio}} = \sum_{i=1}^{n} (E_i + U_i \times \theta_i)$$

where n is the total number of credit facilities in the portfolio.

Furthermore, for revolving credit facilities where borrowers can make multiple withdrawals over the loan life, EAD estimation may require integrating over the expected utilization path. This involves predicting not just a single drawdown, but a sequence of potential utilizations at different points in time, leading to a more dynamic and time-sensitive EAD estimation.

$$\text{EAD} = E_0 + \sum_{t=1}^{T} (U_t \times \theta_t)$$

where E_0 is the initial outstanding balance, U_t is the undrawn credit line at time t, θ_t is the CCF at time t, and T is the total time horizon.

The definition of EAD suggests that it is quite sensitive to the CCF parameter θ. This sensitivity can be characterized using sensitivity analysis, which involves assessing how changes in key parameters, such as the CCF or the undrawn credit line, impact the EAD estimates. For example, an increase in the CCF from 50% to 60% would proportionally increase the EAD by $20,000 in the aforementioned example:

$$\Delta\text{EAD} = U \times (\theta_{new} - \theta_{old}) = 200{,}000 \times (0.60 - 0.50) = 20{,}000$$

3.5 Expected Credit Loss

Let us look at a concrete example of calculating the ECL in a housing mortgage loan. Imagine a bank that provides a mortgage loan to a borrower to purchase a residential property. The key parameters of this loan are as follows: The borrower secures a loan amount of $400,000 to finance a property valued at $500,000, resulting in a loan-to-value ratio (LTV) of 80%. Over time, the borrower makes repayments that add up to $40,000, thus reducing the outstanding loan balance to $360,000. This outstanding balance is calculated by subtracting the repayments made from the initial loan amount. It is the EAD for the bank, representing the total Value at Risk should the borrower default on the loan. This calculation reveals that the lender's exposure at the current time point is $360,000, which consists of both the principal and any accrued interest that remains unpaid.

Next, we look at PD, which measures the likelihood that the borrower will default on the mortgage within a specified time horizon. Based on historical data, suppose that it is observed that one out of four homeowners default on their mortgage loans within a year. This empirical observation serves as an estimate for future PD:

$$\text{PD} = \frac{\text{Number of Defaults}}{\text{Total Number of Loans}} = \frac{1}{4} = 0.25 \text{ or } 25\%$$

This implies a 25% probability that the borrower will default on the loan within the year.

We also look at LGD, which quantifies the proportion of the exposure that is lost when a borrower defaults, after accounting for recoveries from collateral or other credit enhancements. In this example, assume that if the borrower defaults, the lender is able to immediately sell the property for $342,000. The remaining loss incurred by the default event is the difference between the total outstanding loan balance and the recovery amount.

$$L = \text{EAD} - R = 360000 - 342000 = 18000$$

3.5 Expected Credit Loss

LGD is then calculated as the ratio of this loss to the exposure at default:

$$\text{LGD} = \frac{L}{\text{EAD}} = \frac{\$18,000}{\$360,000} = 0.05 \text{ or } 5\%$$

This calculation indicates that, in the event of default, the lender expects to lose 5% of the exposure at default, primarily due to the shortfall between the outstanding balance and the amount of recovery from the property sale.

Finally, let us calculate the ECL by integrating the three components, PD, LGD, and EAD, into a single measure that quantifies the expected average loss from credit exposures via the following:

$$\text{ECL} = \text{PD} \times \text{LGD} \times \text{EAD}$$

Substituting the values from our example:

$$\text{ECL} = 0.25 \times 0.05 \times 360000 = 4500$$

Thus, the bank's ECL is $4,500. This figure represents the expected average loss from the loan, considering both the likelihood of default and the severity of the loss upon default.

Note that the ECL formula is based on the principle of conditional expectation, where the expected loss is the product of the probability of a loss event (PD), the percentage loss given a default (LGD), and the size of the exposure at the time of the event (EAD). This multiplicative relationship ensures that the impact of each component is reflected proportionately in the overall expected loss. In this example, a PD of 25% combined with an LGD of 5% and an EAD of $360,000 yields an ECL of $4,500, highlighting how even relatively low LGD values can result in significant expected losses when combined with substantial exposure and non-negligible default probabilities.

Note that we can further perform sensitivity analysis to analyze the impact of individual components, while assuming the rest is fixed, on the resulting ECL. All of these components have a positive correlation with ECL, meaning that a higher level of PD, LGD, or EAD will tend to increase ECL.

In the following section, we look at a related concept: the risk-weighted asset.

3.5.1 Capital Regulation Using Risk-Weighted Asset

In modern banking, managing credit risk is a crucial function within the risk management space. If not properly managed, credit risk can significantly affect a bank's financial health. To mitigate this risk, many regulatory frameworks have been proposed, such as Basel III, which requires banks to have sufficient capital relative to the level of risk and exposure. This is where the concept of risk-weighted assets (RWAs) comes in.

RWAs provide a mechanism to adjust the total value of bank assets based on the level of risk they carry. Simply put, it is a weighted combination across the value of all available assets. For instance, a government bond may be considered less risky than a corporate loan, and, therefore, it should receive a lower risk weight. By assigning risk weights to different asset classes, RWAs ensure that banks maintain an appropriate capital buffer proportional to the total exposure.

In addition to RWA, we also have a regulatory requirement on the bank's Capital Adequacy Ratio (CAR), a key measure of financial stability used to derive the required amount of capital reserve. Regulatory authorities, through the Basel III framework, have established minimum capital requirements (often set at 8%) to ensure that banks remain resilient in times of economic stress. CAR helps ensure that a bank has enough capital to cover its risks, thereby promoting stability and solvency in the financial system.

The required capital reserve is thus defined as the product of RWA and CAR:

$$\text{Capital} = \text{CAR} \times \text{RWA}$$

where Capital refers to the regulatory capital of a bank, which consists of Tier 1 (core capital, including common equity and retained earnings) and Tier 2 (supplementary capital, such as subordinated debt). Given the regulated CAR and the calculated RWA, we can then derive the amount of capital that the bank needs to reserve.

There are two main methods outlined in the Basel III framework for calculating RWAs for credit risk: the standardized approach (SA) and the internal ratings–based (IRB) approach. Both methods involve assigning risk weights to assets. SA is the simpler method of calculating RWA and is commonly used by smaller banks and financial institutions. This approach uses a fixed set of risk weights predefined by regulators, typically based on the external credit ratings of the counterparty or asset class involved. These credit ratings are then converted to a set of risk weights and further used to calculate RWA through the following:

$$\text{RWA} = \text{EAD} \times \text{Risk Weight}$$

Thus, to calculate the RWA, we would first determine the exposure value of each asset (along with additional adjustments for collateral or guarantees), multiply the exposure value of each asset by its assigned risk weight, and then sum the results across all assets. Consider a bank with the following assets: $200 million in AAA-rated government bonds with a risk weight of 0%, $80 million in BBB-rated corporate loans with a risk weight of 100%, and $50 million in residential mortgages with a risk weight of 50%. The RWA is calculated as $(200 \times 0\%) + (80 \times 100\%) + (50 \times 50\%) = 105$ million. Therefore, the total RWA for credit risk amounts to $105 million.

There are multiple types of asset classes when it comes to risk exposure, including sovereign exposures, corporate loans, residential mortgages, retail exposures, and off-balance sheet items. Each asset class is assigned a specific risk weight based

3.5 Expected Credit Loss

on the credit rating of the counterparty (if available) or the asset type. For example, government bonds, which are AAA rated, can get 0% risk weight, while corporate loans (BBB rated) get 100% risk weight (due to their high risk of default), residential mortgages get 50% risk weight (since the property itself can serve as collateral), and retail loans get 75% risk weight (relatively risky especially for unsecured loans).

Compared to SA, the IRB approach is more advanced and allows banks and financial institutions to use their own risk models to calculate the three risk components (PD, LGD, and EAD). Due to its complexity and a considerable amount of development effort, this method is typically used by larger banks with more complex portfolios and requires regulatory approval from local and/or foreign regulators.

There are two variants of the IRB approach: Foundation IRB (F-IRB), where banks estimate PD with LGD and EAD provided by regulators, and Advanced IRB (A-IRB), where banks estimate all three key components. These parameters, once estimated, are then used in the calculation of the RWA.

Specifically, we first calculate the risk weight parameter K, which represents the capital requirement per unit of EAD. A common calculation is based on the PD, LGD, and asset correlation parameter ρ using the following expression:

$$K = \text{LGD} \times \Phi\left(\frac{\Phi^{-1}(\text{PD}) + \sqrt{\rho}\Phi^{-1}(0.999)}{\sqrt{1-\rho}}\right)$$

This quantity reflects the amount (in percentage) of capital that a bank needs to hold for each unit exposure to cover the unexpected loss (tail risk or extreme loss scenarios beyond the average anticipated loss) with a specified confidence level (99.9%). Φ is the cumulative distribution function of the standard normal distribution (used to map probabilities to the corresponding Z scores), and $\Phi^{-1}(p)$ is the inverse cumulative distribution function (quantile function) of the standard normal distribution, representing the Z score corresponding to a probability p. Note that more advanced models may also consider the maturity of the exposure in the calculation.

Once K is calculated, we can then calculate RWA via RWA $= K \times$ EAD. This process reflects the risk sensitivity of the bank's exposures and helps determine how much capital the bank needs to hold to cover potential losses.

Consider a scenario with the following parameters: an EAD of $120 million, a PD of 5%, an LGD of 55%, an asset correlation (ρ) of 0.2, a CAR of 8%, and a target confidence level 99.9%. To calculate the capital requirement, we first determine K:

$$K = 0.55 \times \Phi\left(\frac{\Phi^{-1}(0.05) + \sqrt{0.2} \times \Phi^{-1}(0.999)}{\sqrt{1-0.2}}\right) \approx 21.12\%$$

Next, the RWA is calculated as follows:

$$\text{RWA} = 0.2112 \times 120{,}000{,}000 = \$25{,}344{,}000$$

Finally, the required capital is computed as follows:

$$\text{Capital} = 0.08 \times 25{,}344{,}000 \approx \$2.03 \quad \text{million}$$

This implies that a bank with an RWA value of $25.344 million must maintain $2.03 million in capital to meet the regulatory CAR of 8%. This calculation highlights the interaction between credit risk parameters and regulatory requirements, ensuring sufficient capital buffers to absorb potential losses.

In the next section, we will look at how to build a PD model using the logistic regression model. We focus on this component due to its important role as a first-level screening between high-risk and low-risk borrowers.

3.6 Building a PD Model

A PD model takes relevant borrower information and outputs the probability of default within the next period of time, which could be one year, two years, etc. There are typically two types of obligor data: one-time application data and recurrent behavioral data. By digesting both application and behavioral data, credit risk models aim to predict the probability of default, which helps to set the interest rate and other risk management guidelines throughout the borrowing period.

Application data refers to the information provided by the borrower at the time of the credit application. It typically includes key demographic and loan-specific characteristics that give an initial indication of the borrower's risk profile. The key attributes in the application data, once approved, include interest rate (which positively correlates with credit risk), credit grade (an internal grade assigned to potential obligors as an indicator of creditworthiness), and loan amount (the total amount of money requested by the borrower).

Behavioral data reflect the borrower's financial status and historical background information. This information is often collected and assessed on a periodic basis, often yearly, after the borrower has taken out a loan. This periodic assessment ensures that the borrower is in good financial condition on a regular basis. Example behavior attributes include employment history (such as length of service and income level), historical default (past default history, which is a key predictor of future default risk), and other demographics such as spending or transaction history.

When developing a PD model, the default definition, or good-bad definition, is typically based on the delinquency status of the borrower in terms of the number of days past the due date. A common definition is that a borrower would be considered as default if it has been more than 90 days past the due date. However, a borrower who has committed fraud may also be considered a default. The default status is often stored in a binary variable where 1 indicates default and 0 indicates non-default. When modeling the default outcome in logistic regression, the log odds of the default probability are modeled as a linear combination of the features.

3.6 Building a PD Model

In the following sections, we first look at common best practices in data processing and exploration, including dealing with outliers and missing data. We then move on to model development using logistic regression and its evaluation.

3.6.1 Data Processing and Exploration

We will look at a credit bureau dataset that contains both application and behavior features. The dataset contains 32,581 rows and 12 columns, as shown in Listing 3-1.

```python
import numpy as np
import pandas as pd
import matplotlib.pyplot as plt
from sklearn.model_selection import train_test_split
from sklearn.linear_model import LogisticRegression
from sklearn.metrics import (
    accuracy_score,
    precision_score,
    recall_score,
    f1_score,
    confusion_matrix,
    roc_curve,
    auc,
    classification_report
)
import seaborn as sns

cr_loan = pd.read_csv("data/cr_loan2.csv")
cr_loan.shape

# Output
(32581, 12)
```

Listing 3-1 Importing data

In this dataset, the *loan_status* variable indicates the default status. As mentioned earlier, banks and financial institutions demand a higher interest for risky obligors whose probability of default is higher than less risky borrowers. We can verify this via Listing 3-2, which shows the average interest rate for each type of *loan_status* and *person_home_ownership*. The resulting table, as shown in Table 3-1, suggests that the average interest rate is the lowest for non-default cases but rises up for default cases.

```python
# Crosstab between 'person_home_ownership' and 'loan_status',
# calculating the mean of 'loan_int_rate' and rounding it to 2
    decimal places
pd.crosstab(
    cr_loan['person_home_ownership'],  # Index: Homeownership
    status
    cr_loan['loan_status'],            # Columns: Loan status
    values=cr_loan['loan_int_rate'],   # Values to aggregate:
    Loan interest rate
```

Table 3-1 Comparing the interest rates across different home ownerships and default status

Loan status	0	1
Person home ownership		
MORTGAGE	10.06	13.43
OTHER	11.41	13.56
OWN	10.75	12.24
RENT	10.75	12.97

```
7     aggfunc='mean'                   # Aggregation function:
      Mean
8 ).round(2)                           # Round the results to 2
      decimal places
```

Listing 3-2 Analyzing interest rate across different home ownerships and default status

3.6.2 Dealing with Outliers

When developing credit risk models, outliers can arise from various sources, such as incorrect data entry, rare but extreme financial behaviors, or unique economic events that lead to significant deviation from the norm. These outliers are typically data points that deviate considerably from the majority of observations and can distort statistical analyses and predictions. For example, exceptionally long or short employment terms, income levels, or loan amounts may not represent typical borrower behavior and can skew the model's understanding of default risk. Thus, it is important to detect and handle these outliers because they can influence the estimation process and lead to biased PD predictions. Once detected, outliers can be treated by either removing them, transforming them, or using robust modeling techniques that reduce their influence.

Let us start by analyzing *person_emp_length* and *loan_int_rate*, where we show the original scatterplot in the left panel of Figure 3-2. Since it is unlikely that a person will have more than 60 years of employment duration, we can identify these rows as outliers and remove them from the original dataframe. This generates the right panel of Figure 3-2.

See Listing 3-3 for details on removing outlier observations.

```
1  # Copy original data to preserve it for "before" plot
2  df_before = cr_loan.copy()
3
4  # Identify outliers: employment length >= 60 months
5  outlier_indices = df_before[df_before['person_emp_length'] >=
       60].index
6
7  # Remove those outliers to create 'after' set
8  df_after = df_before.drop(outlier_indices)
9
10 # Create a 1x2 subplot
```

3.6 Building a PD Model

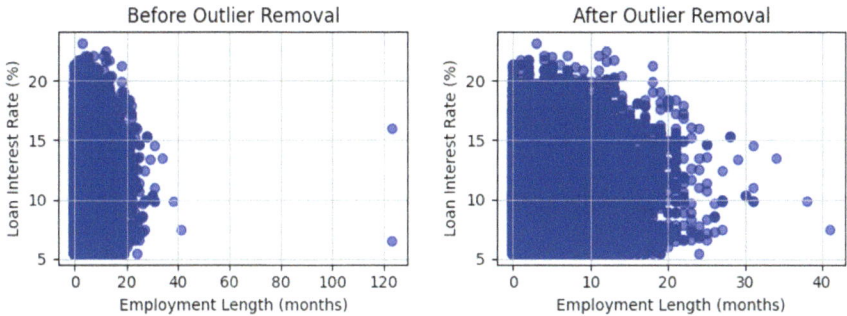

Figure 3-2 Scatter plot of Employment Length vs. Loan Interest Rate. Left: before removing outliers. Right: after removing outliers

```
fig, axes = plt.subplots(nrows=1, ncols=2, figsize=(8, 3))

# -- Plot 1: Before Outlier Removal
axes[0].scatter(df_before['person_emp_length'],
                df_before['loan_int_rate'],
                alpha=0.5,
                color='blue')
axes[0].set_title('Before Outlier Removal')
axes[0].set_xlabel('Employment Length (months)')
axes[0].set_ylabel('Loan Interest Rate (%)')
axes[0].grid(True)

# -- Plot 2: After Outlier Removal
axes[1].scatter(df_after['person_emp_length'],
                df_after['loan_int_rate'],
                alpha=0.5,
                color='blue')
axes[1].set_title('After Outlier Removal')
axes[1].set_xlabel('Employment Length (months)')
axes[1].set_ylabel('Loan Interest Rate (%)')
axes[1].grid(True)

plt.tight_layout()
plt.show()
```

Listing 3-3 Removing outliers

In addition to removing outliers, we can also transform them into meaningful observations so that they can still be used for modeling purposes. For example, applying a log transformation compresses the range of the data by converting large values into a logarithmic scale, which reduces the disproportionate influence of extreme observations and stabilizes variance. Standardization, on the other hand, rescales the data so that each feature has a mean of 0 and a standard deviation of 1, thereby facilitating comparisons across different variables and improving the convergence of many algorithms. Additionally, winsorization involves capping extreme values at specific percentile thresholds, which limits the impact of outliers while preserving the overall distribution of the data. Together, these methods enable us to retain valuable information from outliers while ensuring that they do not unduly distort the modeling process.

3.6.3 Dealing with Missing Data

The handling of missing data is also a critical step in ensuring the integrity and predictive power of the model. Missing data can occur for a variety of reasons, such as incomplete customer applications, data entry errors, or limitations in data collection systems. If not addressed properly, missing values can introduce bias, reduce the efficiency of the model, or even render the model invalid. When a feature has most of the observations missing, the common practice is to remove it. However, when only a few observations are missing, we tend to fill these missing values with some estimate.

There are several techniques for treating missing data in credit risk modeling, each depending on the extent and nature of the missing observations. Common methods include mean or median imputation, where missing values are replaced by the average or median of the observed data, which is simple and often effective for continuous variables. Mode imputation is useful for categorical variables. In some cases, the missing data itself may be informative and indicative of increased risk, in which case creating a separate "missing" category can be useful.

In Listing 3-4, we first count the number of rows with missing data in *loan_int_rate* and *person_emp_length*, followed by mean value replacement and row removal for the latter.

```
cr_loan = df_after.copy()

# Fill missing values in the 'loan_int_rate' column with the mean
    of the non-missing values
cr_loan['loan_int_rate'].fillna(cr_loan['loan_int_rate'].mean(),
    inplace=True)
# Get the indices of rows where 'person_emp_length' is null (NaN)
indices = cr_loan[cr_loan['person_emp_length'].isnull()].index
# Drop the rows with missing 'person_emp_length' values from the
    DataFrame
cr_loan.drop(indices, inplace=True)
```

Listing 3-4 Dealing with missing value

3.6.4 Dealing with Categorical Data

Logistic regression requires numerical input, so any categorical variables in the dataset must be converted to a numerical format. One common method for this

3.6 Building a PD Model

conversion is one-hot encoding, which transforms categorical variables into a series of binary columns, as shown in Listing 3-5.

```
# Identify categorical variables
categorical_vars = ['person_home_ownership', 'loan_intent', '
    loan_grade', 'cb_person_default_on_file']

# Perform dummy encoding on categorical variables, dropping the
    first category to avoid multicollinearity
cr_loan_encoded = pd.get_dummies(cr_loan, columns=
    categorical_vars, drop_first=True)
```

Listing 3-5 One-hot encoding categorical data

By applying one-hot encoding to the identified categorical variables and dropping the first category, we prevent multicollinearity, which can adversely affect the model's performance.

3.6.5 Train-Test Split

As shown in Listing 3-6, after encoding the categorical variables, the next step is to separate the dataset into features and the target variable. The features (X) are all the columns except *loan_status*, which is the target (y) that we aim to predict.

```
# Define feature matrix X and target vector y
X = cr_loan_encoded.drop('loan_status', axis=1)
y = cr_loan_encoded['loan_status']
```

Listing 3-6 Creating features and target variables

To effectively evaluate the performance of the model, it is important to divide the data into training and testing sets. As shown in Listing 3-7, typically, a common split is 70% for training and 30% for testing. This division allows the model to learn from the training data and be evaluated on unseen testing data.

```
# Split the data into training and testing sets (e.g., 70% train,
    30% test)
X_train, X_test, y_train, y_test = train_test_split(
    X, y, test_size=0.3, random_state=42, stratify=y
)
```

Listing 3-7 Performing train-test split

Here, setting *random_state=42* ensures reproducibility of the results, and *stratify=y* maintains the same distribution of the target variable in both training and testing sets.

Now, let us move on to the model development stage.

3.6.6 Developing Logistic Regression Model

With the data prepared, the next step is to build and train the logistic regression model. As shown in Listing 3-8, we will initialize the model with a higher maximum number of iterations to ensure convergence and use the "lbfgs" solver, which is suitable for smaller datasets and supports multinomial loss.

```
# Initialize the Logistic Regression model with increased
    max_iter to ensure convergence
logreg = LogisticRegression(max_iter=1000, solver='lbfgs')
# Fit the model on the training data
logreg.fit(X_train, y_train)
```

Listing 3-8 Building logistic regression model

As shown in Listing 3-9, training the predictive model involves fitting it to the training data, allowing it to learn the relationships between the features and the target variable. After training the model, we use it to make predictions on the test set. This involves predicting both the class labels and the probabilities associated with the positive class, which are useful for evaluating the model's performance using ROC analysis.

```
# Make predictions on the test set
y_pred = logreg.predict(X_test)
y_pred_proba = logreg.predict_proba(X_test)[:, 1]
```

Listing 3-9 Generating model predictions

Here, *y_pred* contains the predicted class labels, while *y_pred_proba* contains the predicted probabilities for the positive class.

3.6.7 Model Evaluation

Evaluating the model's performance is crucial to understand how well it generalizes to new data. As shown in Listing 3-10, we will use several metrics, including accuracy, precision, recall, F1 score, confusion matrix, and the ROC-AUC curve, to assess the model's performance. Specifically, accuracy measures the proportion of correctly predicted instances out of all instances. Precision assesses the correctness of positive predictions, recall evaluates the model's ability to capture all positive instances, and the F1 score balances precision and recall.

```
# Evaluate the model
accuracy = accuracy_score(y_test, y_pred)
precision = precision_score(y_test, y_pred)
recall = recall_score(y_test, y_pred)
f1 = f1_score(y_test, y_pred)

print("Model Evaluation Metrics:")
print(f"Accuracy : {accuracy:.4f}")
print(f"Precision: {precision:.4f}")
print(f"Recall   : {recall:.4f}")
```

3.6 Building a PD Model

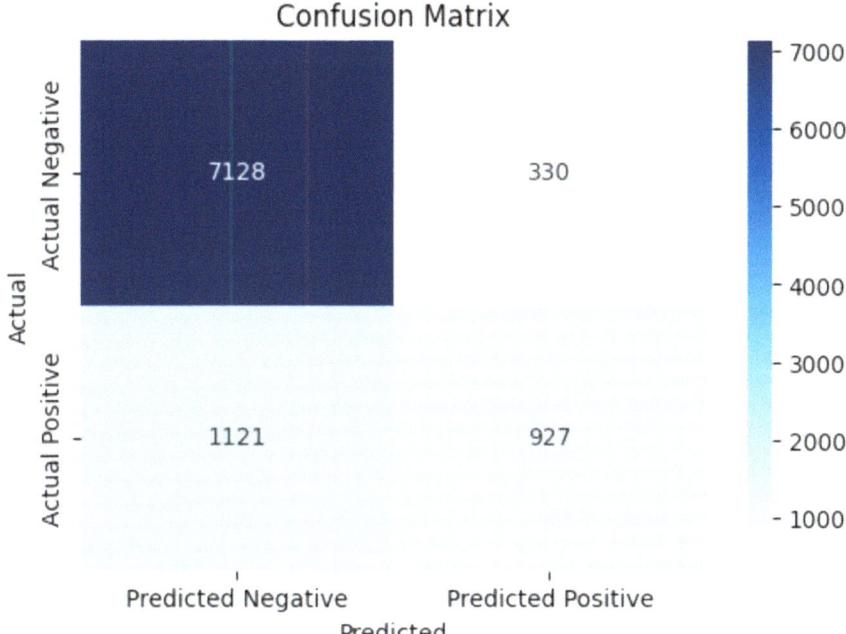

Figure 3-3 Confusion matrix between model predictions and actual targets

```
print(f"F1 Score : {f1:.4f}")

# Output
Accuracy : 0.8474
Precision: 0.7375
Recall   : 0.4526
F1 Score : 0.5610
```

Listing 3-10 Model evaluation

The result suggests that there might be a trade-off between precision and recall. Although the model is good at avoiding false positives (as indicated by the high precision), it is poor at capturing actual defaults (low recall). In credit risk modeling, missing actual defaults can be risky, so recall is often more important than precision.

As shown in Listing 3-11, the confusion matrix provides a more detailed breakdown of the model predictions, showing the number of true positives, true negatives, false positives, and false negatives. This visualization, as shown in Figure 3-3, helps to understand where the model is performing well and where it might be making mistakes.

```
# Display the confusion matrix
conf_matrix = confusion_matrix(y_test, y_pred)
plt.figure(figsize=(6,4))
sns.heatmap(conf_matrix, annot=True, fmt='d', cmap='Blues',
            xticklabels=['Predicted Negative', 'Predicted Positive'],
```

```
            yticklabels=['Actual Negative', 'Actual Positive'])
plt.title('Confusion Matrix')
plt.xlabel('Predicted')
plt.ylabel('Actual')
plt.show()
```

Listing 3-11 Displaying confusion matrix

As shown in Listing 3-12, we can also use the classification report to obtain a comprehensive overview of the model's performance, including precision, recall, F1 score, and support for each class. This report also helps us to understand how the model performs in different categories.

```
# Classification report for detailed metrics
print("Classification Report:")
print(classification_report(y_test, y_pred))

# Output
# Classification Report:
              precision    recall  f1-score   support

           0       0.86      0.96      0.91      7458
           1       0.74      0.45      0.56      2048

    accuracy                           0.85      9506
   macro avg       0.80      0.70      0.73      9506
weighted avg       0.84      0.85      0.83      9506
```

Listing 3-12 Classification report

3.6.8 ROC Curve

Note that such a classification report is based on a threshold value of 0.5 by default. Choosing the appropriate classification threshold is a critical step in building an effective logistic regression model, especially in sensitive applications such as credit risk modeling. The threshold determines how predicted probabilities are converted into class labels (e.g., default or no default), directly impacting the balance between true positives and false positives. In this context, selecting the optimal threshold involves not only statistical considerations but also a deep understanding of the business implications.

The classification threshold is the probability value above which a prediction is classified as the positive class (e.g., loan default) and below which it is classified as the negative class (e.g., loan non-default). Adjusting this threshold affects the model's sensitivity (true positive rate) and specificity (true negative rate).

The Receiver Operating Characteristic (ROC) curve is a graphical representation that illustrates the trade-off between the true positive rate (TPR) and the false positive rate (FPR) in different threshold settings. Each point on the ROC curve corresponds to a specific threshold value and the corresponding trade-off between

3.6 Building a PD Model

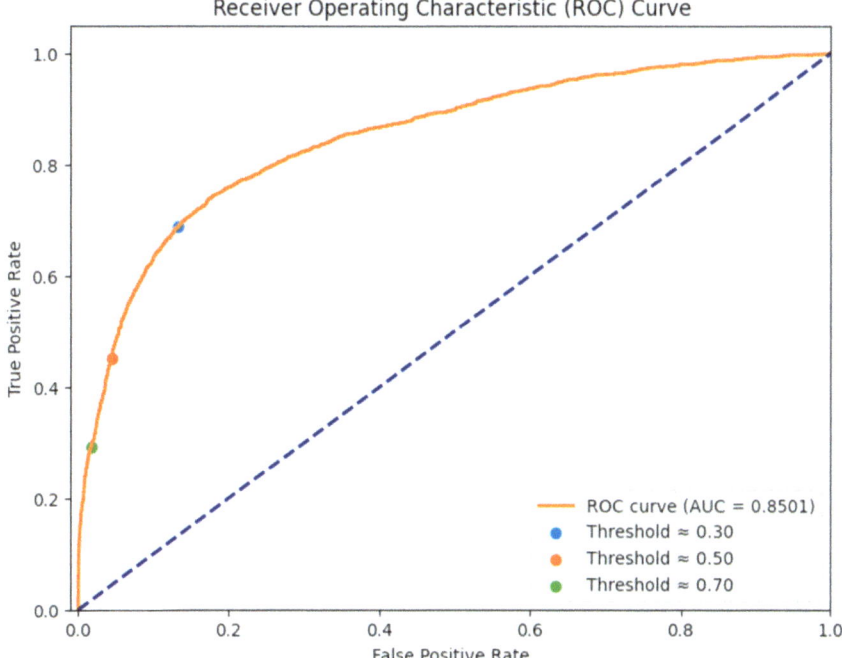

Figure 3-4 ROC curve

precision and recall. By plotting TPR against FPR at various thresholds, the ROC curve provides a comprehensive view of the model's performance. The Area Under the Curve (AUC) then quantifies the overall ability of the model to discriminate between the two classes, with a higher AUC indicating better performance.

However, the ROC curve alone does not specify the best threshold for classification. To determine the optimal threshold, especially in the context of credit risk modeling, it is still essential to consider the specific costs and benefits associated with different types of prediction errors.

To better understand how the threshold impacts model performance and to identify the optimal threshold for credit risk modeling, let us delve deeper into the ROC curve and incorporate additional analyses. In Listing 3-13, we plot the ROC curve and highlight specific threshold points (0.3, 0.5, and 0.7) to visualize how different thresholds affect the true positive and false positive rates, as shown in Figure 3-4. The *find_closest_threshold* function ensures that we select the nearest available threshold value to avoid indexing errors. In addition, we also demonstrate how changing the threshold to 0.7 affects key performance metrics.

```
# ROC Curve and AUC
fpr, tpr, thresholds = roc_curve(y_test, y_pred_proba)
roc_auc = auc(fpr, tpr)

plt.figure(figsize=(8,6))
```

```python
plt.plot(fpr, tpr, color='darkorange', lw=2, label=f'ROC curve (
    AUC = {roc_auc:.4f})')
plt.plot([0, 1], [0, 1], color='navy', lw=2, linestyle='--')

# Define the thresholds you want to highlight
desired_thresholds = [0.3, 0.5, 0.7]

# Function to find the closest threshold
def find_closest_threshold(thresholds, desired_thresh):
    idx = np.argmin(np.abs(thresholds - desired_thresh))
    return idx

# Highlight specific threshold points
for thresh in desired_thresholds:
    idx = find_closest_threshold(thresholds, thresh)
    plt.scatter(fpr[idx], tpr[idx], label=f'Threshold {
        thresholds[idx]:.2f}', marker='o')

plt.xlim([-0.01, 1.0])
plt.ylim([0.0, 1.05])
plt.xlabel('False Positive Rate')
plt.ylabel('True Positive Rate')
plt.title('Receiver Operating Characteristic (ROC) Curve')
plt.legend(loc="lower right")
plt.show()

# Example of threshold impact on predictions
threshold = 0.7
y_pred_threshold = (y_pred_proba >= threshold).astype(int)

# Evaluate performance at the chosen threshold
accuracy = accuracy_score(y_test, y_pred_threshold)
precision = precision_score(y_test, y_pred_threshold)
recall = recall_score(y_test, y_pred_threshold)
f1 = f1_score(y_test, y_pred_threshold)

print(f"Performance Metrics at Threshold = {threshold}:")
print(f"Accuracy : {accuracy:.4f}")
print(f"Precision: {precision:.4f}")
print(f"Recall   : {recall:.4f}")
print(f"F1 Score : {f1:.4f}")

# Output
Performance Metrics at Threshold = 0.7:
Accuracy : 0.8340
Precision: 0.8210
Recall   : 0.2935
F1 Score : 0.4324
```

Listing 3-13 ROC curve and AOC

Assuming that there is no preference between precision and recall, we can use the F1 score to balance the two. The F1 score is the harmonic mean of precision and recall, which can be particularly useful when the classes are imbalanced. In

Listing 3-14, we iterate through all thresholds and calculate the F1 score to select the threshold that achieves the highest balance between precision and recall. In this case, the optimal threshold is 0.34.

```
# Maximizing the F1-Score
f1_scores = []
for thresh in thresholds:
    y_pred_thresh = (y_pred_proba >= thresh).astype(int)
    f1 = f1_score(y_test, y_pred_thresh)
    f1_scores.append(f1)

optimal_idx = np.argmax(f1_scores)
optimal_threshold = thresholds[optimal_idx]
print(f"Optimal Threshold based on F1-Score: {optimal_threshold
    :.2f}")

# Output
Optimal Threshold based on F1-Score: 0.34
```

Listing 3-14 *Maximizing the F1 score*

3.7 Summary

Managing credit risk is a fundamental aspect of financial institutions, who need to assess potential losses due to potential default event. This chapter began with an introduction to credit risk, highlighting its importance in maintaining financial stability and preventing substantial financial losses. The discussion then moved deep into the core components of credit risk assessment: PD, LGD, and EAD. These elements collectively form ECL, a pivotal metric that integrates the likelihood, severity, and magnitude of potential defaults to provide a nuanced estimate of future expected losses.

This chapter also examined advanced concepts such as unexpected loss (UL) and stress loss (SL), which extend the ECL framework to account for extreme and unforeseen adverse events. In addition, the discussion transitioned to capital regulation, explaining how RWA and CAR are used under regulatory frameworks like Basel III to ensure that banks have sufficient capital relative to their risk exposures.

In the realm of predictive modeling, we introduced the construction of a PD model using logistic regression, starting with data preprocessing steps such as outlier detection, handling missing data, and categorical variable encoding. The model development process involves training the logistic regression model, making predictions, and evaluating its performance through metrics like accuracy, precision, recall, F1 score, and the ROC curve. We also discussed the importance of selecting an optimal classification threshold, particularly in credit risk contexts where the balance between true positives and false positives has significant financial implications. As an example, we introduced techniques such as maximizing the F1 score to select the most appropriate threshold.

In general, this chapter provided a framework for understanding and managing credit risk, integrating quantitative methodologies with practical considerations to improve financial institutions' ability to predict, assess, and mitigate potential losses. We further enhanced the discussion by introducing a hands-on example of building a PD model using logistic regression, which serves as an important first-level check on the creditworthiness of potential and existing obligors.

Managing Market Risk

Market risk encompasses the uncertainty and potential financial loss generated by broad-based fluctuations in asset prices, driven by factors such as interest rates, inflation, currency movements, and macroeconomic indicators. Unlike idiosyncratic risk, which pertains to specific firms or sectors and can be minimized through diversification, market risk is systemic throughout the global financial landscape. It can affect the performance of equities, bonds, commodities, and other asset classes simultaneously. The inherent challenge lies in managing this pervasive risk by balancing portfolio construction, hedging strategies, and regulatory oversight to mitigate vulnerabilities while still pursuing returns. For example, we can adopt a market-neutral strategy to bet on the relative difference between two assets rather than focusing on the directional change of a single asset, which is often random and difficult to predict.

Market risk is ubiquitous in multiple asset classes, such as equities, interest rates, foreign exchange rates, and commodity prices. For example, fluctuations in stock prices can result in substantial gains or losses, affecting both individual investors and institutional portfolios. Changes in interest rates affect borrowing costs, savings returns, and the valuations of fixed-income securities, which, in turn, influence investment decisions and overall economic activity. Fluctuations in currency exchange rates can also significantly affect multinational corporations, investors with foreign assets, and economies that depend significantly on imports and exports, such as Singapore. Furthermore, changes in the prices of essential commodities such as oil, gold, and agricultural products can have a profound impact on various industries, consumer prices, and geopolitical stability.

Note that market risk is widespread and cannot be completely eliminated through diversification strategies, which are primarily effective against unsystematic and idiosyncratic risk, which is the risk associated with individual assets or specific sectors. To manage market risk, it is essential to have a thorough understanding of the factors that influence market movements and to implement robust risk management frameworks. On this front, we often use various quantitative metrics to manage and reduce market risk effectively. These metrics offer crucial insights into different aspects of risk, including volatility, the potential scale of tail losses, and the overall exposure of investment portfolios to negative market conditions.

In this chapter, we focus on three fundamental market risk metrics: variance, maximum drawdown, and Value at Risk (VaR). First, variance is a statistical measure that quantifies how asset returns fluctuate from the mean, serving as an indicator of volatility and the level of uncertainty in investment returns. Second, maximum drawdown measures the largest decline from a peak to a trough in the value of an investment portfolio, highlighting the potential for significant losses during unfavorable market conditions. Lastly, VaR is a probabilistic measure that estimates the maximum expected loss of a portfolio over a specified time period at a given confidence level. Each of these metrics offers a distinct perspective on market risk, allowing a comprehensive assessment of potential downside risks for portfolios. These three risk measures jointly provide a benchmark for assessing risk levels and can be used together to guide capital allocation.

We examine each risk measure in detail in the following sections.

4.1 Variance

Variance is an important statistical metric that measures how much variability or dispersion exists within a dataset. In statistics, it is the second moment that is used to describe the distribution of the data. In finance, it is also a crucial tool for evaluating an asset's volatility, showing how much the asset's returns differ from the expected average over a specific timeframe. A high variance indicates greater uncertainty and risk, as the asset's returns fluctuate widely. In contrast, a low variance suggests more stable and, therefore, more predictable returns.

High volatility should not be universally considered a negative characteristic. In fact, a highly volatile asset can offer the potential for large gains, which can be particularly appealing to investors with a strong appetite for risk or those targeting substantial returns. At the same time, this elevated volatility carries an equally heightened possibility of severe losses. Consequently, such assets are generally not suitable for risk-averse individuals or those seeking more stable and predictable returns.

The variance of a series of returns can be calculated as the average of the squared differences between each return and the mean return. Here, we would differentiate between sample variance and population variance, where the former denotes the variance for the current limited sample, and the latter refers to the whole population (which we may not have access to). Specifically, for an asset with a series of returns

4.1 Variance

$R = \{R_1, R_2, \ldots, R_n\}$, the sample variance ($s^2$) is determined using the following formula:

$$s^2 = \frac{1}{n-1} \sum_{i=1}^{n} (R_i - \bar{R})^2$$

where R_i represents the return of the asset in the i-th period, $\bar{R}$ denotes the mean return calculated as $\bar{R} = \frac{1}{n} \sum_{i=1}^{n} R_i$, and n is the total number of observations.

Note that squaring the deviations from the mean ensures that both positive and negative differences contribute to the total variability, preventing them from canceling each other out. Furthermore, using $n-1$ in the denominator, known as Bessel's correction, adjusts for the bias that occurs when estimating the population variance from a sample. This adjustment ensures that the calculated variance is an unbiased estimator of the true variance of the population.

Let us look at an example of how to calculate the variance of a stock. Suppose a collection of monthly returns valued at 3%, −2%, and 4%. The average return is $\bar{R} = \frac{3+(-2)+4}{3} \approx 1.67\%$. Next, the squared deviations from the mean are computed: $(3 - 1.67)^2 \approx 1.77$, $(-2 - 1.67)^2 \approx 13.44$, and $(4 - 1.67)^2 \approx 5.44$. Summing these squared deviations gives approximately 20.65. Applying Bessel's correction by dividing by $n - 1 = 2$ yields a sample variance of $\frac{20.65}{2} \approx 10.33\%$. This indicates that the monthly returns of the stock fluctuate considerably around the average return of 1.67%, implying higher volatility and, therefore, a higher level of risk and the potential for significant gains or losses.

4.1.1 Unbiasedness in Sample Variance

When estimating the variance from a sample of data, it is important to use an unbiased estimator. This means that the expected value of the estimator should equal the true population variance as the number of observations gets bigger. To achieve this, the formula for sample variance uses a denominator of $n - 1$ instead of n. This adjustment, known as Bessel's correction, addresses the bias that can occur when estimating the population variance from a finite sample.

Consider a set of independently and identically distributed (i.i.d.) random variables $R_1, R_2, \ldots, R_n$ with a mean μ and variance σ^2. The sample mean $\bar{R}$ serves as an unbiased estimator of the population mean μ, as indicated by the fact that $E[\bar{R}] = \mu$ according to the law of large numbers. Recall the definition of sample variance s^2:

$$s^2 = \frac{1}{n-1} \sum_{i=1}^{n} (R_i - \bar{R})^2$$

Now we would also like to have $E[s^2] = \sigma^2$, which means that s^2 is an unbiased estimator of σ^2 in expectation. We begin by expanding the squared deviations by adding and subtracting μ.

$$\sum_{i=1}^{n}(R_i - \bar{R})^2 = \sum_{i=1}^{n}(R_i - \mu + \mu - \bar{R})^2$$

Now, we expand the squared term inside the summation:

$$\sum_{i=1}^{n}\left[(R_i - \mu) + (\mu - \bar{R})\right]^2 = \sum_{i=1}^{n}\left[(R_i - \mu)^2 + 2(R_i - \mu)(\mu - \bar{R}) + (\mu - \bar{R})^2\right]$$

We can break the expanded expression into three separate sums:

$$\sum_{i=1}^{n}(R_i - \bar{R})^2 = \sum_{i=1}^{n}(R_i - \mu)^2 + 2(\mu - \bar{R})\sum_{i=1}^{n}(R_i - \mu) + \sum_{i=1}^{n}(\mu - \bar{R})^2$$

Note that the first term $\sum_{i=1}^{n}(R_i - \mu)^2$ is the sum of squared deviations from the population mean. For the second term, we know that

$$\sum_{i=1}^{n}(R_i - \mu) = n\bar{R} - n\mu = n(\bar{R} - \mu)$$

Therefore, the second term becomes

$$2(\mu - \bar{R}) \cdot n(\bar{R} - \mu) = -2n(\bar{R} - \mu)^2$$

The third term is $\sum_{i=1}^{n}(\mu - \bar{R})^2 = n(\mu - \bar{R})^2$; since $\mu - \bar{R}$ is constant with respect to i, it can be factored out.

Putting it all together, we have

$$\sum_{i=1}^{n}(R_i - \bar{R})^2 = \sum_{i=1}^{n}(R_i - \mu)^2 - 2n(\bar{R} - \mu)^2 + n(\bar{R} - \mu)^2$$

Further simplifying, we have the following:

$$\sum_{i=1}^{n}(R_i - \bar{R})^2 = \sum_{i=1}^{n}(R_i - \mu)^2 - n(\bar{R} - \mu)^2$$

4.1 Variance

Now we can take the expected value of both sides:

$$E\left[\sum_{i=1}^n (R_i - \bar{R})^2\right] = E\left[\sum_{i=1}^n (R_i - \mu)^2\right] - E\left[n(\bar{R} - \mu)^2\right]$$

For the first term, since R_i are i.i.d. with variance σ^2, we have

$$E\left[\sum_{i=1}^n (R_i - \mu)^2\right] = \sum_{i=1}^n E\left[(R_i - \mu)^2\right] = n\sigma^2$$

For the second term, since the variance of the sample mean $\bar{R}$ is $\text{Var}(\bar{R}) = \frac{\sigma^2}{n}$, thus

$$E\left[n(\bar{R} - \mu)^2\right] = n \cdot E\left[(\bar{R} - \mu)^2\right] = n \cdot \text{Var}(\bar{R}) = n \cdot \frac{\sigma^2}{n} = \sigma^2$$

Substituting the expected values back gives

$$E\left[\sum_{i=1}^n (R_i - \bar{R})^2\right] = n\sigma^2 - \sigma^2 = (n-1)\sigma^2$$

Recall that

$$s^2 = \frac{1}{n-1} \sum_{i=1}^n (R_i - \bar{R})^2$$

Taking the expected value gives

$$E[s^2] = \frac{1}{n-1} E\left[\sum_{i=1}^n (R_i - \bar{R})^2\right] = \frac{1}{n-1} \cdot (n-1)\sigma^2 = \sigma^2$$

Thus, we have shown that the sample variance s^2 is an unbiased estimator of the population variance σ^2. This result indicates that using n as the denominator can lead to an underestimation of the true population variance, especially when the sample size n is small. That is

$$E\left[\frac{1}{n}\sum_{i=1}^n (R_i - \bar{R})^2\right] = \frac{n-1}{n}\sigma^2 < \sigma^2$$

which would underestimate the true population variance. Thus, Bessel's correction addresses this bias by using $n-1$ the denominator, ensuring that the sample variance serves as an unbiased estimator of the population variance.

4.1.2 Variance in Practice

Let us use Python to demonstrate how to compute the variance using real stock price data. In this example, we will retrieve historical stock prices, calculate monthly returns, and determine both sample and population variance. We first download daily adjusted closing prices for Apple (AAPL), covering the period from January 1, 2024, to December 1, 2024. The adjusted closing prices are used because they account for dividends and stock splits, providing a more accurate representation of the stock's true value over time.

We then calculate the returns after obtaining the data. First, we compute the daily returns by measuring the percentage change between consecutive trading days using the "pct_change()" function, which effectively assesses the day-to-day performance of the stock. To gain a broader understanding of the stock's performance, we then aggregate these daily returns into monthly returns. The aggregation is done by selecting the last available price for each month and calculating the percentage change from the previous month (also for the last day). Such aggregation smooths out daily volatility and highlights longer-term trends in the stock's performance.

As shown in Listing 4-1, the next step is to calculate the variance, which includes both sample variance and population variance. The sample variance is calculated with the degree of freedom (known as "ddof") set to 1. This means that the denominator in the variance formula is $n - 1$. As discussed earlier, this adjustment helps ensure that the sample variance is an unbiased estimator of the population variance. On the other hand, the population variance is calculated with "ddof" set to 0, which is the default setting, using n as the denominator. This approach assumes that the dataset represents the entire population rather than just a sample. Although this results in a biased estimator, it is useful for understanding how variance is computed when considering the entire population.

```
import pandas as pd
import numpy as np
import yfinance as yf
import matplotlib.pyplot as plt

# Suppress warnings for clean output
import warnings
warnings.filterwarnings('ignore')

# Step 1: Fetch Historical Stock Data
ticker = 'AAPL'    # Example: Apple Inc.
start_date = '2024-01-01'
end_date = '2024-12-01'

# Download daily adjusted closing prices
stock_data = yf.download(ticker, start=start_date, end=end_date,
    progress=False)['Adj Close']

# Display the first few rows
print("Historical Adjusted Closing Prices:")
print(stock_data.head())
```

4.1 Variance

```python
# Step 2: Calculate Daily Returns
daily_returns = stock_data.pct_change().dropna()

# Display the first few daily returns
print("\nDaily Returns:")
print(daily_returns.head())

# Step 3: Resample to Monthly Returns
monthly_returns = stock_data.resample('M').ffill().pct_change().
    dropna()

# Display the monthly returns
print("\nMonthly Returns:")
print(monthly_returns)

# Step 4: Calculate Sample Variance (Unbiased Estimator)
sample_variance = monthly_returns.var(ddof=1)  # ddof=1 for
    sample variance

# Step 5: Calculate Population Variance (Biased Estimator)
population_variance = monthly_returns.var(ddof=0)  # ddof=0 for
    population variance

print(f"\nSample Variance (Unbiased Estimator): {sample_variance
    :.4%}")
print(f"Population Variance (Biased Estimator): {
    population_variance:.4%}")

# Step 6: Visualization (Optional)
plt.figure(figsize=(10, 5))
plt.plot(stock_data.index, stock_data, label='Adjusted Close
    Price')
plt.title(f'{ticker} Adjusted Close Price in 2024')
plt.xlabel('Date')
plt.ylabel('Price ($)')
plt.legend()
plt.show()

# Output
Sample Variance (Unbiased Estimator): 0.3275%
Population Variance (Biased Estimator): 0.2947%
```

Listing 4-1 Downloading stock data and calculating variance

Figure 4-1 shows the daily adjusted close price of Apple in 2024.

4.1.3 Limitations of Variance As a Risk Measure

Although it is a commonly used metric for measuring volatility, variance has its own limitations. One major drawback is its increased sensitivity to outliers. Because variance is calculated by squaring the deviations from the mean, it tends

Figure 4-1 Daily adjusted close price of Apple in 2024

to exaggerate the effects of extreme values. This means that outliers—whether exceptionally high or low data points—can distort the variance, possibly resulting in misleading conclusions about the true variability of the dataset.

The Python code in Listing 4-2 demonstrates the impact of outliers on variance. By adding two extreme returns of 20% and −20% to the dataset, the population variance increases from approximately 0.0021 to 0.0028.

```
import numpy as np
import matplotlib.pyplot as plt

# Generate a dataset with normal returns
np.random.seed(42)
returns = np.random.normal(loc=0.02, scale=0.05, size=100)

# Calculate initial variance
initial_variance = np.var(returns, ddof=1)
print(f"Initial Variance: {initial_variance:.4f}")

# Introduce outliers
outliers = np.array([0.2, -0.2])  # Extreme positive and negative returns
returns_with_outliers = np.concatenate((returns, outliers))

# Calculate variance after adding outliers
variance_with_outliers = np.var(returns_with_outliers, ddof=1)
print(f"Variance with Outliers: {variance_with_outliers:.4f}")

# Visualization
plt.figure(figsize=(12, 6))

plt.subplot(1, 2, 1)
```

4.1 Variance

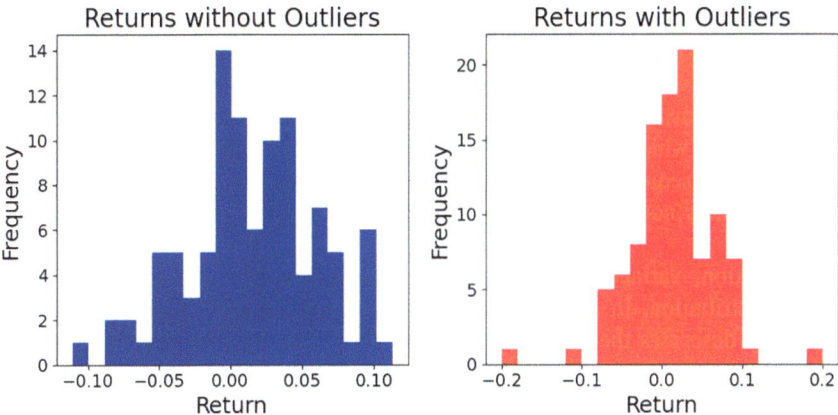

Figure 4-2 Distribution of returns before and after adding outliers

```
plt.hist(returns, bins=20, color='blue', alpha=0.7)
plt.title('Returns without Outliers')
plt.xlabel('Return')
plt.ylabel('Frequency')

plt.subplot(1, 2, 2)
plt.hist(returns_with_outliers, bins=20, color='red', alpha=0.7)
plt.title('Returns with Outliers')
plt.xlabel('Return')
plt.ylabel('Frequency')

plt.tight_layout()
plt.show()

# Output
Initial Variance: 0.0021
Variance with Outliers: 0.0028
```

Listing 4-2 Assessing the impact of outliers to variance

To further illustrate the distorting impact of outliers on the distribution, we plot the histograms before and after including extreme returns. As shown in Figure 4-2, the scale of the x-axis doubles, highlighting how outliers can skew the variance measure and alter the perceived distribution of returns. Specifically, the left histogram displays the distribution of returns without outliers, showing a concentration around the mean with relatively few extreme values. However, the right histogram includes outliers that extend the range of returns and increase the overall variance. Therefore, when extreme values are present or likely, relying only on variance alone can result in misleading risk assessments. On this front, it is often helpful to use additional risk measures, such as the median absolute deviation or the interquartile range, which are more resilient to the influence of outliers.

Another limitation of using variance as a risk measure is its treatment of non-symmetric returns. Variance treats both positive and negative deviations from the mean equally, which may not align with the specific risk preferences of most investors. In particular, a typical investor would be more concerned with the downside risk, which refers to the negative deviations, rather than fluctuations in the upside. Consequently, the equal weighting of upward and downward movements in variance may not adequately capture the types of risks that are most relevant to investors.

In addition, variance also depends on the assumption that returns follow a normal distribution. In a normal distribution, represented by $\mathcal{N}(\mu, \sigma^2)$, variance accurately describes the spread of the data. However, financial returns frequently show skewness and kurtosis, which indicate asymmetry and fat tails, respectively, thus deviating from normality. Skewness (γ_1) measures the asymmetry of the distribution and is defined as follows:

$$\gamma_1 = \frac{E[(R-\mu)^3]}{\sigma^3}$$

Kurtosis (γ_2) measures the heaviness of the distribution's tails and is defined as

$$\gamma_2 = \frac{E[(R-\mu)^4]}{\sigma^4} - 3$$

These higher-order moments provide additional insights that variance alone cannot capture. Since variance does not take into account the asymmetry or the tendency for extreme values in the distribution of returns, using these higher-order moments could better reflect the actual risk.

Besides, another important limitation of variance as a risk measure is that it assumes that asset returns do not depend on each other over time. As mentioned earlier, variance is based on the idea that returns are independent and identically distributed (i.i.d.). This means that the return R_t at any time t does not affect the returns at other times $t' \neq t$. This independence can be formally stated as

$$P(R_t \mid R_{t-1}, R_{t-2}, \ldots, R_1) = P(R_t)$$

This equation implies that past returns do not influence the probability distribution of future returns. In addition, each return R_t is assumed to follow the same probability distribution with constants μ and σ^2:

$$E[R_t] = \mu \quad \text{and} \quad \text{Var}(R_t) = \sigma^2 \quad \forall t$$

This uniformity ensures that the statistical properties of the returns remain consistent over various time periods. However, empirical observations in financial markets frequently show deviations from these assumptions, leading to time dependence in

4.1 Variance

return series. Two main forms of time dependence are autocorrelation (or serial correlation) and volatility clustering.

Autocorrelation refers to intercorrelation between observations at different time points in a time series. It could also pose modeling challenges, especially when current returns are correlated with past returns. The autocorrelation function (ACF) at lag k quantifies this relationship and is defined as

$$\rho_k = \frac{\text{Cov}(R_t, R_{t+k})}{\text{Var}(R_t)}$$

Here, $\text{Cov}(R_t, R_{t+k})$ is the covariance between the returns at times t and $t + k$, and ρ_k quantifies the (linear) correlation between R_t and R_{t+k}. When $\rho_k \neq 0$ for any k, it means that the time series data are autocorrelated, suggesting that past returns can be used to predict future returns. Positive autocorrelation ($\rho_k > 0$) means that high returns in the future are likely to be observed by high returns observed now, and vice versa.

When returns have autocorrelation, the assumption of independence is no longer valid. Positive autocorrelation can underestimate true variance because groups of high or low returns make consecutive periods less varied. However, negative autocorrelation can overestimate variance since the alternating high and low returns create a perception of greater variability.

In terms of volatility clustering, it is a commonly observed phenomenon in financial markets. It often occurs when periods of high volatility are followed by more high volatility, and similarly, periods of low volatility tend to follow other low volatility periods. This indicates that the variance of returns is not constant over time; instead, it fluctuates in response to past volatility. To model this behavior, we can use Autoregressive Conditional Heteroskedasticity (ARCH) or Generalized ARCH (GARCH) models. These models allow the variance σ_t^2 at a given time to depend on past squared returns and variances by the following:

$$\sigma_t^2 = \alpha_0 + \alpha_1 R_{t-1}^2 + \beta_1 \sigma_{t-1}^2$$

Here, α_0, α_1, and β_1 are the parameters to be estimated. The term $\alpha_1 R_{t-1}^2$ captures the impact of past squared returns (information about recent volatility), while $\beta_1 \sigma_{t-1}^2$ accounts for the persistence of volatility from previous periods.

As shown in Listing 4-3, to empirically investigate the time dependence of financial returns, we can analyze Apple's daily returns by computing the autocorrelation coefficients to evaluate the presence of serial correlation.

```
import matplotlib.pyplot as plt
from statsmodels.graphics.tsaplots import plot_acf, plot_pacf
from statsmodels.tsa.stattools import acf

# Create a figure with two subplots side by side
fig, axes = plt.subplots(1, 2, figsize=(14, 6))

# Autocorrelation Function (ACF) Plot
```

```python
 9  plot_acf(daily_returns, lags=30, alpha=0.05, ax=axes[0])
10  axes[0].set_xlabel('Lag')
11  axes[0].set_ylabel('Autocorrelation')
12
13  # Partial Autocorrelation Function (PACF) Plot
14  plot_pacf(daily_returns, lags=30, alpha=0.05, ax=axes[1])
15  axes[1].set_xlabel('Lag')
16  axes[1].set_ylabel('Partial Autocorrelation')
17
18  # Adjust layout
19  plt.tight_layout()
20  plt.show()
21
22  # Calculate and print autocorrelation coefficients for
        verification
23  autocorr_coeffs = acf(daily_returns, nlags=30, fft=False)
24  print("\nAutocorrelation Coefficients (First 30 Lags):")
25  print(autocorr_coeffs)
26
27  # Output
28  Autocorrelation Coefficients (First 30 Lags):
29  [ 1.00000000e+00  5.37236795e-02 -3.70519869e-02 -8.65535152e-02
30    7.83734376e-02 -1.05379582e-01  1.68068543e-02  3.55114712e-02
31    1.81508577e-02 -2.04299197e-03 -5.55866151e-02 -9.83094485e-03
32    4.56800420e-03  5.31590184e-02 -9.50762751e-02  6.75666460e-02
33   -4.03906304e-02  1.89938306e-02  2.36953557e-02  3.23774660e-02
34    5.57144925e-03  4.98538062e-03  7.48970516e-02  4.48094570e-05
35   -1.34294058e-02 -8.26390596e-02  4.67667504e-02  9.16426999e-02
36    4.78552297e-02 -5.53208738e-02 -1.74259679e-02]
```

Listing 4-3 Assessing autocorrelation

The ACF plot of daily returns, shown in Figure 4-3, illustrates the correlation between returns at various time lags. For Apple's daily returns in 2024, the autocorrelation coefficients for the first 30 lags are nearly zero, indicating minimal serial correlation. This suggests that the returns are approximately independent over time, supporting the assumption of i.i.d. returns. As a result, this validates the use of variance as a risk measure in this context.

However, this observation may not apply universally to all assets or in different time periods. For example, the value at lag 5 is very close to the threshold at the 95% confidence interval, suggesting a potential autocorrelation at this specific lag. The 95% confidence interval indicates that there is a 95% probability that the true autocorrelation coefficient for each lag falls within this range, assuming that the data follow a white noise process (i.e., no autocorrelation).

Financial markets are inherently dynamic, and during times of market stress or significant economic events, characteristics such as volatility clustering can become more pronounced. For example, at the onset of a financial crisis, returns may show high autocorrelation and persistent volatility. This situation requires more advanced risk measures that go beyond just variance. To address these limitations, variance is frequently combined with other risk measures such as Value at Risk (VaR)

4.2 Maximum Drawdown (Max Drawdown)

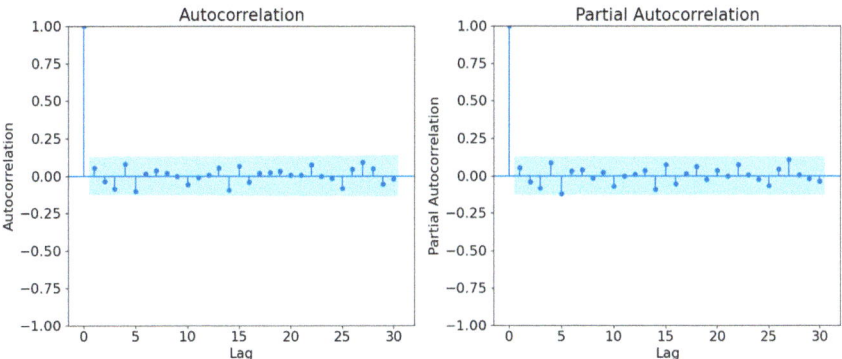

Figure 4-3 ACF and PACF plots of Apple's daily returns

and maximum drawdown. These downside risk measures offer a more thorough assessment of market risk, capturing elements that variance alone may miss. By using measures that consider time dependence and asymmetric risks, investors can gain a clearer and more comprehensive understanding of the risks involved in the investment portfolios.

4.2 Maximum Drawdown (Max Drawdown)

Unlike variance, which places equal weight on both upside and downside risk, the maximum drawdown (or Max Drawdown) measure specifically focuses on the download risk in an extreme case. It identifies the largest up-to-date decline in a portfolio's value from its peak to its lowest point before recovering. This measure represents the worst potential loss an investor could experience over a specific time frame. By focusing on the most significant drop in value, Max Drawdown highlights the potential severity of losses during challenging market conditions, offering valuable insights into the investment's risk and resilience. Formally, for a series of portfolio values $P = \{P_1, P_2, \ldots, P_n\}$, the Max Drawdown ($MDD$) is defined as

$$MDD = \max_{1 \leq i \leq j \leq n} \left(\frac{P_i - P_j}{P_i} \right) \times 100\%$$

In this equation, P_i represents the portfolio value at its peak time i, and P_j is the value at the trough time j that occurs after the peak i. The fraction $\frac{P_i - P_j}{P_i}$ calculates the percentage decline from the peak P_i to the trough P_j. Essentially, Max Drawdown identifies the most significant loss during the investment period, which is unlike variance that measures average volatility. This focused approach provides a clear view of downside risk, presenting a better view of the potential substantial losses in the portfolios.

To illustrate the calculation of Max Drawdown, consider an investor monitoring the monthly portfolio values over a four-month period, as shown below:

Month	Portfolio Value (P)
1	$800
2	$850
3	$830
4	$810

To calculate the Max Drawdown, first, we need to identify all the peak-trough pairs within the four-month period. A peak refers to a portfolio value that is followed by a decline, while a trough is the lowest portfolio value that occurs after that peak before a new peak is reached. In this case, we identify the first peak at Month 2 ($850), with toughs at Month 3 ($830) and Month 4 ($810).

Next, for each peak-trough pair, we can calculate the drawdown as follows:

$$\text{Drawdown} = \left(\frac{P_{\text{peak}} - P_{\text{trough}}}{P_{\text{peak}}} \right) \times 100\%$$

Here, P_{peak} is the portfolio (or asset) value at the peak, and P_{trough} is the value at the trough. Specifically, from Peak Month 2 ($850) to Trough Month 3 ($830), we have

$$\text{Drawdown} = \left(\frac{850 - 830}{850} \right) \times 100\% = \left(\frac{20}{850} \right) \times 100\% \approx 2.35\%$$

From Peak Month 2 ($850) to Trough Month 4 ($810), we have

$$\text{Drawdown} = \left(\frac{850 - 810}{850} \right) \times 100\% = \left(\frac{40}{850} \right) \times 100\% \approx 4.71\%$$

Among these daily drawdowns, the largest is 4.71%, which comes from Peak Month 2 ($850) to Trough Month 4 ($810). Thus, this value represents the maximum drawdown for the portfolio over the four-month period, indicating the deepest decline experienced. Since Max Drawdown is typically reported as a negative percentage, it would be -4.71% in this case.

4.2.1 Distinctive Features of Maximum Drawdown

Max Drawdown measures the largest loss from a peak to a trough during an investment period, giving us a clear perspective on potential extreme downside risk. In contrast to variance, which assesses average volatility, Max Drawdown focuses specifically on extreme losses. It allows us to grasp the potential for significant declines in the portfolio. With Max Drawdown, we can evaluate the possible severity

4.2 Maximum Drawdown (Max Drawdown)

of losses and make informed decisions about risk management and investment strategies. For example, a profiting strategy may not be so attractive if it comes with a big Max Drawdown. This metric is especially valuable for assessing portfolio performance during turbulent market conditions and for comparing the risk profiles of different investment options.

Specifically, Max Drawdown is notable for its focus on the sequence of returns, distinguishing it from variance. Although variance sums all deviations from the mean regardless of their order, Max Drawdown specifically identifies the largest decline from a peak to a trough in a portfolio's history. This means that Max Drawdown indicates not only how much a portfolio can lose but also when those losses occur. For example, a sharp decline following a high peak results in a higher Max Drawdown compared to a gradual decrease, even if the total loss is the same. This ability to take into account the order of returns allows Max Drawdown to provide a clearer understanding of extreme loss events, which is essential for effective risk management.

In addition, Max Drawdown is a non-parametric measure, meaning it does not assume that investment returns follow a specific distribution. This characteristic makes it versatile and applicable across various market conditions and asset types. Unlike variance, which is most effective when returns are normally distributed, Max Drawdown remains relevant even when returns are skewed or exhibit heavy tails. This is especially important in financial markets, where returns often deviate from normal patterns and can display irregular behaviors and extreme values. Therefore, it can provide an accurate assessment of downside risk without being constrained by rigid statistical models, thus being able to cater to a more realistic perspective on investment risks.

Instead of reporting separate measures, Max Drawdown can complement other risk measures, with variance included. Although variance provides an average assessment of volatility by considering all deviations from the mean, Max Drawdown focuses on the most significant losses. This combination gives investors a comprehensive understanding of both regular and extreme risks. For example, a portfolio with a low variance but a high Max Drawdown may indicate that it typically experiences manageable volatility but is at risk of substantial losses during unfavorable market conditions. Conversely, a portfolio with a high variance but a low Max Drawdown suggests frequent fluctuations without severe declines, which might appeal to investors seeking stability.

We can also use Max Drawdown to identify the maximum potential loss an investment could experience, thus assessing how much capital we should retain as reserves for significant downturns. Including Max Drawdown in capital allocation ensures that portfolios maintain sufficient liquidity and buffers during periods of market stress. For example, if a portfolio has a Max Drawdown of 10%, we may decide to hold additional reserves or implement hedging strategies to mitigate the impact of similar future losses. This proactive approach improves the durability of the portfolio and protects against challenging market conditions, which further aligns investment strategies with individual risk tolerance.

However, we should note that the Max Drawdown is highly sensitive to the time period chosen for calculation. The size of Max Drawdown can vary significantly based on the duration of the measurement. Shorter periods may reflect temporary market fluctuations, resulting in greater variability in Max Drawdown. In contrast, longer periods incorporate larger market movements, leading to more stable and accurate Max Drawdown values. This sensitivity is related to the time frame used to identify peaks and troughs. For example, calculating Max Drawdown over six months may reveal different risks compared to a one-year period due to varying exposure to market cycles and volatility. Therefore, selecting the appropriate time horizon is an important decision when assessing the risk associated with a given portfolio strategy.

The time scale we choose for calculating Max Drawdown, whether daily or monthly, can also affect the results. Daily data capture quick market changes, showing sharp declines that occur in just a few trading days. This often leads to higher or more frequent drawdowns, as daily prices react quickly to news and market events. In contrast, using monthly data smooths out these daily ups and downs, focusing on longer-term trends. This typically results in smaller or fewer declines. In practice, short-term traders may favor daily Max Drawdown to manage immediate risks, while long-term investors may prefer monthly Max Drawdown to understand overall performance and how well they can withstand longer market downturns.

4.2.2 Calculating Max Drawdown

To better appreciate how Max Drawdown is calculated and why it is important, let us consider an example that calculates total returns over time, identifies daily declines, and determines the largest drop (i.e., the Max Drawdown).

```python
# Step 1: Calculate Cumulative Returns
cumulative_returns = (1 + daily_returns).cumprod()

# Step 2: Calculate Running Maximum
running_max = cumulative_returns.cummax()

# Step 3: Calculate Drawdown
drawdown = (cumulative_returns - running_max) / running_max

# Step 4: Calculate Max Drawdown
max_drawdown = drawdown.min() * 100   # Convert to percentage

print(f"\nMaximum Drawdown: {max_drawdown:.2f}%")

# Step 5: Visualization of Cumulative Returns and Drawdown
plt.figure(figsize=(12, 6))   # Increased figsize for better readability
plt.plot(cumulative_returns, label='Cumulative Returns')
plt.plot(running_max, label='Running Maximum', linestyle='--')
plt.fill_between(cumulative_returns.index, cumulative_returns,
    running_max,
```

4.2 Maximum Drawdown (Max Drawdown)

```
                        color='red', alpha=0.3, label='Drawdown')

# Uncomment and set 'ticker' if needed
# plt.title(f'{ticker} Cumulative Returns and Drawdown (Jan-Jun
    2023)')

plt.xlabel('Date')
plt.ylabel('Cumulative Returns')
plt.legend()

# Rotate x-axis labels for better readability
plt.xticks(rotation=45)

# Adjust layout to prevent clipping of tick-labels
plt.tight_layout()

plt.show()

# Step 6: Plot Drawdown Over Time
plt.figure(figsize=(12, 6))   # Increased figsize for consistency
plt.plot(drawdown, label='Drawdown', color='red')

# Uncomment and set 'ticker' if needed
# plt.title(f'{ticker} Drawdown Over Time (Jan-Jun 2023)')

plt.xlabel('Date')
plt.ylabel('Drawdown')
plt.legend()

# Rotate x-axis labels for better readability
plt.xticks(rotation=45)

# Adjust layout to prevent clipping of tick-labels
plt.tight_layout()

plt.show()

# Output
Maximum Drawdown: -15.35%
```

Listing 4-4 Calculating max drawdown

In Listing 4-4, we first calculate the cumulative returns by multiplying the daily returns over a specific period. We then monitor the highest value that the returns have reached up to each day. Following this, we assess how much the current returns have decreased from this peak value. The smallest value in the drawdown series is identified and converted into a percentage, which represents a Max Drawdown of −15.35% in this example.

Figure 4-4 shows the total returns alongside the highest value reached. The shaded area indicates the periods when the returns were below the peak, which denotes drawdowns.

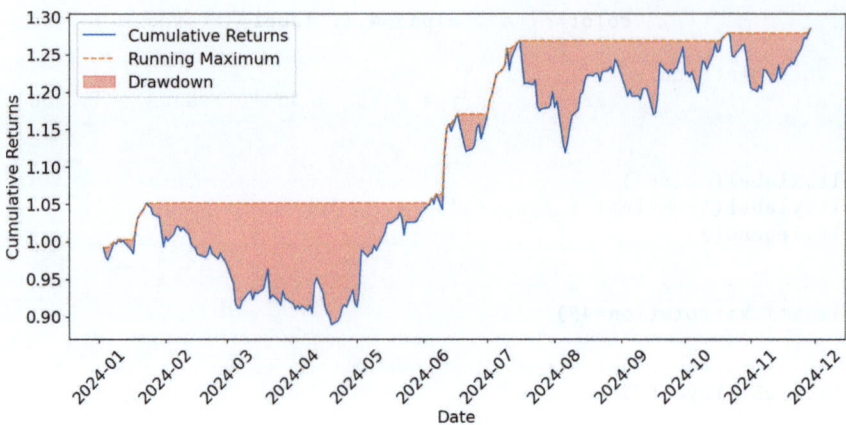

Figure 4-4 Daily cumulative returns and running maximum

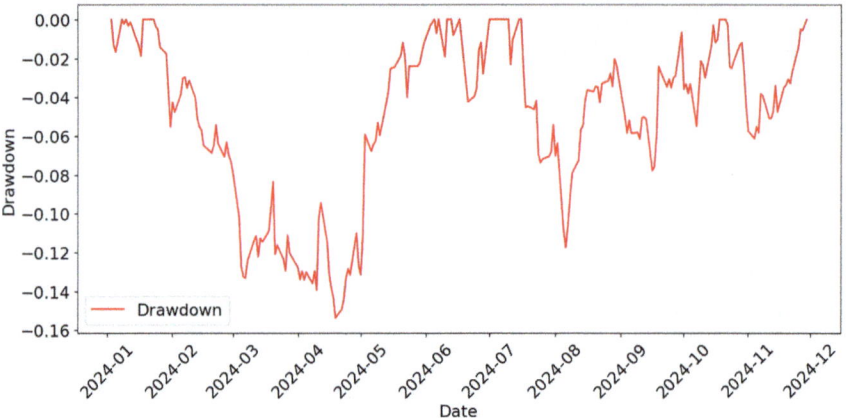

Figure 4-5 Daily drawdown

Figure 4-5 displays the daily drawdowns over time, illustrating the extent and duration of each decline. The Max Drawdown is then identified around mid-April 2024.

Max Drawdown is an important measure of risk, but it is most effective when used alongside other risk metrics to provide a comprehensive view of portfolio risk. For example, combining Max Drawdown with measures like VaR and Expected Shortfall (ES) offers insight into both the probability and magnitude of potential losses. Additionally, examining the rolling Max Drawdown over various time periods can reveal the frequency and duration of drawdowns, which is valuable for managing risk dynamically. Understanding the recovery time from drawdowns is also crucial, as it indicates the portfolio's ability to rebound from losses and impacts long-term investment performance. Integrating it into Monte Carlo simulations and stress testing can also enhance risk assessments by evaluating how the portfolio may perform under different adverse conditions.

The next section introduces another commonly used downside risk measure: Value at Risk (VaR).

4.3 Value at Risk

Value at Risk, commonly known as VaR, is a key measure used in finance to assess the risk associated with an investment portfolio. It is an estimate of the maximum potential loss that a portfolio could experience over a specific time period, such as a day, week, or month, at a certain confidence level. For example, a daily VaR of 1% at a 95% confidence level indicates that there is only a 5% chance that the portfolio will lose more than 1% of its value in a single day.

VaR is formally defined as the smallest loss that will not be exceeded with a given probability over a specified time frame. Formally, for a portfolio with returns $R = \{R_1, R_2, \ldots, R_n\}$, the VaR at a confidence level α over a time horizon T is expressed as

$$VaR_\alpha = \inf\{x \in \mathbb{R} : P(L \leq x) \geq \alpha\}$$

Here, $L = P_0 - P_T$ represents the loss, where P_0 is the initial value of the portfolio and P_T is its value at time T. This definition ensures that there is at most $(1 - \alpha)$ probability that the loss L exceeds the VaR.

Note that VaR is essentially a quantile measure, meaning it identifies the threshold loss value below which a specific percentage of losses occur. It represents the inverse of the cumulative distribution function (CDF) of the loss distribution at a given confidence level.

$$VaR_\alpha = F_L^{-1}(1 - \alpha)$$

where F_L^{-1} is the quantile function of the loss distribution.

Regulatory bodies, including the Basel Committee on Banking Supervision, recognize and require the use of VaR to assess market risk in financial institutions. VaR can be applied to portfolios of various sizes and complexities, from straightforward stock holdings to complex combinations of assets. This flexibility allows many investors and financial professionals to evaluate and manage risk in a wide range of investment products.

In terms of mathematical properties, although VaR has several desirable properties, such as being monotonic and positively homogeneous, it does not always meet the requirement of subadditivity. Subadditivity means that the VaR of a combined portfolio should be less than or equal to the sum of the VaRs of the individual portfolios. That is, for two portfolios A and B, we would like to see

$$VaR_\alpha(A+B) \leq VaR_\alpha(A) + VaR_\alpha(B)$$

However, in cases where portfolios exhibit heavy-tailed return distributions or have high levels of dependency, this property may not be valid. As a result, VaR might not always promote diversification, since the VaR of a combined portfolio can sometimes exceed the sum of the individual VaRs. This makes VaR much less appealing compared to improved measures such as conditional VaR, since diversification is the only free lunch in finance.

Besides, VaR only considers extreme risk up to the specified quantile level when it comes to capturing the tail risk while ignoring further extreme losses that occur beyond the VaR threshold. To address this limitation, Expected Shortfall (ES) is often used alongside VaR. ES measures the average loss that occurs when losses exceed the VaR level, offering a more comprehensive understanding of potential extreme losses. It is defined as

$$ES_\alpha = E[L \mid L > VaR_\alpha]$$

When it comes to calculation, VaR can be calculated using various methods, including Historical Simulation, the Variance-Covariance (or parametric) approach, and Monte Carlo simulation. Each method is based on different mathematical principles and assumptions, providing unique perspectives and varying levels of accuracy depending on the portfolio's characteristics and the data available.

4.3.1 Historical Simulation Approach

The Historical Simulation approach is a simple method for calculating VaR that does not require any specific statistical distribution for returns. Instead, it relies entirely on historical return data, operating under the premise that past returns can help predict future performance.

To start, we first collect a series of past portfolio returns $R = \{R_1, R_2, \ldots, R_n\}$ collected over the time period of analysis. We then sort the returns from lowest to highest to create an ordered list, $R_{(1)} \leq R_{(2)} \leq \ldots \leq R_{(n)}$. The next step is to identify the return that corresponds to the $(1-\alpha)$ percentile of this sorted list, which represents the VaR at a confidence level α. Mathematically, VaR at confidence level α is calculated as

$$VaR_\alpha = R_{(\lceil(1-\alpha)n\rceil)}$$

Here, $R_{(k)}$ refers to the k-th return in the sorted list. The ceiling function $\lceil \cdot \rceil$ ensures that we select the smallest integer greater than or equal to $(1-\alpha)n$, which accurately captures the desired percentile in the dataset.

4.3 Value at Risk

For example, to determine 95% VaR using the Historical Simulation method, we would look for the return at the fifth percentile of the sorted historical returns. This process is illustrated in Listing 4-5.

```
# Historical Simulation VaR
confidence_level = 0.95
VaR_hist = np.percentile(daily_returns, (1 - confidence_level) *
    100)

print(f"Historical Simulation VaR at {confidence_level*100}%
    confidence level: {VaR_hist:.2%}")

# Visualization
plt.figure(figsize=(10, 6))
plt.hist(daily_returns, bins=50, alpha=0.7, color='blue',
    edgecolor='black')
plt.axvline(x=VaR_hist, color='red', linestyle='dashed',
    linewidth=2, label=f'VaR at {confidence_level*100}%')
plt.title(f'Histogram of {ticker} Daily Returns with VaR ({
    confidence_level*100}%)')
plt.xlabel('Daily Return')
plt.ylabel('Frequency')
plt.legend()
plt.show()

# Output
Historical Simulation VaR at 95.0% confidence level: -2.18%
```

Listing 4-5 Calculating VaR using the historical simulation approach

Running this code reveals that Apple's VaR at a 95% confidence level for the year 2024 (until the first of December) is -2.18%. This means there is a 95% confidence that the daily loss will not exceed 2.18%. Figure 4-6 displays a histogram of Apple's daily returns for 2024, highlighting the VaR threshold with a red dashed line. The histogram illustrates the distribution of returns and indicates where VaR falls within this distribution. Again, this method does not consider losses that exceed the VaR threshold, and we can use ES to measure the average loss that occurs beyond the VaR level.

In summary, the Historical Simulation approach offers a straightforward and intuitive method for estimating VaR using historical return data. Although this method effectively illustrates potential losses based on past performance, it may not account for extremely rare or severe losses.

The next section introduces the second approach for the VaR calculation: the Variance-Covariance (parametric) approach.

4.3.2 Variance-Covariance (Parametric) Approach

The Variance-Covariance method, also known as the parameter approach, is another technique to calculate VaR. This method assumes that portfolio returns follow a

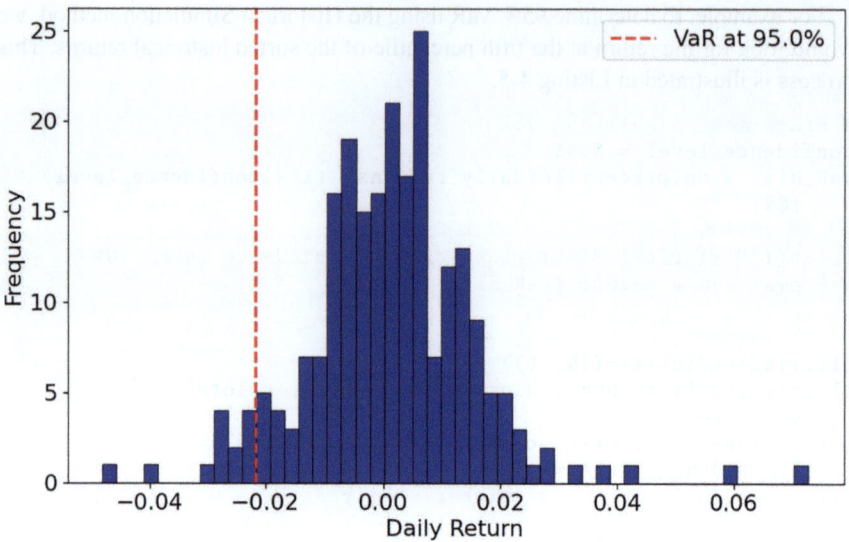

Figure 4-6 Histogram of daily returns with VaR at 95%

normal distribution, which simplifies the analytical computation of VaR by using the mean and standard deviation of the returns.

Specifically, consider portfolio returns denoted by R, which are normally distributed as $R \sim N(\mu, \sigma^2)$, where μ represents the mean return and σ is the standard deviation. The loss over the time horizon can be expressed as $L = -P_0 R$, where P_0 is the initial portfolio value. Our objective is to determine VaR_α, the VaR at a confidence level α.

We begin by writing the probability that the loss exceeds the VaR:

$$P(L > VaR_\alpha) = 1 - \alpha$$

Substituting $L = -P_0 R$ into the equation gives

$$P(-P_0 R > VaR_\alpha) = 1 - \alpha$$

Since P_0 is positive, dividing both sides of the inequality $-P_0 R > VaR_\alpha$ by $-P_0$ reverses the inequality:

$$P\left(R < -\frac{VaR_\alpha}{P_0}\right) = 1 - \alpha$$

Given that R is normally distributed, we can standardize it using the z-score transformation:

$$Z = \frac{R - \mu}{\sigma}$$

4.3 Value at Risk

This allows the probability statement to be rewritten in terms of the standard normal distribution:

$$P\left(Z < \frac{-\frac{VaR_\alpha}{P_0} - \mu}{\sigma}\right) = 1 - \alpha$$

Let $z_{1-\alpha}$ denote the z-score corresponding to the cumulative probability $1 - \alpha$. Therefore, the equation becomes

$$\frac{-\frac{VaR_\alpha}{P_0} - \mu}{\sigma} = z_{1-\alpha}$$

Recognizing that the standard normal distribution is symmetric, $z_{1-\alpha}$ is equal to $-z_\alpha$, where z_α is the z-score corresponding to the cumulative probability α. Substituting this into the equation yields

$$\frac{-\frac{VaR_\alpha}{P_0} - \mu}{\sigma} = -z_\alpha$$

We proceed with the simplification to solve for VaR_α:

$$-\frac{VaR_\alpha}{P_0} - \mu = -\sigma z_\alpha$$

$$\frac{VaR_\alpha}{P_0} + \mu = \sigma z_\alpha$$

$$VaR_\alpha = P_0(\sigma z_\alpha - \mu)$$

This formula adjusts the mean return μ by multiplying the standard deviation σ and the z-score z_α, thus capturing the risk-adjusted threshold for potential losses.

For instance, consider a portfolio with an initial value $P_0 = \$1,000$, an average daily return $\mu = 0.2\%$, a standard deviation $\sigma = 1.5\%$, and a confidence level $\alpha = 99\%$ (so $z_\alpha = 2.33$). The VaR can be computed as follows:

$$VaR_{0.99} = 1,000 \times (0.015 \times 2.33 - 0.002) = \$32.95$$

This means that there is a 1% chance that the portfolio will lose more than $32.95 in a single day. In other words, among the worst 1% of trading days, losses could exceed this amount, which is crucial information for risk management and capital allocation decisions.

Listing 4-6 demonstrates how to calculate VaR using the Variance-Covariance (parametric) approach. We normalize the portfolio value by setting $P_0 = 1$ to express VaR as a percentage.

```python
from scipy.stats import norm

# Variance-Covariance VaR
confidence_level = 0.95
mu = daily_returns.mean()
sigma = daily_returns.std()
z_score = norm.ppf(confidence_level)  # z-score for the given
    confidence level

# Portfolio Value (normalized)
P0 = 1

# VaR Calculation
VaR_var_cov = P0 * (sigma * z_score - mu)

print(f"Variance-Covariance VaR at {confidence_level*100}%
    confidence level: -{VaR_var_cov:.2%}")

# OutputVariance-Covariance VaR at 95.0% confidence level: -2.26%
```

Listing 4-6 Calculating VaR using the parametric approach

Here, we set *confidence_level* to 0.95 to reflect a 95% confidence level. The variables *mu* and *sigma* represent the mean and standard deviation of the daily returns, respectively. The *z_score* is calculated using the inverse cumulative distribution function of the normal distribution for the specified confidence level. By setting the portfolio value P_0 to 1, the VaR is expressed as a percentage. Running this code yields a VaR of approximately -2.26%, indicating a 5% chance that the portfolio will lose more than 2.26% of its value in a day using the parametric approach. This VaR is slightly higher than the one obtained using the Historical Simulation method, reflecting a greater potential loss based on the assumption of a normal distribution.

Note that the z-score z_α is a key element in this calculation, as it indicates how many standard deviations a data point is from the mean for a given cumulative probability. For a 95% confidence level with $\alpha = 0.95$, we have $z_\alpha \approx 1.645$. This z-score directly connects VaR to the characteristics of the normal distribution, allowing for a straightforward calculation based on the portfolio's mean and standard deviation.

Also, note that the parametric approach depends on the assumption that return distributions are normal. This assumption may not always hold, particularly in financial markets, where returns can show large deviations from a normal distribution. Although this method provides an analytical solution for VaR, making it computationally efficient, its accuracy is based on how well the normality assumption fits the actual return distribution. In situations where the return distribution has long tails or high levels of autocorrelation, the VaR estimates may be inaccurate, and extreme events might not be adequately captured. Therefore, despite its usefulness, the Variance-Covariance approach has limitations and should be applied with an understanding of its underlying assumptions and potential inaccuracies.

4.3 Value at Risk

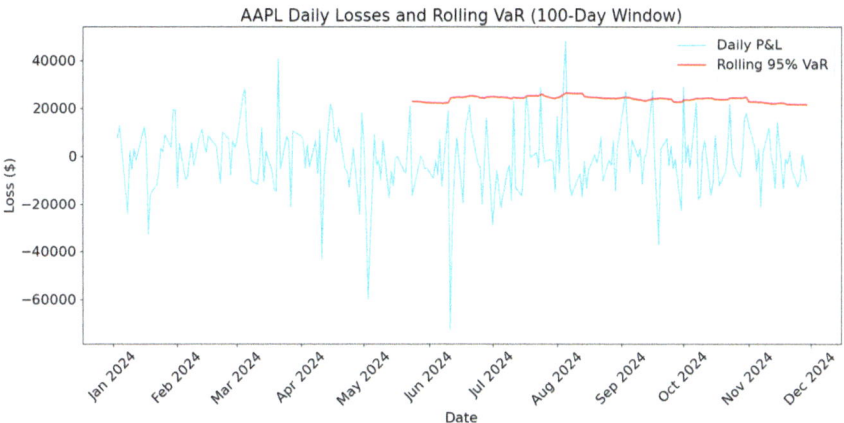

Figure 4-7 Daily P&L and rolling VaR using the Variance-Covariance approach

Figure 4-7 plots the daily P&L and rolling VaR at the confidence level 95% with a window size of 100 days, along with the code snippet shown in Listing 4-7. Plotting the running VaR gives us an idea of the long-term trend of extreme loss metrics.

```python
from scipy.stats import norm
import numpy as np
import pandas as pd
import matplotlib.pyplot as plt
import matplotlib.dates as mdates

window_size = 100  # Number of days in the rolling window

# Calculate Rolling VaR using Variance-Covariance Approach
mu_rolling = daily_returns.rolling(window=window_size).mean()
sigma_rolling = daily_returns.rolling(window=window_size).std()
z_score = norm.ppf(0.95)  # 95% confidence level

# Portfolio Value
P0 = 1_000_000  # $1,000,000

# Calculate Rolling VaR
rolling_VaR = P0 * (sigma_rolling * z_score - mu_rolling)

# Calculate Daily Losses in Dollar Terms
daily_losses = -P0 * daily_returns

# Plot Overlay of Daily Losses and Rolling VaR
plt.figure(figsize=(14, 7))
plt.plot(daily_losses.index, daily_losses, label='Daily P&L',
    alpha=0.5)
plt.plot(rolling_VaR.index, rolling_VaR, label='Rolling 95% VaR',
    color='red')
plt.title(f'{ticker} Daily Losses and Rolling VaR ({window_size}-
    Day Window)')
```

```
28  plt.xlabel('Date')
29  plt.ylabel('Loss ($)')
30  plt.legend()
31
32  # Format x-axis to show monthly ticks
33  ax = plt.gca()
34  ax.xaxis.set_major_locator(mdates.MonthLocator())   # Set major
      ticks to monthly intervals
35  ax.xaxis.set_major_formatter(mdates.DateFormatter('%b %Y'))  #
      Format ticks as 'Month Year'
36  plt.xticks(rotation=45)   # Rotate x-axis labels for better
      readability
37
38  plt.tight_layout()   # Adjust layout to prevent clipping of tick-
      labels
39  plt.show()
```

Listing 4-7 Plotting daily P&L and rolling VaR

Next, we look at the third approach to calculate VaR.

4.3.3 Monte Carlo Simulation

The Monte Carlo simulation method calculates VaR by generating numerous simulated portfolio returns based on statistical models. This approach is highly flexible, enabling the modeling of complex return distributions and the relationships between assets without relying on strict assumptions of normality.

To calculate VaR using Monte Carlo simulation, we first define the statistical properties of the portfolio returns, including the mean vector and the covariance matrix. Next, we generate a large number N of random return scenarios based on these statistical parameters. For each simulation test, we compute the corresponding loss and then determine the VaR at the $(1 - \alpha)$ percentile of the loss distribution. This identified loss represents the VaR at the specified confidence level.

Formally, if portfolio returns follow a multivariate normal distribution $R \sim \mathcal{N}(\mu, \Sigma)$, we simulate N returns $R_1, R_2, \ldots, R_N$. For each simulated return R_i, we compute the loss $L_i = -P_0 R_i$, where P_0 is the initial portfolio value. The VaR at the confidence level α is then calculated as

$$VaR_\alpha = \text{Percentile}(L, 100 \times (1 - \alpha))$$

where $L = \{L_1, L_2, \ldots, L_N\}$ represents the set of simulated losses.

Listing 4-8 demonstrates how to calculate VaR using the Monte Carlo simulation approach.

```
1  # Monte Carlo Simulation of Returns
2  np.random.seed(42)   # For reproducibility
3  num_simulations = 1000
4  simulated_returns = np.random.normal(mu, sigma, num_simulations)
5
```

4.3 Value at Risk

```
# Calculate Simulated Losses
simulated_losses = -P0 * simulated_returns

# Calculate VaR from Simulated Losses
VaR_monte_carlo = np.percentile(simulated_losses, 100 * (1 -
    confidence_level))

print(f"Monte Carlo Simulation VaR at {confidence_level*100}%
    confidence level: {VaR_monte_carlo:.2%}")

# Output
Monte Carlo Simulation VaR at 95.0% confidence level: -2.54%
```

Listing 4-8 Calculating VaR using the Monte Carlo approach

In this code listing, we first set the random seed to ensure that the results can be reproduced. The *simulated_returns* are generated using a normal distribution with a specified mean and standard deviation, simulating a defined number of returns (*num_simulations*). The *simulated_losses* are then calculated by multiplying each simulated return by $-P_0$, where P_0 represents the initial portfolio value. Finally, *VaR_monte_carlo* is computed using the Monte Carlo method by identifying the percentile of the simulated losses that corresponds to $100 \times (1 - \alpha)$.

The result shows that the VaR calculated using the Monte Carlo simulation approach is approximately -2.54%, which is the highest potential loss compared to the Historical Simulation and Variance-Covariance methods. Figure 4-8 shows the simulated daily returns/losses along with the associated VaR at 95%.

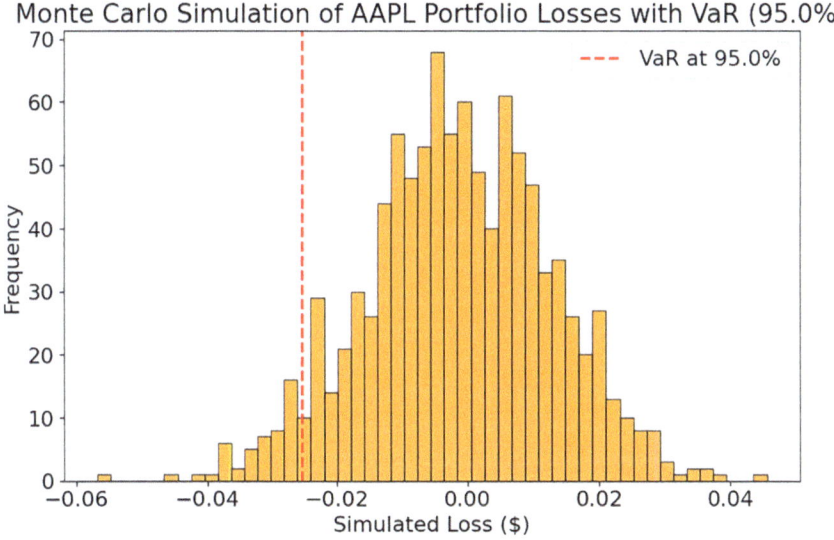

Figure 4-8 Monte Carlo simulation of daily P&L with VaR at 95%

Overall, the Monte Carlo simulation approach provides considerable flexibility by accommodating more complex return distributions and asset dependencies within a portfolio. However, this method can be computationally intensive, as we need to generate a large number of simulated returns. The computation becomes more involved, particularly for large portfolios or when a high number of simulations are required. In practice, financial institutions typically employ a combination of methods, including Historical Simulation, Variance-Covariance, and Monte Carlo simulation, to cross-validate VaR estimates. This approach ensures that estimates are robust under various market scenarios.

4.4 Summary

In this chapter, we explored market risk, which is a crucial type of systematic risk that can result in financial losses due to fluctuations in market factors throughout the entire financial system. We also introduced several metrics to help quantify, manage, and mitigate market risk, including Variance, Max Drawdown, and VaR.

Variance measures the variability of asset returns by calculating the average of the squared deviations from the mean return. This provides insight into the volatility and risk associated with an asset or portfolio. A higher variance indicates a greater spread of returns, which in turn signifies a higher risk. However, variance has several drawbacks. It is sensitive to outliers, treats positive and negative deviations equally, assumes a normal distribution, and assumes that returns are independent and identically distributed. These assumptions may not always hold in real financial markets.

Maximum drawdown measures the largest observed loss from a portfolio's peak value to its lowest point before a new peak is reached. This metric highlights the severity of potential losses, which makes it especially useful for understanding worst-case scenarios that investors may face. Unlike variance, maximum drawdown is path dependent, meaning it does not rely on any specific distribution of returns. This attribute makes it a robust measure under different market conditions. However, it is sensitive to the chosen time horizon.

VaR is a measure that estimates the maximum expected loss over a specified time period at a given confidence level. It provides a probabilistic assessment of potential losses. Essentially, VaR is a quantile measure that indicates the threshold loss value below which a certain percentage of losses is expected to fall. It is versatile and can be applied to different time horizons and portfolio sizes, making it a valuable tool for evaluating risk. However, it does not capture risks that exist beyond the specified confidence level, is sensitive to underlying model assumptions, and lacks the subadditive property. These shortcomings can reduce the advantages of diversification.

VaR can be calculated through various methods, each with different mathematical foundations. The Historical Simulation approach is non-parametric and relies on historical return data, effectively reflecting market behavior but assuming that past returns predict future performance. In contrast, the Variance-Covariance (para-

4.4 Summary

metric) approach assumes returns are normally distributed, allowing for analytical VaR calculations based on the mean and standard deviation, but it strongly relies on the normality assumption. The Monte Carlo simulation approach generates many hypothetical return scenarios using statistical models, providing flexibility for complex distributions; however, it is computationally intensive and requires accurate specification. Each method has its own strengths and weaknesses, making it important to choose the right one based on the context and available data.

Integrating these risk metrics provides a comprehensive view of market risk. For example, variance measures the average volatility, while Max Drawdown focuses on the most extreme losses. VaR estimates potential losses within a specified confidence interval. Considering additional measures such as Expected Shortfall, stress testing, and dynamic models such as GARCH can further enhance risk assessment by addressing tail risks and accounting for time-varying volatility. All methods are frequently used to cross-validate VaR estimates and ensure their robustness against various market scenarios.

Risk Management Using Financial Derivatives 5

A key and recurring theme in finance is the pervasive uncertainty surrounding the performance of almost every tradable asset, which can manifest itself as increased volatility in prices, interest rates, and exchange rates. This volatility naturally poses substantial risks to portfolios and financial positions, prompting the need for robust strategies to mitigate potential losses. One widely discussed approach is diversification, a tactic that implicitly offers a "free lunch," as demonstrated in Chapter 1, by dispersing individual asset risk across a wider set of holdings. However, diversification primarily shields against idiosyncratic or unsystematic risk, and when the entire market changes downward, it proves insufficient to protect portfolios from broad market declines.

Among the various techniques for managing risk, hedging stands out as a particularly effective method to minimize unwanted exposures in a portfolio. In essence, it involves taking positions, often through financial instruments such as options, futures, or swaps, that can offset potential losses arising from adverse market movements. This approach may involve letting go of some potential upside profit, similar to paying an "insurance premium," to guard against severe downside outcomes. By carefully calibrating these hedging strategies, we can aim for a steadier and more predictable financial outcome, one that remains neutral to market fluctuations. In practical terms, this resembles purchasing insurance against the damaging effects of sudden price changes, interest rate changes, or currency fluctuations, thus providing an additional layer of protection and contributing to a more balanced risk-return profile.

Hedging can be executed with a wide range of financial instruments, commonly via financial derivatives such as futures and options. By definition, derivatives derive their value from underlying assets, such as stocks, bonds, commodities, or currencies, offering a degree of risk management without requiring direct ownership of the underlying. This inherent flexibility makes them especially attractive for hedging, where one pays a relatively small premium to shield against the potential for severe losses. In practice, this means that investors can strategically construct positions that offset adverse moves in the market, thereby mitigating portfolio volatility and preserving more stable returns.

In this chapter, we examine two prominent derivatives, futures and options, that are central to hedging strategies. Futures contracts, in particular, are standardized agreements that are used to buy or sell an underlying asset at a predetermined price on a specific future date. Because the price is locked in at the time the contract is created, subsequent market fluctuations no longer affect the agreed-upon transaction value, ensuring a degree of certainty in otherwise volatile conditions. This feature is particularly advantageous for commodity market participants such as farmers, who may use futures to lock in the selling price of their crops, and manufacturers, who can stabilize the cost of raw materials purchased at later dates. More generally, futures contracts provide a practical means of protecting against price fluctuations in a variety of markets, including commodities, interest rates, and other financial products. Traded on regulated exchanges, these contracts benefit from high liquidity, making them accessible for many hedging scenarios. In addition, their standardized terms, governed by centralized exchanges, enhance transparency and reduce counterparty risk through margin requirements and clearing mechanisms, thus simplifying the implementation of hedging strategies.

When holding option contracts, we gain the right, but not the obligation, to buy (in the case of a call option) or sell (in the case of a put option) an underlying asset at a specified strike price within a predetermined time frame. This fundamental distinction from futures, where both parties are obligated to transact, gives option holders the flexibility to simply let the contract expire if the market outlook becomes unfavorable. Consequently, investors can limit their downside while retaining the ability to capture upside gains should prices move in a beneficial direction. This asymmetry in risk and return helps protect against adverse market moves and preserves the potential for profit, making options one of the most popular and versatile hedging instruments in financial markets.

Options, as financial instruments, also experience price fluctuations driven by changes in the underlying asset, time to expiration, and implied volatility. A well-known hedging technique to manage these fluctuations is delta hedging, which involves quantifying how an option's price responds to small changes in the price of the underlying asset, such as stock. This sensitivity is called the delta of the option (Δ). Achieving a "delta neutral" position means compensating for this sensitivity by adjusting the number of underlying assets or related derivatives held, thus reducing exposure to the movements of the underlying price. Because market conditions can change rapidly, maintaining a delta-neutral stance requires continuous monitoring and frequent rebalancing of positions, making this a dynamic and complex strategy to implement. Nonetheless, the systematic approach of delta hedging presents significant opportunities to manage risk effectively, as we will explore in the following sections.

In this chapter, we will explore hedging strategies that use futures and options, paying special attention to the principles and applications of delta hedging. We begin by dissecting the mechanics underpinning these derivatives—covering contract specifications, pricing, and market conventions—to establish a solid foundation.

Building on this groundwork, we then examine various hedging tactics and the theoretical underpinnings that make them effective.

Let us start with the futures contract.

5.1 Hedging with Futures Contracts

Futures contracts are widely used to mitigate exposure to price fluctuations in commodities, currencies, and other financial instruments. They are standardized legal agreements that require two parties to buy or sell a specified quantity of an underlying asset at a set price on a predetermined future date. Crucially, exchanges govern the terms, such as contract size, expiration date, and quality or delivery specifications, ensuring consistency between trades and supporting a liquid market. Although these contracts outline a physical delivery process, market participants aiming to hedge can opt to close or "roll over" their positions rather than receive or deliver the physical asset. In this way, futures serve as a versatile tool, allowing investors and commercial entities to lock in future prices without necessarily incurring the logistical burden of actual commodity exchange.

5.1.1 Hedging Mechanism Using Futures

The fundamental concept behind futures hedging is to establish a position in the futures market that is counter to one's position in the spot (cash) market, helping to offset adverse price movements in the underlying asset. For example, if you already hold an asset and fear a drop in its price, you can sell (short) futures contracts, known as a short hedge, to protect against potential losses. Conversely, if you anticipate buying an asset in the future and worry about rising prices, you can buy (go long) futures contracts to lock in a predetermined price. This so-called long hedge ensures that you can secure the asset at a set cost, effectively insulating your budget from market volatility.

In both cases, movements in the futures market tend to counterbalance fluctuations in the spot market, reducing overall risk. Thus, these offsetting positions offer a practical and cost-effective means of stabilizing cash flows and mitigating the impact of unpredictable price changes. The net effect is to reduce exposure to unfavorable price movements in the underlying asset. However, note that some residual discrepancy, often referred to as "basis risk," may persist because of differences between the price of the spot and futures.

To illustrate the hedging process, consider the following scenario. Let S_t denote the spot price of an asset at time t, and Q represent the total quantity of that asset either held (in a selling context) or required (in a buying context). The value of the spot position at time t, denoted by V_{spot}, can be expressed as

$$V_{\text{spot}} = Q \times S_t$$

which captures the portion of a portfolio that depends directly on the current market price of the asset. Next, let F_t be the futures price at time t, N the number of futures contracts (positive if taking a long position, negative if short), and q the contract size, which specifies how many units of the underlying are covered by each contract. The value of this futures position, V_{futures}, is thus given by

$$V_{\text{futures}} = N \times q \times F_t$$

By examining both V_{spot} and V_{futures} in tandem, we can see how changes in the spot price can be counterbalanced by gains or losses in the futures position, thus forming the core mechanism behind many hedging strategies.

When we enter into a futures contract at the initiation time ($t = 0$), the net value of our portfolio from both spot and futures positions (aside from any margin requirements) at any time t can be expressed as

$$V_{\text{total}} = V_{\text{spot}} + V_{\text{futures}} = Q \times S_t + N \times q \times F_t$$

The profit or loss (Π) from the hedged position during the hedging period, from $t = 0$ to $t = T$, can then be calculated by evaluating changes in both the spot and future positions. That is

$$\Pi = \left[V_{\text{spot}}(T) - V_{\text{spot}}(0)\right] + \left[V_{\text{futures}}(T) - V_{\text{futures}}(0)\right]$$

Since the initial value of the futures position is $V_{\text{futures}}(0) = N \times q \times F_0$, the change in the futures position value becomes

$$\Delta V_{\text{futures}} = V_{\text{futures}}(T) - V_{\text{futures}}(0) = N \times q \times (F_T - F_0)$$

Similarly, we can write the change in the spot position as

$$\Delta V_{\text{spot}} = S_T - S_0$$

Substituting this into Π gives

$$\Pi = \Delta V_{\text{spot}} + \Delta V_{\text{futures}} = Q \times (S_T - S_0) + N \times q \times (F_T - F_0)$$

At the contract's maturity, the futures price F_T converges to the spot price S_T, meaning $F_T = S_T$. Plugging this into Π simplifies to

$$\Pi = Q \times (S_T - S_0) + N \times q \times (S_T - F_0)$$

It is important to note that the sign of N, the number of futures contracts, gives an indication of the nature of the hedge. A negative N indicates a short position, which means that you have sold futures contracts, while a positive N indicates a long position, meaning you have bought futures contracts.

5.1 Hedging with Futures Contracts

Let us consider the case of a short hedge, where we long the spot position and short the futures position as a hedge. Specifically, we hold Q units of the underlying asset and want protection against a potential drop in its price. To do so, we sell (short) futures contracts, where the number of contracts N is typically chosen so that $N \times q \approx Q$. As discussed above, during the hedging period, the value of the spot position changes by $Q(S_T - S_0)$, while the futures position changes by $Nq(F_T - F_0)$. With $N < 0$ (due to short position in futures contract) and $N \times q = -Q$, these changes combine to

$$\Pi = Q(S_T - S_0) + Nq(F_T - F_0) = Q(S_T - S_0) - Q(F_T - F_0).$$

At maturity, assume F_T converges to S_T (which is often the case based on the no arbitrage argument), so substituting $F_T = S_T$ eliminates the dependence on the final spot price S_T, yielding

$$\Pi = Q(F_0 - S_0).$$

This fixed payoff means that we have eliminated the exposure to the asset's price movements due to independence with S_T. Therefore, the short position in futures is considered a perfect hedge in the sense of removing price risk, although the final profit or loss Π can still be positive, negative, or zero depending on the initial difference $(F_0 - S_0)$.

5.1.2 Optimal Hedge Ratio

The effectiveness of a futures hedge largely hinges on how closely the movement in futures prices tracks the corresponding spot price of the asset. Although the idealized assumption $F_T = S_T$ implies that the futures price converges precisely to the terminal spot price, real-world factors, such as carrying costs, delivery specifications, and timing mismatches, can create a nonzero discrepancy known as basis risk at any time point in between $t = 0$ and $t = T$. As a result, the profit or loss of the hedged portfolio (Π_t) may be positive or negative at any time, rather than strictly zero. In practice, rather than enforcing $\Pi_t = 0$, a common objective is to minimize the variance σ_Π^2 of the portfolio's returns. One way to achieve this is to determine the optimal hedge ratio h^*, which specifies the proportion of the underlying position to hedge. Under the assumption that the returns of the spot and futures follow a joint normal distribution, the optimal ratio can be derived as

$$h^* = -\rho_{SF} \frac{\sigma_S}{\sigma_F},$$

where ρ_{SF} is the correlation coefficient between the changes in the price of the spot and futures, σ_S is the standard deviation of the changes in spot price, and σ_F is the standard deviation of the changes in futures price. This formula highlights the key role of both correlation and relative volatility in designing an effective hedge.

To derive this formula, we analyze the variance of the hedged position and determine the value of the hedge ratio (while treating other variables as constant) that minimizes this variance. Recall that the hedged position consists of both the spot position and the futures position, and the change in the value of the hedged position Π over a short time interval can be expressed as follows:

$$\Pi = \Delta V_{\text{spot}} + \Delta V_{\text{futures}} = Q \times \Delta S + N \times q \times \Delta F$$

where Q is the quantity of the asset held or required, N is the number of futures contracts held (again, positive for a long position and negative for a short position), and q is the quantity of the asset per futures contract.

We define the hedge ratio h as a relative ratio:

$$h = \frac{N \times q}{Q}$$

This allows us to express N as

$$N = h \times \frac{Q}{q}$$

Substituting this into the expression for Π gives

$$\Pi = Q \times (\Delta S + h \times \Delta F)$$

The variance of the hedged position is then

$$\sigma_\Pi^2 = \text{Var}(\Pi) = Q^2 \times \text{Var}(\Delta S + h \times \Delta F)$$

Noting that the random variables are ΔS and ΔF, expanding the variance gives

$$\sigma_\Pi^2 = Q^2 \left[\text{Var}(\Delta S) + h^2 \text{Var}(\Delta F) + 2h \, \text{Cov}(\Delta S, \Delta F) \right]$$

Dividing both sides by Q^2 simplifies the equation to

$$\frac{\sigma_\Pi^2}{Q^2} = \sigma_S^2 + h^2 \sigma_F^2 + 2h \rho_{SF} \sigma_S \sigma_F$$

To find the hedge ratio that minimizes the variance σ_Π^2, we can take the derivative of σ_Π^2 with respect to h (now we treat other variables as fixed) and set it to zero:

$$\frac{d\sigma_\Pi^2}{dh} = 2h\sigma_F^2 + 2\rho_{SF}\sigma_S\sigma_F = 0$$

5.1 Hedging with Futures Contracts

Solving for h^* gives

$$h^* = -\rho_{SF} \frac{\sigma_S}{\sigma_F}$$

The negative sign indicates that the futures position should be opposite to the spot position to effectively minimize risk. This means that if we have a long position in the spot market, we should take a short position in futures contract and vice versa. However, since N is already defined as negative for a short position, the optimal hedge ratio can be expressed without the negative sign:

$$h^* = \rho_{SF} \times \frac{\sigma_S}{\sigma_F}$$

Thus, this expression determines the proportion of the exposure (percentage of total number of spot assets) that should be hedged to achieve minimal variance in the hedged position.

For example, assume $\sigma_S = 2$, $\sigma_F = 1.5$, and $\rho_{SF} = 0.5$. The optimal hedge ratio can be calculated using these values as follows:

$$h^* = 0.5 \times \frac{2}{1.5} \approx 0.6667$$

This result indicates that approximately 66.67% of the exposure should be hedged. Generally, a lower correlation coefficient leads to a lower hedge ratio because the effectiveness of the futures contract in hedging the spot position diminishes as the correlation between their price changes weakens.

Once the optimal hedge ratio is determined, the number of futures contracts N^* that is required to hedge the exposure can be calculated via

$$N^* = -h^* \times \frac{Q}{q}$$

The negative sign reflects taking a position opposite to the spot position. If, for instance, the exposure is $Q = 100{,}000$ units and each futures contract covers $q = 1{,}000$ units, then

$$N^* = -0.6667 \times \frac{100{,}000}{1{,}000} = -0.6667 \times 100 = -66.67$$

Since trading a fraction of a contract is not feasible, we typically round to the nearest whole number, resulting in selling 67 futures contracts to hedge the exposure.

Again, note that even with an optimal hedge ratio, perfect hedging is rarely achievable due to basis risk, which refers to the potential risk that futures prices do not move in sync with spot prices. This discrepancy can arise from differences in the underlying asset, contract specifications, or timing mismatches. Furthermore, implementing a hedge comes with transaction costs that should be considered along with the benefits of hedging.

5.1.3 Scenario Analysis at Maturity

To illustrate how the hedge ratio and the correlation factor influence the effectiveness of a hedge and the terminal payoff, let us look at a scenario analysis. We will examine two possible outcomes at maturity: one in which the spot price decreases, leading to $S_T < S_0$, and another in which it increases, leading to $S_T > S_0$. This analysis will reveal how the hedged position responds in each scenario.

Consider the initial condition with a spot price of $S_0 = \$50$ per unit and futures price of $F_0 = \$50$ per unit (which may not necessarily be a realistic assumption due to other considerations on the cost of carry, such as financing costs, storage costs, convenience yields, and dividends). Assume that the quantity of the asset is $Q = 100{,}000$ units and that each futures contract covers $q = 1{,}000$ units. Also, assume that the optimal hedge ratio is $h^* = 0.4$. Using the optimal hedge ratio, we calculate the number of futures contracts needed as

$$N^* = -h^* \times \frac{Q}{q} = -0.4 \times \frac{100{,}000}{1{,}000} = -40 \text{ contracts}$$

The negative sign indicates a short position in futures contracts.

First, we analyze the situation where the spot price S_T drops to \$45 at maturity. The change in the spot market is calculated as

$$\Delta V_{\text{spot}} = Q \times (S_T - S_0) = 100{,}000 \times (\$45 - \$50) = -\$500{,}000$$

which represents a loss of \$500,000 due to the decrease in the spot price.

Next, we assume that the futures price at maturity is $F_T = \$43$, reflecting an imperfect correlation between the spot and futures prices (an example of basis risk where spot and futures prices do not move in perfect lockstep). The change in the futures price is

$$\Delta F = F_T - F_0 = \$43 - \$50 = -\$7$$

Thus, the gain from the futures position is then

$$\Delta V_{\text{futures}} = N^* \times q \times \Delta F = (-40) \times 1{,}000 \times (-\$7) = \$280{,}000$$

The total profit or loss Π from the hedged position is

$$\Pi = \Delta V_{\text{spot}} + \Delta V_{\text{futures}} = -\$500{,}000 + \$280{,}000 = -\$220{,}000$$

5.1 Hedging with Futures Contracts

In this scenario, the loss in the spot market is partially offset by the gain in the futures market, leading to a net loss of $220,000. This indicates that while the hedge has reduced the overall risk, it has not completely eliminated it. This is due to the imperfect correlation between the markets and the fact that only 40% of the exposure was hedged.

Let us look at another scenario where the spot price now rises to $55 at maturity. The change (gain) in the spot market is now

$$\Delta V_{\text{spot}} = Q \times (S_T - S_0) = 100,000 \times (\$55 - \$50) = \$500,000$$

which represents a gain of $500,000 due to the increase in the spot price. Now assuming the futures price at maturity is $F_T = \$54$, the change in the futures price is

$$\Delta F = F_T - F_0 = \$54 - \$50 = \$4$$

The loss from the futures position is then

$$\Delta V_{\text{futures}} = N^* \times q \times \Delta F = (-40) \times 1,000 \times \$4 = -\$160,000$$

The total profit or loss Π for the hedged position is

$$\Pi = \Delta V_{\text{spot}} + \Delta V_{\text{futures}} = \$500,000 - \$160,000 = \$340,000$$

In this scenario, the gain in the spot market is partially offset by the loss in the futures market, resulting in a net profit of $340,000. This outcome shows that the hedged position limits potential gains, which is an expected result when taking up a hedging strategy.

In general, hedging reduces the downside risk by limiting the upside gain. It does not entirely eliminate the risk due to the imperfect correlation between the spot and futures prices. Specifically, only 40% of the exposure was hedged. Because the futures price does not move perfectly in line with the spot price, this leads to what is known as basis risk. Moreover, since only a portion of the exposure is hedged, gains and losses in the spot market are only partially offset by the futures position. This analysis emphasizes the importance of understanding the limitations of hedging strategies and the factors that influence their effectiveness.

5.1.4 Consideration of Basis Risk

The basis at any given time t is defined as the difference between the spot price and the futures price of an asset, which can be expressed as

$$\text{Basis}_t = S_t - F_t$$

At maturity ($t = T$), the basis is expected to be zero because the futures price F_T should converge to the spot price S_T; otherwise, arbitrage activities can occur. This convergence is a fundamental principle in futures markets, ensuring that the futures contract and the underlying asset are priced consistently as the contract approaches expiration. However, in reality, the basis may not be exactly zero at maturity. This discrepancy arises because of an imperfect correlation between the spot and futures prices and various market inefficiencies. For example, it could be due to differences in the characteristics of the underlying asset, variations in the specifications of the contract, or the timing of the hedge being closed out before the futures contract matures. When the futures price does not move in sync with the spot price, the hedge fails to eliminate risk, leaving some residual exposure completely. This residual basis risk leads to $F_T \neq S_T$.

The effectiveness of a hedge can be assessed by comparing the variance of the hedged position to that of the unhedged position, where the variance is calculated based on the entire duration from contract initiation to maturity. This comparison is quantified by the reduction in variance, which is expressed via

$$\Delta \sigma^2 = \sigma_{\text{unhedged}}^2 - \sigma_{\text{hedged}}^2$$

Here, $\sigma_{\text{unhedged}}^2$ denotes the variance of the spot position alone, and we would expect it to be higher than σ_{hedged}^2, which represents the variance of the combined positions in both the spot and futures markets. Ideally, a perfect hedge would eliminate all risk, resulting in $\sigma_{\text{hedged}}^2 = 0$ and thus $\Delta \sigma^2 = \sigma_{\text{unhedged}}^2$. However, due to basis risk, the reduction in variance $\Delta \sigma^2$ is typically less than the total variance of the spot position. This echoes our previous message that, while the hedge reduces the overall risk, it does not completely eliminate it.

Basis risk affects the effectiveness of a hedge because a futures contract may not completely offset the price changes of the underlying asset. As a result, even when using an optimal hedge ratio, some level of risk persists. Therefore, this residual risk needs to be recognized and managed, as it can influence the stability and predictability of the performance of the hedged position.

5.1.5 Implementing the Dynamic Hedging Strategy

In previous sections, we covered the fundamentals of hedging with futures contracts and the use of the optimal hedge ratio to minimize the variance of a hedged position. However, financial markets are dynamic, with volatilities, correlations, and other parameters changing over time. To adapt to these changes, we introduced dynamic hedging, which involves periodically adjusting the hedge position in response to evolving market conditions. In this section, we will illustrate the implementation of a dynamic futures hedging strategy using Python. We first use the Geometric Brownian Motion (GBM) process to simulate asset prices, then apply linear

5.1 Hedging with Futures Contracts

regression to estimate/forecast the optimal hedge ratios. Finally, we dynamically adjust the hedge over time.

To create realistic simulations of price movements, we use GBM, a continuous-time stochastic process commonly applied in financial modeling. GBM effectively captures key characteristics of asset price dynamics, including the log-normal distribution of prices and the important fact that prices cannot fall below zero. The stochastic differential equation (SDE) for GBM representing the asset price S_t is

$$dS_t = \mu_S S_t \, dt + \sigma_S S_t \, dW_t^S$$

where μ_S is the expected return (drift) of the asset, σ_S is the volatility of the asset, and dW_t^S is the increment of a Wiener process (standard Brownian motion).

Similarly, we can model the SDE of the futures price F_t as

$$dF_t = \mu_F F_t \, dt + \sigma_F F_t \, dW_t^F$$

where μ_F and σ_F are the drift and volatility of the futures price, and dW_t^F is another Wiener process. To model the correlation between the asset and futures prices, we assume the dependence structure:

$$dW_t^S \, dW_t^F = \rho_{SF} \, dt$$

where ρ_{SF} is the correlation coefficient between changes in asset price S_t and futures F_t. For numerical simulation, we can discretize these SDEs to obtain the closed-form pricing formula for the next period:

$$S_{t+\Delta t} = S_t \times \exp\left(\left(\mu_S - \frac{\sigma_S^2}{2}\right)\Delta t + \sigma_S \epsilon_S \sqrt{\Delta t}\right)$$

$$F_{t+\Delta t} = F_t \times \exp\left(\left(\mu_F - \frac{\sigma_F^2}{2}\right)\Delta t + \sigma_F \epsilon_F \sqrt{\Delta t}\right)$$

where ϵ_S and ϵ_F are standard normal random variables with correlation ρ_{SF}. Note that all asset prices are positive (or zero, theoretically), and this constraint is satisfied in these pricing formulas.

As time passes and the market moves, the optional hedge ratio h^* also changes. To dynamically estimate h^*, we can perform a linear regression to model the changes in S_t as a function of changes in F_t based on the simulated changes at each time step. The starting point is to consider a spot position in an asset with price changes ΔS_t and a futures position with price changes ΔF_t. If we define the hedge ratio h as the number of futures contracts (scaled appropriately) held per unit of the underlying asset, then the total change in the value of the hedged portfolio can be written as $\Pi = \Delta S_t - h \Delta F_t$ when the underlying is long and the futures position is short. As introduced earlier, to determine h that minimizes risk, we can seek to minimize the variance of Π, denoted $\text{Var}(\Pi)$. By expanding this variance and treating ΔS_t and ΔF_t as jointly normal random variables, it follows that $\text{Var}(\Pi) = \text{Var}(\Delta S_t - h\,\Delta F_t) = \text{Var}(\Delta S_t) + h^2\,\text{Var}(\Delta F_t) - 2h\,\text{Cov}(\Delta S_t, \Delta F_t)$. Differentiating this expression with respect to h and setting it to zero yields $h^* = \frac{\text{Cov}(\Delta S_t, \Delta F_t)}{\text{Var}(\Delta F_t)}$. Because the covariance between ΔS_t and ΔF_t can be written in terms of the correlation ρ_{SF} and the product of the respective standard deviations σ_S and σ_F, the hedge ratio that minimizes variance becomes $h^* = \rho_{SF} \frac{\sigma_S}{\sigma_F}$.

To connect this result with the linear regression approach, consider a simple ordinary least squares (OLS) regression of ΔS_t on ΔF_t. Here, we often write

$$\Delta S_t = \alpha + \beta\,\Delta F_t + \varepsilon_t$$

where α is an intercept, β is a slope coefficient, and ε_t is the error term. It is a standard OLS result that the optimal estimated β is given by the ratio of the sample covariance of ΔS_t and ΔF_t to the sample variance of ΔF_t. Specifically, $\beta = \frac{\overline{\text{Cov}}(\Delta S_t, \Delta F_t)}{\overline{\text{Var}}(\Delta F_t)}$ by solving the following:

$$\min_{\beta,\alpha} \sum_{t=1}^{T} (\Delta S_t - \beta\Delta F_t - \alpha)^2$$

In the idealized population limit, this converges to the true ratio of covariance to variance, namely, $\frac{\text{Cov}(\Delta S_t, \Delta F_t)}{\text{Var}(\Delta F_t)}$. That quantity is precisely the hedge ratio derived by minimizing the variance of the hedged portfolio.

The equivalence arises because the slope coefficient in a regression of one random variable on another is the quantity that best explains, in a least squares sense, how changes in the independent variable co-move with changes in the dependent variable. In a hedging context, spot price changes ΔS_t are viewed as the outcome to be "covered," and futures price changes ΔF_t are the tool used to hedge. The slope β telling us how ΔS_t scales with ΔF_t is the same parameter that appears in the variance-minimizing portfolio, since the variance-minimization problem also requires knowledge of how ΔS_t and ΔF_t move together. Even if the regression contains a nonzero intercept α, that term does not affect the slope and thus does not alter the hedge ratio; the intercept reflects an average drift or level effect that does not change the ratio needed to offset price fluctuations. Hence, whether one directly solves for h^* via differentiation of the hedged portfolio's variance or estimates β via an OLS regression of ΔS_t on ΔF_t, both frameworks produce the same formula for the optimal hedge ratio in a setting where returns (or price changes) follow a joint normal distribution.

Now, we can come to the dynamic hedging strategy using the futures contract for each period. The process consists of several key steps. First, we simulate price paths for both the asset and futures prices using the GBM model. At each time step, we estimate the optimal hedge ratios through linear regression, enabling the strategy to dynamically adjust hedge positions based on these ratios. Throughout this process,

5.1 Hedging with Futures Contracts

we calculate the profit and loss for both the asset and the futures positions. Finally, we evaluate the effectiveness of the hedging strategy by comparing the P&L distributions and risk metrics of the hedged and unhedged positions. This comparison provides insights into the performance and risk reduction achieved through the hedging approach.

As shown in Listing 5-1, we begin by importing the necessary libraries and setting simulation parameters, including the time horizon, time steps, and number of simulations.

```python
import numpy as np
import pandas as pd
import matplotlib.pyplot as plt
import seaborn as sns
from sklearn.linear_model import LinearRegression

# Simulation parameters
np.random.seed(42)        # For reproducibility
T = 0.5                   # Time to maturity in years (6 months)
dt = 1/252                # Time step (daily)
N_steps = int(T / dt)     # Number of time steps
N_simulations = 5000      # Number of simulated price paths

# Asset price parameters
S0 = 50                   # Initial spot price of the asset
mu_S = 0.05               # Expected annual return of the asset
sigma_S = 0.25            # Annual volatility of the asset

# Futures price parameters
F0 = 50                   # Initial futures price
mu_F = 0.05               # Expected annual return of the futures
sigma_F = 0.25            # Annual volatility of the futures

# Correlation between asset and futures price changes
rho_SF = 0.9

# Quantity parameters
Q = 5000                  # Quantity of the asset
q = 50                    # Contract size of the futures
transaction_cost = 0.001  # Transaction cost per unit
```

Listing 5-1 Setting up parameters for simulation

Next, we simulate correlated asset and futures price paths using GBM.

```python
# Time array
time_grid = np.linspace(0, T, N_steps + 1)

# Preallocate arrays
S_paths = np.zeros((N_simulations, N_steps + 1))
F_paths = np.zeros((N_simulations, N_steps + 1))

# Set initial prices
S_paths[:, 0] = S0
F_paths[:, 0] = F0
```

```python
# Cholesky decomposition for correlated random variables
cov_matrix = np.array([[1, rho_SF], [rho_SF, 1]])
chol_matrix = np.linalg.cholesky(cov_matrix)

for i in range(N_simulations):
    for t in range(1, N_steps + 1):
        # Generate standard normal random variables
        z = np.random.normal(size=2)
        correlated_z = chol_matrix @ z

        # Simulate asset price
        S_paths[i, t] = S_paths[i, t - 1] * np.exp(
            (mu_S - 0.5 * sigma_S**2) * dt + sigma_S *
    correlated_z[0] * np.sqrt(dt)
        )

        # Simulate futures price
        F_paths[i, t] = F_paths[i, t - 1] * np.exp(
            (mu_F - 0.5 * sigma_F**2) * dt + sigma_F *
    correlated_z[1] * np.sqrt(dt)
        )
```

Listing 5-2 Simulating GBM processes

Here, we used the Cholesky decomposition to generate correlated random variables, ensuring that the simulated asset and futures prices reflect the desired correlation. At each time step, we can estimate the optimal hedge ratio using linear regression.

```python
hedge_ratios = []

for t in range(N_steps):
    # Calculate price changes
    delta_S = S_paths[:, t + 1] - S_paths[:, t]
    delta_F = F_paths[:, t + 1] - F_paths[:, t]

    # Reshape delta_F for regression
    delta_F = delta_F.reshape(-1, 1)

    # Perform linear regression
    model = LinearRegression().fit(delta_F, delta_S)
    h_star = model.coef_[0]

    hedge_ratios.append(h_star)
```

Listing 5-3 Estimating optimal hedge ratio via linear regression

We then roll out the dynamic hedging process using futures contracts by adjusting the futures position on the basis of the estimated optimal hedge ratios.

```python
# Initialize arrays
position_futures = np.zeros((N_simulations, N_steps + 1))
cash_flows = np.zeros((N_simulations, N_steps + 1))

for t in range(N_steps):
    h_star = hedge_ratios[t]
```

5.1 Hedging with Futures Contracts

```python
    N_star = -h_star * (Q / q)

    if t == 0:
        # Initial position
        position_futures[:, t] = N_star
    else:
        # Adjust position
        delta_N = N_star - position_futures[:, t - 1]
        position_futures[:, t] = N_star

        # Transaction costs
        cash_flows[:, t] -= np.abs(delta_N * F_paths[:, t] * q *
    transaction_cost)
```

Listing 5-4 Rolling out dynamic hedge using futures contract

In this code, we calculate the number of futures contracts needed at each time step and account for transaction costs incurred due to adjustments. We also compute the P&L for both the hedged and unhedged positions.

```python
# Final futures position remains the same as the last adjustment
position_futures[:, -1] = position_futures[:, -2]

# P&L from spot position
pnl_spot = Q * (S_paths[:, -1] - S0)

# P&L from futures position
pnl_futures = position_futures[:, -1] * q * (F_paths[:, -1] -
    F_paths[:, 0])

# Total transaction costs
total_transaction_costs = np.sum(cash_flows, axis=1)

# Total P&L
pnl_hedged = pnl_spot + pnl_futures + total_transaction_costs
pnl_unhedged = pnl_spot
```

Listing 5-5 Comparing PnL of hedged and unhedged positions

We then calculate common downside risk metrics such as Value at Risk (VaR) and Expected Shortfall (ES).

```python
def calculate_risk_metrics(pnl, confidence_level=0.95):
    pnl_sorted = np.sort(pnl)
    index = int((1 - confidence_level) * len(pnl_sorted))
    VaR = -pnl_sorted[index]
    ES = -np.mean(pnl_sorted[:index])
    return VaR, ES

# Hedged position risk metrics
VaR_hedged, ES_hedged = calculate_risk_metrics(pnl_hedged)

# Unhedged position risk metrics
VaR_unhedged, ES_unhedged = calculate_risk_metrics(pnl_unhedged)
```

Listing 5-6 Calculating downside risk measures

Now we can visualize the P&L distributions and the hedge ratios over time.

```
# P&L Distribution Plot
plt.figure(figsize=(12, 6))
sns.kdeplot(pnl_unhedged, label='Unhedged Position', shade=True)
sns.kdeplot(pnl_hedged, label='Hedged Position', shade=True)
plt.title('P&L Distribution of Hedged vs. Unhedged Positions')
plt.xlabel('Profit and Loss ($)')
plt.ylabel('Density')
plt.legend()
plt.show()

# Hedge Ratios Over Time
plt.figure(figsize=(10, 4))
plt.plot(np.arange(N_steps) * dt, hedge_ratios)
plt.title('Optimal Hedge Ratio Over Time')
plt.xlabel('Time (Years)')
plt.ylabel('Hedge Ratio')
plt.show()
```

Listing 5-7 Plotting P&L and hedge ratios

The P&L distribution plot (left panel of Figure 5-1) shows that the hedged position has less variability compared to the unhedged position, indicating a reduced risk. The hedge ratio plot (right panel of Figure 5-1) illustrates how the hedge ratio fluctuates over time, reflecting adjustments made in response to changing market conditions.

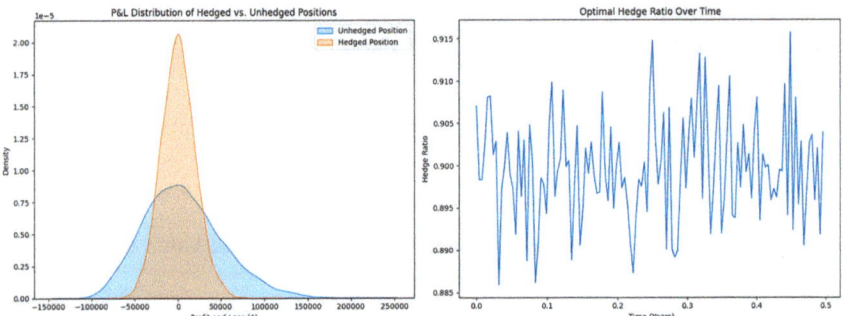

Figure 5-1 Illustrating hedging effectiveness. The left panel shows the P&L distribution of hedged and unhedged positions. The right panel shows the estimated optimal hedge ratio over time

5.2 Hedging with Option Contracts

Finally, we print the risk metrics as shown in Listing 5-8.

```
print(f"Hedged Position VaR at 95% confidence: ${VaR_hedged:,.2f}
    ")
print(f"Hedged Position Expected Shortfall at 95% confidence: ${
    ES_hedged:,.2f}\n")
print(f"Unhedged Position VaR at 95% confidence: ${VaR_unhedged
    :,.2f}")
print(f"Unhedged Position Expected Shortfall at 95% confidence: $
    {ES_unhedged:,.2f}")

# Output
Hedged Position VaR at 95% confidence: $31,761.44
Hedged Position Expected Shortfall at 95% confidence: $39,471.00

Unhedged Position VaR at 95% confidence: $63,486.41
Unhedged Position Expected Shortfall at 95% confidence: $75
    ,266.29
```

Listing 5-8 Printing risk metrics

The results indicate that a hedged position has considerably lower VaR and ES compared to an unhedged position, which means a reduction in risk. By adopting a dynamic hedging strategy that adjusts the hedge ratio over time based on current market data, we can more effectively manage risk in changing market conditions.

5.2 Hedging with Option Contracts

Option contracts are a common instrument for hedging and offer greater flexibility and adaptability than futures contracts. As mentioned earlier, an option gives the holder the right, but not the obligation, to buy or sell an underlying asset at a predetermined price within a specific time frame (typically on or before the expiration date). An option contract is a type of derivative, which means that its value is derived on the basis of an underlying asset such as stocks, commodities, or currencies. In this section, we explore how options can be used for hedging, describe key hedging strategies, and offer detailed frameworks and examples to illustrate their practical usage. We will focus mainly on European options.

There are two main types of options: call options and put options. A call option allows the holder to buy the underlying asset at a predetermined price known as the strike price (denoted K) on the expiration date. In contrast, a put option grants the holder the right to sell the underlying asset at the strike price K on the expiration date. The cost of purchasing an option is referred to as the premium paid to the other party (ignoring middlemen such as exchanges or brokers). Options can be traded on exchanges, where contracts are standardized, or in over-the-counter markets, where contracts can be customized to meet specific needs.

Options present particularly versatile hedging opportunities by virtue of their asymmetric payoff profiles, which allow potential gains and losses to be managed differently compared to linear instruments like futures. Two widely used option-based hedging strategies are the protective put and the covered call. The protective put involves buying a put option on an asset already held, thereby placing a "floor" on potential losses if the asset price falls below the strike. Meanwhile, the covered call involves selling (writing) a call option on an asset that one owns, generating immediate premium income but capping upside gains if the asset's price rises substantially. Both of these strategies illustrate how options can be used to fine-tune a portfolio's risk-return profile, balancing downside risk mitigation against foregone opportunities for higher profits.

These hedging techniques harness the mathematically distinctive payoff structures of options to manage risk in a precise and adaptable manner. By carefully selecting the strike price and accounting for the option premium, we can construct tailored hedges that align with specific risk preferences, market outlooks, and time horizons. Consequently, the resulting strategies offer both reliable downside protection and the flexibility to accommodate different market conditions, making them a powerful tool for controlling exposure to adverse price movements.

Let us look at these two common hedging strategies in detail, starting with the protective put strategy.

5.2.1 Protective Put Strategy

The protective put strategy serves as a mechanism to protect against potential declines in the value of an asset while preserving the opportunity to gain should the value of the asset appreciate. Conceptually, it mirrors the principle behind futures-based hedges, but with the added flexibility due to the asymmetric payoff of the option. Specifically, say that we have Q units of an asset priced at S_0 and wish to shield the investment from downside risk at a future time T. We can purchase N put option contracts, each covering q units, at a chosen strike price K. This approach effectively places a floor limit on how much we can lose if the asset price falls below K, while allowing for upside potential if market prices rise. The trade-off is the premium paid for the put options, which slightly reduces any potential gain. Mathematically, the total initial outlay, reflecting both the spot holding and the premium expenditure, is given by

$$\text{Initial Outlay} = Q \times S_0 + N \times q \times \text{Premium}_{\text{put}},$$

where the terms ensure that the hedging cost is applicable and the downside protection is in place. Here, the premium is calculated per share of the underlying asset. At the expiration date of the option T, the value of our protective put position depends on the price of the asset at that time S_T. The payoff from holding the asset is

$$\text{Payoff}_{\text{asset}} = Q \times (S_T - S_0)$$

which represents the gain or loss due to ownership of the asset over the period.

On the other hand, the payoff per share from each put option is

$$\text{Payoff}_{\text{put}} = \max(K - S_T, 0)$$

5.2 Hedging with Option Contracts

So, the total payoff from all $N \times q$ put options is

$$\text{Total Payoff}_{\text{put}} = N \times q \times \max(K - S_T, 0)$$

Therefore, the total profit or loss $\Pi_{\text{protective put}}$ of our portfolio at maturity (time T) is

$$\Pi_{\text{protective put}} = \text{Payoff}_{\text{asset}} + \text{Total Payoff}_{\text{put}} - N \times q \times \text{Premium}_{\text{put}}$$

This formula calculates the net profit or loss from the hedged position, considering the change in the asset's value, the payoff from the put options, and the premium paid.

Note that an equivalent way to express the protective put payoff is to compare the final value of the combined position to the initial outlay. Specifically, at maturity, the final value consists of two parts: the value of the underlying asset, $Q\,S_T$, plus the value of the put options, $N\,q\,\max(K - S_T, 0)$. The total initial outlay is simply the cost of acquiring the asset, $Q\,S_0$, plus the premium paid for the puts, $N\,q\,\text{Premium}_{\text{put}}$. Thus, we can write

$$\Pi_{\text{protective put}} = \underbrace{\left(Q\,S_T + N\,q\,\max(K - S_T, 0)\right)}_{\text{Final Value}} - \underbrace{\left(Q\,S_0 + N\,q\,\text{Premium}_{\text{put}}\right)}_{\text{Initial Outlay}},$$

which is mathematically equivalent to the previous expression as the sum of the change in the price of the asset plus the return of the put and minus the premium of the put.

The protective put strategy effectively sets a minimum price level (the strike price K minus the premium paid per share) below which you will not lose more money, while still allowing for unlimited gains if the asset's price rises. In other words, the protective put strategy offers a form of "insurance" for the asset, ensuring that its value cannot drop below a certain floor while preserving the upside potential. By holding the underlying asset and simultaneously purchasing put options with strike price K, the investor gains the contractual right (but not the obligation) to sell the asset at K. In practice, this creates a lower limit on losses: if the asset's market price falls well below K, put options can be exercised (or sold at an intrinsic value) to offset further declines, effectively limiting downside. The main cost of this downside protection is the option premium, which reduces the net payoff by a fixed amount per share. Consequently, if the asset's price is above K at expiration, the put options can expire worthless, allowing the investor to capture all the upside gains of the asset minus the initial premium paid.

As shown in Figure 5-2, a put option produces a skewed payoff line that flattens below K (reflecting limited loss) and rises in tandem with the asset price above K (preserving the profit potential). Hence, the strategy secures a minimum effective selling price around $K - $ Premium per share, while still offering open-ended gains if the market moves favorably. The graph illustrates the payoff curves for three

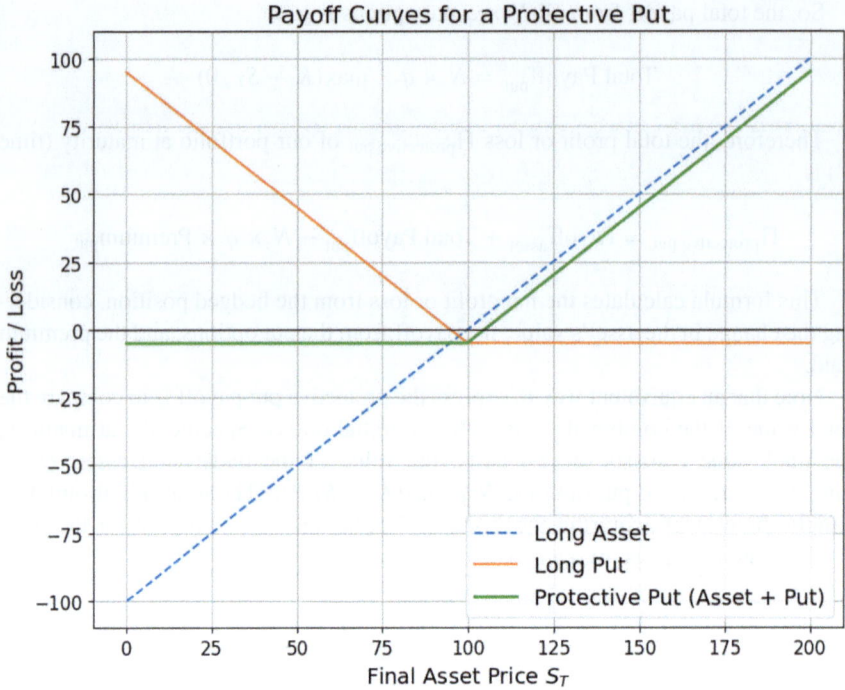

Figure 5-2 P&L of a protective put option

positions: (1) owning the underlying asset alone, (2) buying a put option, and (3) combining both into a protective put. The asset payoff we own has a slope of $+1$ (i.e., the profit or loss increases one-for-one with the underlying's price S_T), crossing the horizontal axis at $S_T = S_0$. The put payoff remains at $-$ Premium as long as $S_T > K$ (since the option expires worthless in that region), then slopes upward as $K - S_T -$ Premium when $S_T < K$. When these two positions are combined, the resulting protective put payoff matches the asset payoff above the strike K but flattens out below K, effectively placing a floor on losses. Specifically, for $S_T < K$, the intrinsic value of the put compensates for any further decline in the asset's price, limiting downside exposure to approximately $(K - S_0 - \text{Premium})$. Above K, the position behaves much like a simple long stock, retaining unlimited upside minus the fixed cost of the put premium. This asymmetry, limited loss, and open-ended gains make a protective put an attractive hedging strategy for investors who wish to preserve significant upside potential while insuring against catastrophic losses.

Listing 5-9 is used to generate the plot.

```
1  import numpy as np
2  import matplotlib.pyplot as plt
3
4  # Adjust global font size for all text elements
5  plt.rcParams.update({
6      'font.size': 14,           # Main text font size
```

5.2 Hedging with Option Contracts

```python
    'axes.titlesize': 16,    # Axes title font size
    'axes.labelsize': 14,    # Axes label font size
    'legend.fontsize': 14,   # Legend font size
    'xtick.labelsize': 12,   # X tick label size
    'ytick.labelsize': 12    # Y tick label size
})

# Parameters
S0 = 100.0          # Initial price of the asset
K = 100.0           # Put option strike
put_premium = 5     # Cost of the put option (per share)

# Generate a range of possible final asset prices (S_T)
S_T = np.linspace(0, 200, 201)

# Payoff 1: Long asset (bought at S0).
#     P&L = (S_T - S0)
payoff_asset = S_T - S0

# Payoff 2: Long put option
#     Gross payoff = max(K - S_T, 0)
#     Net payoff after premium = max(K - S_T, 0) - put_premium
payoff_put = np.maximum(K - S_T, 0) - put_premium

# Combined payoff: Protective put = Long asset + Long put
payoff_protective = payoff_asset + payoff_put

# Plot the results
plt.figure(figsize=(9, 7))

# Plot each component payoff
plt.plot(S_T, payoff_asset, label='Long Asset', linestyle='--')
plt.plot(S_T, payoff_put, label='Long Put')
plt.plot(S_T, payoff_protective, label='Protective Put (Asset + Put)', linewidth=2)

# Reference line at zero P&L
plt.axhline(y=0, color='black', linewidth=1)

# Labeling
plt.xlabel('Final Asset Price $S_T$')
plt.ylabel('Profit / Loss')
plt.title('Payoff Curves for a Protective Put')
plt.legend()
plt.grid(True)

# Display the figure
plt.show()
```

Listing 5-9 Generating payoff curves for the protective put strategy

For example, suppose we own 500 shares ($Q = 500$) of a stock currently priced at $S_0 = \$80$ per share. We are concerned about a potential decline in the stock price over the next few months. To hedge this risk, we can purchase put options with a strike price of $K = \$80$. Assume the premium per share is $\text{Premium}_{put} = \$3$. Since each option contract typically covers 100 shares ($q = 100$), we need

$$N = \frac{Q}{q} = \frac{500}{100} = 5 \text{ contracts}$$

The total premium paid is

$$\text{Total Premium}_{put} = N \times q \times \text{Premium}_{put} = 5 \times 100 \times \$3 = \$1{,}500$$

The total initial investment outlay is

$$\text{Initial Outlay} = 500 \times \$80 + 5 \times 100 \times \$3 = \$40{,}000 + \$1{,}500 = \$41{,}500$$

If the stock price falls to $S_T = \$65$, the payoff from the asset is

$$\text{Payoff}_{asset} = 500 \times (\$65 - \$80) = 500 \times (-\$15) = -\$7{,}500$$

which represents a loss due to the decrease in the stock price.

Next, the payoff from the put options is:

$$\text{Total Payoff}_{put} = 5 \times 100 \times (\$80 - \$65) = 500 \times \$15 = \$7{,}500$$

These put options are "in the money" and thus provide a gain that offsets the loss from the asset.

The total profit or loss becomes

$$\Pi_{\text{protective put}} = -\$7{,}500 + \$7{,}500 - \$1{,}500 = -\$1{,}500$$

which shows that the net loss is equal to the premium paid for the put options. In other words, the loss from the asset's price decline is fully offset by the gain from the put options, except for the premium paid.

On the other hand, if the stock price rises to $S_T = \$90$, the payoff from the asset becomes

$$\text{Payoff}_{asset} = 500 \times (\$90 - \$80) = 500 \times \$10 = \$5{,}000$$

5.2 Hedging with Option Contracts

Table 5-1 Payoff and profit/loss table

Stock price at maturity (S_T)	Payoff from asset	Payoff from put options	Premium paid	Total P&L
$65	− $7,500	$7,500	− $1,500	− $1,500
$90	$5,000	$0	− $1,500	$3,500

which is the gain from the increase in the stock price. As for the payoff of the put options, since $S_T > K$, the put options expire worthless:

$$\text{Total Payoff}_{\text{put}} = 0$$

Thus, the total profit or loss is

$$\Pi_{\text{protective put}} = \$5{,}000 + \$0 - \$1{,}500 = \$3{,}500$$

The net profit is the gain from the asset minus the premium paid for the put options. Thus, we benefit from the asset's price increase, but incur the cost of the premium.

Table 5-1 summarizes the P&L of each component and the overall portfolio of the protective put strategy in each scenario. This strategy essentially limits our downside risk to the premium paid while allowing for upside potential if the asset price increases.

The next section looks at implementing this strategy and observing its effect via simulations.

5.2.2 Implementing the Protective Put Strategy

Now that we understand the protective put strategy, let us implement it using Python. We will simulate asset price movements, calculate option premiums, and evaluate payoffs to see how effective the hedge is in different scenarios. We will again use GBM to simulate asset price movements and the Black-Scholes-Merton (BSM) model to price the options. As introduced earlier, GBM can be used to capture both the predictable trend (drift) and random fluctuations (volatility) when simulating how the asset price changes over time. Recall that we discretize the GBM using the following equation:

$$S_{t+\Delta t} = S_t \times \exp\left(\left(\mu - \frac{\sigma^2}{2}\right)\Delta t + \sigma \epsilon_t \sqrt{\Delta t}\right)$$

where Δt is the time step size, and ϵ_t is a standard normal random variable ($\epsilon_t \sim N(0, 1)$).

To price European put options, we can use the Black-Scholes-Merton model:

$$P = Ke^{-r(T-t)}N(-d_2) - S_t N(-d_1)$$

where

$$d_1 = \frac{\ln\left(\frac{S_t}{K}\right) + \left(r + \frac{\sigma^2}{2}\right)(T-t)}{\sigma\sqrt{T-t}}$$

$$d_2 = d_1 - \sigma\sqrt{T-t}$$

In these equations, $N(\cdot)$ is the cumulative distribution function of the standard normal distribution, S_t is the asset price at time t, K is the strike price, r is the risk-free interest rate, and T is the time to maturity. Recall that at maturity T, the payoff of the put option is

$$\text{Payoff}_{\text{put}} = \max(K - S_T, 0)$$

We can now simulate the protective put strategy by modeling asset price paths using GBM, calculating option premiums with the BSM model, and evaluating the payoffs from both the asset and the put options.

First, we import the necessary packages and define the parameters for our simulation as shown in Listing 5-10.

```python
import numpy as np
import pandas as pd
import matplotlib.pyplot as plt
from scipy.stats import norm

# Simulation parameters
np.random.seed(42)          # For reproducibility
S0 = 100                    # Initial asset price ($100)
K = 100                     # Strike price of the put option ($100)
T = 0.5                     # Time to maturity in years (6 months)
r = 0.02                    # Risk-free interest rate (2%)
sigma = 0.25                # Volatility of the asset (25%)
mu = 0.10                   # Expected return of the asset (10%)
N_simulations = 5000        # Number of simulation paths
N_steps = 126               # Number of time steps (approx. 6 months of trading days)
dt = T / N_steps            # Time step size
Q = 2000                    # Quantity of the asset held
q = 100                     # Quantity per option contract
N_options = Q // q          # Number of option contracts
```

Listing 5-10 Defining simulation parameters

5.2 Hedging with Option Contracts

Next, we calculate the premium of the put option at time $t = 0$.

```python
def black_scholes_put(S, K, T, r, sigma):
    d1 = (np.log(S / K) + (r + 0.5 * sigma**2) * T) / (sigma * np
    .sqrt(T))
    d2 = d1 - sigma * np.sqrt(T)
    put_price = K * np.exp(-r * T) * norm.cdf(-d2) - S * norm.cdf
    (-d1)
    return put_price

# Calculate the premium per option
premium_per_option = black_scholes_put(S0, K, T, r, sigma)
print(f"Premium per Put Option: ${premium_per_option:.2f}")

# Total premium paid
total_premium = N_options * q * premium_per_option
print(f"Total Premium Paid: ${total_premium:.2f}")

# Output
Premium per Put Option: $6.52
Total Premium Paid: $13043.66
```

Listing 5-11 Calculating option premium

Now we can simulate multiple asset price paths over the time horizon T.

```python
# Time array
time_grid = np.linspace(0, T, N_steps + 1)

# Preallocate array for asset prices
S_paths = np.zeros((N_simulations, N_steps + 1))
S_paths[:, 0] = S0

# Simulate price paths
for t in range(1, N_steps + 1):
    Z = np.random.standard_normal(N_simulations)
    S_paths[:, t] = S_paths[:, t - 1] * np.exp((mu - 0.5 * sigma
    **2) * dt + sigma * Z * np.sqrt(dt))
```

Listing 5-12 Simulating asset price paths

At maturity, we can calculate the payoffs from both the asset and the put options.

```python
# Asset price at maturity
S_T = S_paths[:, -1]

# Payoff from the asset
payoff_asset = Q * (S_T - S0)

# Payoff from the put options
payoff_put = N_options * q * np.maximum(K - S_T, 0)

# Total profit or loss
total_pnl = payoff_asset + payoff_put - total_premium
```

Listing 5-13 Calculating payoffs

Now we can analyze the hedging effectiveness by comparing the protective put strategy to holding the asset without hedging as shown in Listing 5-14.

```
# Profit or loss without hedging
pnl_unhedged = payoff_asset

# Create a DataFrame for comparison
results = pd.DataFrame({
    'Asset_Price_T': S_T,
    'Payoff_Asset': payoff_asset,
    'Payoff_Put': payoff_put,
    'Total_PnL_Hedged': total_pnl,
    'PnL_Unhedged': pnl_unhedged
})

# Calculate descriptive statistics
stats = results[['Total_PnL_Hedged', 'PnL_Unhedged']].describe()
print(stats)

# OutputTotal_PnL_Hedged      PnL_Unhedged
count          5000.000000      5000.000000
mean           6833.195431      9698.512913
std           26862.596609     37183.472059
min          -13043.659498    -91149.304063
25%          -13043.659498    -17461.066383
50%           -6159.277399      6884.382098
75%           19882.797212     32926.456709
max          178995.442071    192039.101569
```

Listing 5-14 Comparing strategies

We can also plot the distribution of the profits and losses for both hedged and unhedged positions:

```
# Plot P&L distributions
plt.figure(figsize=(12, 6))
plt.hist(total_pnl, bins=100, alpha=0.6, label='Hedged Position')
plt.hist(pnl_unhedged, bins=100, alpha=0.6, label='Unhedged
    Position')
plt.title('Distribution of Profit and Loss', fontsize=18)
plt.xlabel('Profit and Loss ($)', fontsize=16)
plt.ylabel('Frequency', fontsize=16)
plt.legend(fontsize=16)
plt.show()
```

The plot, as shown in Figure 5-3, shows that the hedged position reduces downside risk, with losses capped at the premium paid. The unhedged position has a wider distribution, indicating higher potential losses and gains.

5.2 Hedging with Option Contracts

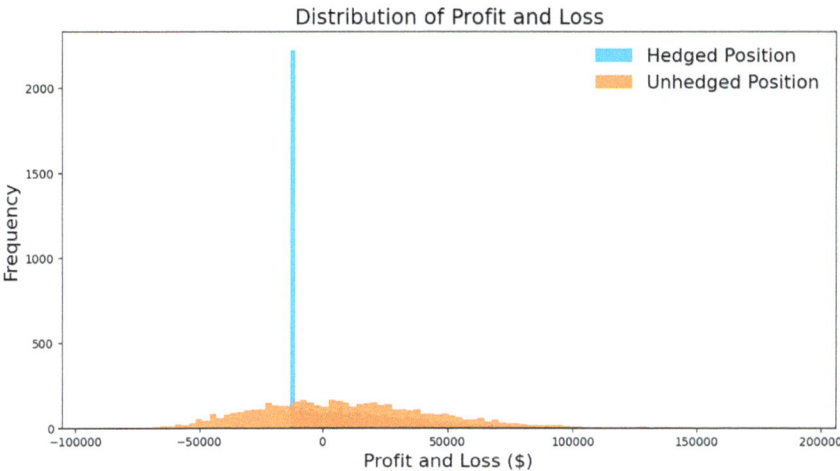

Figure 5-3 Distribution of profit and loss for hedged vs. unhedged positions

Finally, we examine specific scenarios to see how the protective put strategy performs under different market conditions:

```
# Scenario where asset price falls to $70
scenario_loss = results[results['Asset_Price_T'] <= 70].iloc[0]
print("Scenario: Asset price falls to $70")
print(f"Asset Price at Maturity: ${scenario_loss['Asset_Price_T']:.2f}")
print(f"Payoff from Asset: ${scenario_loss['Payoff_Asset']:.2f}")
print(f"Payoff from Put Options: ${scenario_loss['Payoff_Put']:.2f}")
print(f"Total P&L (Hedged): ${scenario_loss['Total_PnL_Hedged']:.2f}")
print(f"P&L (Unhedged): ${scenario_loss['PnL_Unhedged']:.2f}")

# Scenario where asset price rises to $130
scenario_gain = results[results['Asset_Price_T'] >= 130].iloc[0]
print("\nScenario: Asset price rises to $130")
print(f"Asset Price at Maturity: ${scenario_gain['Asset_Price_T']:.2f}")
print(f"Payoff from Asset: ${scenario_gain['Payoff_Asset']:.2f}")
print(f"Payoff from Put Options: ${scenario_gain['Payoff_Put']:.2f}")
print(f"Total P&L (Hedged): ${scenario_gain['Total_PnL_Hedged']:.2f}")
print(f"P&L (Unhedged): ${scenario_gain['PnL_Unhedged']:.2f}")

# Output
Scenario: Asset price falls to $70
Asset Price at Maturity: $61.64
Payoff from Asset: $-76714.94
Payoff from Put Options: $76714.94
```

```
 24 Total P&L (Hedged): $-13043.66
 25 P&L (Unhedged): $-76714.94
 26
 27 Scenario: Asset price rises to $130
 28 Asset Price at Maturity: $140.75
 29 Payoff from Asset: $81504.28
 30 Payoff from Put Options: $0.00
 31 Total P&L (Hedged): $68460.62
 32 P&L (Unhedged): $81504.28
```

In the scenario where the asset price falls to $70, the loss from the asset is fully offset by the gain from the put options, except for the premium paid, resulting in a net loss equal to the premium. In the scenario where the asset price rises to $130, the gain from the asset is reduced by the premium paid for the put options, but we still achieve a significant profit. By examining these scenarios, we see how the protective put strategy limits losses while still allowing for potential gains, offering a practical method to manage risk.

Next, we turn to the covered call strategy.

5.2.3 Covered Call Strategy

A covered call strategy involves owning the underlying asset and simultaneously writing (selling) call options on the same asset. Also called a yield-enhancement strategy, this approach can generate additional income by receiving the option premium, but limit the upside if the asset price rises well above the strike price. The received premium can act as a buffer against minor price declines in the underlying asset, although protection is limited and risk mitigation is only partial. If the underlying asset drops significantly, the writer still assumes most of the downside risk beyond the premium.

Specifically, suppose that we have Q units of an asset priced at S_0. To implement a covered call, we write (sell) N call option contracts, each covering q units (each standard contract typically covers $q = 100$ shares), at a chosen strike price K. Because we receive a premium for writing these calls, we earn extra cash flow up front, which can partially offset minor price declines in the underlying asset. However, should the underlying price increase substantially above K, our additional gains on the asset are capped by the short call position, making this a trade-off between enhanced current yield and limited upside potential.

Since we receive the call premium rather than pay it, the net initial outlay is

$$\text{Initial Outlay} = Q S_0 - (N \times q \times \text{Premium}_{\text{call}}),$$

which reflects the fact that the call premium provides an immediate cash inflow that partially offsets the asset's purchase cost. Often, one chooses $N = \frac{Q}{q}$ so that every share held in the spot market is "covered" by exactly one corresponding short call share.

5.2 Hedging with Option Contracts

Now, let S_T be the asset's price at option expiration T. The covered call strategy's P&L (the terminal payoff) then depends on two components: asset in a long position and call option in a short position. For the long asset payoff, if we purchased Q shares at S_0, the change in the asset's value over the period is

$$\text{Payoff}_{\text{asset}} = Q(S_T - S_0).$$

For the short call payoff, writing the call grants the buyer the right to purchase the asset at price K. If $S_T \leq K$, the option expires worthless, and our payoff from the short call position is simply the premium received: $N\,q\,\text{Premium}_{\text{call}}$. However, if $S_T > K$, the call is exercised, and we must deliver the asset at K. The intrinsic loss on the short call is $\max(S_T - K, 0)$ per share, multiplied by $N\,q$ total shares. Factoring in the premium, the net payoff from the short call can be expressed as

$$\text{Payoff}_{\text{short call}} = N\,q\,\text{Premium}_{\text{call}} - N\,q\,\max(S_T - K, 0).$$

Combining these two payoffs gives the covered call portfolio's P&L at maturity:

$$\Pi_{\text{covered call}} = \underbrace{Q(S_T - S_0)}_{\text{Asset}} + \underbrace{\left[N\,q\,\text{Premium}_{\text{call}} - N\,q\,\max(S_T - K, 0)\right]}_{\text{Short Call}}.$$

Again, an equivalent way to write this is to compare the final value of the portfolio to the initial outlay:

$$\Pi_{\text{covered call}} = \underbrace{(Q\,S_T - N\,q\,\max(S_T - K, 0))}_{\text{Final Value}} - \underbrace{(Q\,S_0 - N\,q\,\text{Premium}_{\text{call}})}_{\text{Initial Outlay}},$$

which clarifies that any gains above K on the asset are effectively "given up" to the call buyer, while the premium is ours to keep regardless of the outcome.

In essence, the short call "covers" part of our cost by adding immediate premium income, thus providing a small buffer against price declines. On the other hand, once S_T rises above K, we cease to benefit from additional upside, as we must sell the asset at K. However, below K, we bear the downside risk almost in full (minus the premium). As a result, a covered call strategy is moderately bullish, in the sense that

- It performs best in scenarios where the underlying price stays below or moderately above K.
- If the asset surges well beyond K, our gains become capped relative to holding the asset alone.
- If the asset plummets, we still incur losses similar to an unhedged position, offset slightly by the option premium.

5 Risk Management Using Financial Derivatives

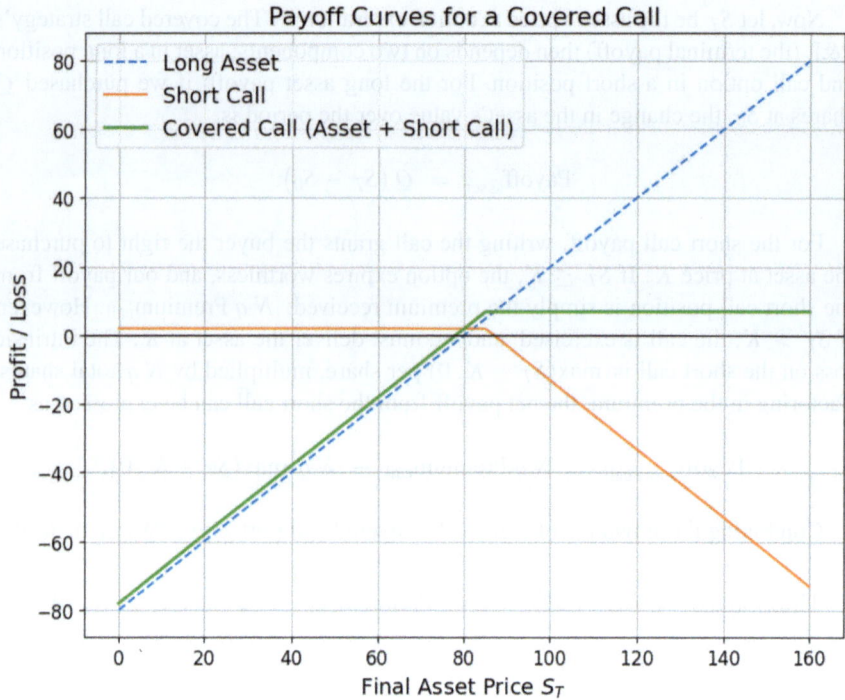

Figure 5-4 Payoff diagram for a covered call strategy compared to its components

Figure 5-4 presents the payoff diagram that consists of a long asset alone, a short call alone, and the combined covered call. For the short call position, the payoff is simply Premium $-\max(S_T - K, 0)$, which remains at the premium received when $S_T \leq K$ and declines linearly for $S_T > K$. The covered call adds this short-call payoff to the long-asset payoff, resulting in a payoff curve that is identical to the long-asset payoff up to $S_T = K$, then flattens out beyond K. That flat portion indicates the foregone upside. Meanwhile, the initial premium from writing the call acts as a cushion against mild price dips.

Listing 5-15 shows how to generate this graph.

```
import numpy as np
import matplotlib.pyplot as plt

# Adjust global font size for all text elements
plt.rcParams.update({
    'font.size': 14,            # Main text font size
    'axes.titlesize': 16,       # Axes title font size
    'axes.labelsize': 14,       # Axes label font size
    'legend.fontsize': 14,      # Legend font size
    'xtick.labelsize': 12,      # X tick label size
    'ytick.labelsize': 12       # Y tick label size
})
```

5.2 Hedging with Option Contracts

```python
# Parameters
S0 = 100.0          # Initial price of the asset
K = 100.0           # Put option strike
put_premium = 5     # Cost of the put option (per share)

# Generate a range of possible final asset prices (S_T)
S_T = np.linspace(0, 200, 201)

# Payoff 1: Long asset (bought at S0).
#      P&L = (S_T - S0)
payoff_asset = S_T - S0

# Payoff 2: Long put option
#     Gross payoff = max(K - S_T, 0)
#     Net payoff after premium = max(K - S_T, 0) - put_premium
payoff_put = np.maximum(K - S_T, 0) - put_premium

# Combined payoff: Protective put = Long asset + Long put
payoff_protective = payoff_asset + payoff_put

# Plot the results
plt.figure(figsize=(9, 7))

# Plot each component payoff
plt.plot(S_T, payoff_asset, label='Long Asset', linestyle='--')
plt.plot(S_T, payoff_put, label='Long Put')
plt.plot(S_T, payoff_protective, label='Protective Put (Asset +
    Put)', linewidth=2)

# Reference line at zero P&L
plt.axhline(y=0, color='black', linewidth=1)

# Labeling
plt.xlabel('Final Asset Price $S_T$')
plt.ylabel('Profit / Loss')
plt.title('Payoff Curves for a Protective Put')
plt.legend()
plt.grid(True)

# Display the figure
plt.show()
```

Listing 5-15 Generating payoff curves for covered call strategy

Let us look at a specific example. Suppose we hold $Q = 500$ shares of a stock currently priced at $S_0 = \$80$. We sell call options at strike $K = \$85$, each option covering $q = 100$ shares. Assume the call premium per share is Premium$_{call} = \$2$. The required number of call contracts to cover 500 shares is

$$N = \frac{Q}{q} = \frac{500}{100} = 5 \text{ contracts.}$$

The total premium received from writing these five contracts is

$$\text{Total Premium}_{\text{call}} = N \times q \times \text{Premium}_{\text{call}} = 5 \times 100 \times \$2 = \$1{,}000.$$

Hence, our net initial outlay is the cost of buying (or holding) the 500 shares minus the premium income:

$$\text{Initial Outlay} = 500 \times \$80 - \$1{,}000 = \$40{,}000 - \$1{,}000 = \$39{,}000.$$

Now consider two scenarios at option expiration. When $S_T = \$90$ (above the strike), the short calls will be exercised, forcing us to sell the stock at \$85 per share. We still own 500 shares, but our effective sale price is \$85. The resulting payoffs will be

- $\text{Payoff}_{\text{asset}} = 500 \times (85 - 80) = \$2{,}500.$
- $\text{Payoff}_{\text{short call}} = +\$1{,}000 - 500 \times (90 - 85) = +\$1{,}000 - \$2{,}500 = -\$1{,}500.$
- Total P&L $= \$2{,}500 + (-\$1{,}500) = \$1{,}000.$

Thus, compared to simply holding the shares (which would have gained \$5,000 if sold at \$90), our extra income is capped once S_T exceeds \$85, resulting in only \$1,000 net profit plus the difference in initial outlay.

When $S_T = \$75$ (below the strike), the calls expire worthless ($S_T < K$), so we keep the shares plus the entire \$1,000 premium. The resulting payoffs will be

- $\text{Payoff}_{\text{asset}} = 500 \times (75 - 80) = -\$2{,}500.$
- $\text{Payoff}_{\text{short call}} = +\$1{,}000 - 0 = +\$1{,}000.$
- Total P&L $= -\$2{,}500 + \$1{,}000 = -\$1{,}500.$

The short call cushions our loss by \$1,000, but we still incur a net loss if the stock falls significantly.

Table 5-2 summarizes these outcomes. While the call premium provides some downside protection, large price drops still lead to notable losses, and substantial price increases only yield limited gains once S_T exceeds the strike K.

In general, a covered call strategy suits investors with a neutral to moderately bullish outlook who wish to improve the yield through premium income but accept a cap on gains if the asset's price rises beyond strike. Although it offers partial (limited) protection against small price declines, it leaves the investor exposed to large downward moves aside from the modest premium cushion.

Table 5-2 Covered call payoff in two scenarios

S_T	Asset P&L	Short call P&L	Net premium	Total P&L
\$75	-\$2,500	\$0	\$1,000	-\$1,500
\$90	\$2,500	-\$2,500	\$1,000	\$1,000

5.2.4 Implementing the Covered Call Strategy

This section demonstrates how to implement the covered call strategy. As introduced earlier, the covered call strategy involves owning an underlying asset and simultaneously writing call options on it to earn premium income. Although this strategy improves returns when the asset price remains stable or increases moderately, it also caps potential profits if the price rises well above the strike price.

Consider owning $Q = 1,000$ shares of a stock currently priced at $S_0 = \$70$ per share. We write call options with a strike price $K = \$75$. Since each contract covers $q = 100$ shares, the number of contracts is $N = Q/q = 1,000/100 = 10$. We assume a time to maturity of $T = 1$ year, a risk-free interest rate $r = 0.03$, a volatility $\sigma = 0.3$, and an expected return of the asset $\mu = 0.12$. We simulate $N_{\text{simulations}} = 5,000$ price paths over $N_{\text{steps}} = 252$ time steps, resulting in $\Delta t = T/N_{\text{steps}}$.

The Black-Scholes formula for a European call option gives the call price as

$$d_1 = \frac{\ln\left(\frac{S_0}{K}\right) + \left(r + \frac{\sigma^2}{2}\right)T}{\sigma\sqrt{T}}, \quad d_2 = d_1 - \sigma\sqrt{T}$$

$$\text{Call Price} = S_0 N(d_1) - Ke^{-rT} N(d_2)$$

where $N(\cdot)$ is the cumulative distribution function of the standard normal distribution.

The codes in Listing 5-16 is the Python code that implements this strategy. We first calculate the call premium using the Black-Scholes model, then simulate asset price paths under a geometric Brownian motion, compute the terminal payoffs, and finally compare the covered call strategy against holding the asset unhedged.

```python
import numpy as np
import pandas as pd
import matplotlib.pyplot as plt
from scipy.stats import norm

# Parameters
np.random.seed(42)
S0 = 70
K = 75
T = 1.0
r = 0.03
sigma = 0.3
mu = 0.12
N_simulations = 5000
N_steps = 252
dt = T / N_steps
Q = 1000
q = 100
N_options = Q // q
```

```python
def black_scholes_call(S, K, T, r, sigma):
    d1 = (np.log(S / K) + (r + 0.5 * sigma**2)*T) / (sigma * np.
        sqrt(T))
    d2 = d1 - sigma * np.sqrt(T)
    call_price = S * norm.cdf(d1) - K * np.exp(-r*T) * norm.cdf(
        d2)
    return call_price

# Compute the call option premium
premium_per_option = black_scholes_call(S0, K, T, r, sigma)
total_premium = N_options * q * premium_per_option
print(f"Premium per Call Option: ${premium_per_option:.2f}")
print(f"Total Premium Received: ${total_premium:.2f}")

# Simulate asset price paths
time_grid = np.linspace(0, T, N_steps + 1)
S_paths = np.zeros((N_simulations, N_steps + 1))
S_paths[:, 0] = S0

for t in range(1, N_steps + 1):
    Z = np.random.standard_normal(N_simulations)
    S_paths[:, t] = S_paths[:, t-1] * np.exp((mu - 0.5*sigma**2)*
        dt + sigma*Z*np.sqrt(dt))

# Compute payoffs at maturity
S_T = S_paths[:, -1]
payoff_asset = Q * (S_T - S0)
payoff_call_seller = -N_options * q * np.maximum(S_T - K, 0)
total_pnl = payoff_asset + payoff_call_seller + total_premium

pnl_unhedged = payoff_asset
results = pd.DataFrame({
    'Asset_Price_T': S_T,
    'Payoff_Asset': payoff_asset,
    'Payoff_Call_Seller': payoff_call_seller,
    'Total_PnL_Covered_Call': total_pnl,
    'PnL_Unhedged': pnl_unhedged
})

stats = results[['Total_PnL_Covered_Call', 'PnL_Unhedged']].
    describe()
print(stats)

# Plot the P&L distributions
plt.figure(figsize=(12,6))
plt.hist(total_pnl, bins=100, alpha=0.6, label='Covered Call
    Strategy')
plt.hist(pnl_unhedged, bins=100, alpha=0.6, label='Unhedged
    Position')
plt.title('Distribution of Profit and Loss', fontsize=18)
plt.xlabel('Profit and Loss ($)', fontsize=16)
plt.ylabel('Frequency', fontsize=16)
plt.legend(fontsize=16)
```

5.2 Hedging with Option Contracts

```
plt.show()

# Output
Premium per Call Option: $7.19
Total Premium Received: $7191.96
       Total_PnL_Covered_Call    PnL_Unhedged
count              5000.000000    5000.000000
mean               4688.877238    8350.378168
std               10405.567618   23757.218489
min              -39000.394164  -46192.358760
25%               -1173.264159   -8365.228754
50%               12191.964596    5187.967171
75%               12191.964596   21884.387136
max               12191.964596  153288.458197
```

Listing 5-16 Implementing the covered call strategy

The result shows that the mean profit for the covered call strategy is lower than the unhedged position, reflecting the capped upside. The standard deviation is lower for the covered call, indicating reduced volatility. The minimum loss is similar for both, but the covered call provides some income to offset losses. This observation is further illustrated in Figure 5-5.

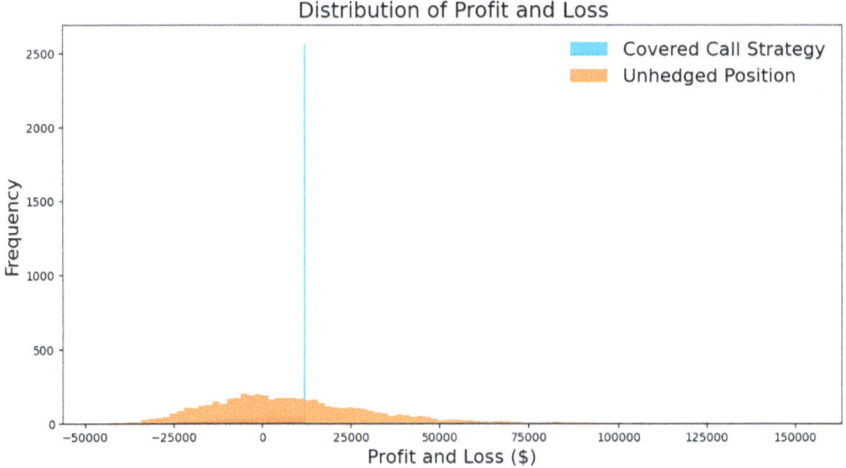

Figure 5-5 Distribution of profit and loss for covered call strategy vs. unhedged position

Finally, let us examine specific scenarios to illustrate the strategy's performance.

```
# Scenario where asset price ~ $70
scenario_70 = results.iloc[(results['Asset_Price_T'] - 70).abs().
    argsort()[0]]
print("Scenario: Asset price near $70")
print(f"Asset Price at Maturity: ${scenario_70['Asset_Price_T
    ']:.2f}")
print(f"Payoff from Asset: ${scenario_70['Payoff_Asset']:.2f}")
print(f"Payoff from Call Options (Seller): ${scenario_70['
    Payoff_Call_Seller']:.2f}")
print(f"Total P&L (Covered Call): ${scenario_70['
    Total_PnL_Covered_Call']:.2f}")
print(f"P&L (Unhedged): ${scenario_70['PnL_Unhedged']:.2f}")

# Scenario where asset price ~ $85
scenario_85 = results.iloc[(results['Asset_Price_T'] - 85).abs().
    argsort()[0]]
print("\nScenario: Asset price near $85")
print(f"Asset Price at Maturity: ${scenario_85['Asset_Price_T
    ']:.2f}")
print(f"Payoff from Asset: ${scenario_85['Payoff_Asset']:.2f}")
print(f"Payoff from Call Options (Seller): ${scenario_85['
    Payoff_Call_Seller']:.2f}")
print(f"Total P&L (Covered Call): ${scenario_85['
    Total_PnL_Covered_Call']:.2f}")
print(f"P&L (Unhedged): ${scenario_85['PnL_Unhedged']:.2f}")

# Output
Scenario: Asset price near $70
Asset Price at Maturity: $70.00
Payoff from Asset: $-0.72
Payoff from Call Options (Seller): $-0.00
Total P&L (Covered Call): $7191.24
P&L (Unhedged): $-0.72

Scenario: Asset price near $85
Asset Price at Maturity: $85.00
Payoff from Asset: $14995.35
Payoff from Call Options (Seller): $-9995.35
Total P&L (Covered Call): $12191.96
P&L (Unhedged): $14995.35
```

The result shows that, when the asset price is near $70, which is below the strike price, the call options are not used. The investor retains the entire premium, resulting in a profit that comes solely from the initial option income. There is no asset-based gain or loss since the asset price ends where it started and no obligation to sell the shares arises. In this scenario, the covered call strategy outperforms simply holding the asset, as the unhedged position would show little to no profit, while the covered call earns the premium.

When the asset price ends near $85, which is above the strike price, the call options are exercised. The investor must sell the shares at the strike price, capturing the difference between the strike and the initial price plus the premium received.

Although this scenario shows a substantial gain, it is less than what the unhedged position would have earned if the shares had been sold at a higher market price without option obligations. Thus, the covered call strategy provides additional income over small price increases, but sacrifices some of the upside potential, capping the maximum profit achievable.

5.3 Summary

In this chapter, we explored the foundational concepts and practical implementations of risk management techniques using financial derivatives. Beginning with an overview of the importance of hedging in uncertain and volatile markets, we highlighted the necessity for strategies that reduce unwanted exposure while still preserving the potential for gains where possible.

Futures contracts were introduced as a straightforward tool for hedging price risk. Their standardized nature and high liquidity make them suitable for mitigating uncertainty in commodities, currencies, and financial products. We discussed the mechanics of setting up a hedge with futures and derived the mathematical relationship between spot and futures positions. This included examining the optimal hedge ratio, which minimizes variance, and demonstrating the effectiveness of futures-based hedging through scenario analysis. Although such hedges can significantly reduce risk, we emphasize that risk and imperfect correlations remain persistent challenges, preventing complete elimination of uncertainty.

We then moved on to options-based hedging strategies, focusing on protective put and covered call strategies. By purchasing a protective put, an investor establishes a safety net against adverse price movements while still retaining the opportunity to benefit from price increases. In contrast, the covered call strategy allows an investor who already owns an asset to generate additional income from premiums, albeit at the cost of capping potential upside if prices rise substantially. Through several examples of scenario analysis, we show how these strategies strike different balances between risk reduction, cost, and forgone opportunities.

To provide a deeper understanding, we implemented these hedging strategies in Python. By simulating asset and futures price paths with Geometric Brownian Motion and pricing options using the Black-Scholes-Merton model, we illustrated how changes in underlying parameters, market conditions, and hedge ratios affect the outcomes of various strategies. Dynamic hedging approaches, which require continual monitoring and adjustment of hedge positions, were introduced to better reflect the evolving nature of real-world markets.

In summary, this chapter demonstrated that while no hedge is perfect, the informed use of futures and option contracts allows for more controlled exposure to market volatility. By thoughtfully selecting hedge ratios, strike prices, and maturities, and embracing dynamic adjustments in response to changing conditions, practitioners can significantly reduce risk and improve the predictability of portfolio performance. The techniques presented here form the foundation for more advanced risk management frameworks and guide the practical application of financial derivatives as essential instruments in modern finance.

Static and Dynamic Hedging 6

Effective risk management is essential to preserve the stability and resilience of financial markets, institutions, and individual portfolios, as unmanaged exposures can lead to significant losses or systemic disruptions due to various types of risks. One prominent method to mitigate these risks is hedging with derivatives, as discussed in Chapter 5. This involves the systematic deployment of instruments such as options, futures, forwards, and swaps to compensate for adverse fluctuations in underlying asset prices, thus cushioning the negative impact. For example, Chapter 5 introduced the use of futures contracts to lock in future transaction prices and protective puts to protect against sudden declines in asset prices.

When we invest in options, another commonly used hedging technique is delta hedging, which is aimed at stabilizing the option price due to fluctuations in the price of the underlying asset. Options are powerful vehicles for both leverage and hedging, yet their prices often display high sensitivity to the respective underlying. The goal of delta hedging is thus to construct portfolios that are locally insensitive to small changes in the price of the underlying asset; that is, setting the derivative of the portfolio value with respect to the asset price (the delta) to zero. In other cases, hedging approaches may involve minimizing portfolio variance by solving optimization problems where the objective is to minimize the quadratic risk measure subject to the constraints imposed by the derivative contracts, thus stabilizing returns and securing the portfolios against unfavorable price movements.

In modern finance, derivatives are acknowledged as versatile instruments that serve both hedging and leveraging functions, and their efficacy can often be analyzed using mathematical frameworks. For example, options provide the holder with the right, though not the obligation, to buy or sell an underlying asset at a predetermined strike price before or on a specified expiration date. These instruments are often modeled using the Black-Scholes framework, which uses stochastic differential equations and assumes a geometric Brownian motion to derive closed-form pricing solutions. In contrast, futures contracts impose a compulsory obligation to transact at a future date, with their valuation frequently based on cost-of-carry models that integrate factors such as interest rates and storage costs to enforce no-arbitrage conditions. Similarly, forward contracts extend this concept into over-the-counter agreements, allowing for customized contractual terms that accommodate unique risk profiles. In addition, swaps facilitate the exchange of cash flows or other financial variables—such as fixed vs. floating interest rates or different currencies—by applying fixed-for-floating exchange models that help mitigate specific exposures. All these vehicles can be further calibrated by formulating different optimization problems and using variance minimization techniques, aiming at effectively managing risk and optimizing returns.

Hedging is fundamentally a risk mitigation strategy that aims to eliminate or significantly reduce exposure to adverse market movements rather than to generate profit. Often, such risk mitigation comes at the cost of potential upside gain. One example is to take offsetting positions in derivative products, such as futures and options, thus neutralizing the portfolio's sensitivity to fluctuations in underlying asset prices. As discussed in the previous chapter, an investor with a substantial position in a particular asset can choose to purchase put options (called the protective put strategy), using models such as Black-Scholes to calculate the option delta and determine the optimal hedge ratio to offset potential declines in the asset value. Similarly, a corporation that expects to earn income in a foreign currency may use currency swaps to stabilize its cash flows and minimize volatility. All of these hedging techniques aim to protect against unforeseen market fluctuations to obtain more stable and predictable outcomes in both investment portfolios and corporate financial operations.

To further elaborate on the concept of delta hedging, consider an option priced at $V(S, t)$, where S denotes the underlying asset's price and t represents the current time, which also relates to the residual time to expiration. The option's delta, Δ, is then defined as $\Delta = \frac{\partial V}{\partial S}$, which is the first derivative (instantaneous rate of change) of V against S. In a delta-neutral hedging strategy, the objective is to construct a portfolio (an additional position on top of the current option) in which the aggregate delta will be zero, thereby neutralizing the sensitivity of the option price to small fluctuations in the underlying asset's price. To achieve this, we can adjust a position in the underlying asset that has a hedge ratio of $-\Delta$; that is, for every unit of delta exposure in the option, an opposing position of equal magnitude is taken in the underlying asset. Given that Δ is inherently a function of both the asset price S and time t (owing to the dynamic nature of the option's payoff structure and market volatility), continuous or frequent rebalancing is required to maintain the hedge. For example, if an investor holds a call option and the underlying stock currently trades at \$100 with $\Delta = 0.5$, the corresponding hedge would be to short 0.5 unit of shares per option. Should the stock price increase to \$101, and the resulting delta become 0.55, the hedge must be adjusted by shorting an additional 0.05 shares per option to restore delta neutrality. This example illustrates the dynamic and mathematically intensive nature of delta hedging, where the principles of differential calculus and continuous-time finance underpin the iterative process of risk mitigation in volatile markets.

Hedging strategies can be broadly classified into dynamic and static approaches, each displaying different methodologies, benefits, and inherent trade-offs. Dynamic hedging involves continuously or frequently rebalancing portfolio positions to stabilize portfolio value and adapt to changing market conditions, so that the portfolio is less sensitive to fluctuations in the price of the underlying asset. However, this method requires one to continuously monitor the underlying asset price and make a proper adjustment, which would incur a high transaction cost. In contrast, static hedging promotes the construction of the hedge at the inception of a strategy and maintaining such hedging position throughout its duration, thus simplifying portfolio management. However, such a static nature may potentially fail to cater to rapid market shifts.

In contrast, static hedging involves establishing a hedge at the beginning of a position that remains unchanged until maturity, thus preventing the need for continuous rebalancing of the hedging position. Instead, it relies on the upfront selection of financial instruments that are engineered to replicate the target payoff profile from the beginning, ensuring that the hedge remains relatively stable and demands minimal monitoring throughout its duration. This approach, while operationally simpler and less burdened by transaction costs associated with frequent adjustments, inherently sacrifices flexibility because it does not adjust to unforeseen market movements or shifts in underlying risk factors, thereby potentially exposing the portfolio to residual risks (the portion of risk that remains after implementing the hedge) that may deviate from the original expectations. For example, consider the static replication of a European put option using put-call parity: by combining a position in the underlying asset, a bond that replicates the risk-free component (often represented as Ke^{-rT} in the pricing formula), and a call option with the same strike and maturity, one can replicate the eventual payoff of the put option according to the central put-call parity relationship $P + S = C + Ke^{-rT}$. This mathematically elegant construction illustrates how a static hedge is designed to mirror the desired payoff without necessitating ongoing adjustments, yet it also underscores the inherent trade-off between the simplicity and operational efficiency of static replication and the potential exposure to market dynamics that a more flexible, dynamic strategy might mitigate.

Both dynamic and static hedging methods approach risk management in contrasting yet complementary ways, reflecting distinct trade-offs between flexibility and operational simplicity. Dynamic hedging, for example, provides fine-tuned adaptability by continuously rebalancing positions in response to evolving market conditions and adjusting for sensitivities encapsulated by the option Greeks, such as delta, gamma, and vega, thus allowing practitioners to mitigate risk exposures in real time; however, this precision comes at the cost of increased complexity and higher transaction costs associated with frequent trading. In contrast, static hedging simplifies the risk management process by constructing a replicating portfolio at the inception of the strategy, which is then held constant until maturity, effectively minimizing transaction costs and reducing the need for constant supervision, yet at the expense of limited responsiveness to unexpected market movements or volatility shifts. In this chapter, we delve into the nuances of these methodologies by examining dynamic hedging techniques such as continuous rebalancing and the explicit use of the option Greeks to adjust for market risk. We will also explore static methods that involve the careful construction of replicating portfolios, thus providing a comprehensive framework that underscores both the theoretical foundations and practical implications of these complementary approaches to risk management.

Let us start with dynamic hedging.

6.1 Dynamic Hedging

Dynamic hedging focuses on continuously adapting a hedging position in response to evolving sensitivities of an option, collectively known as Greeks, that quantify the derivatives of the option price with respect to various underlying parameters. These parameters include Δ (delta), which measures the first-order sensitivity to changes in the underlying asset's price; Γ (gamma), representing the second-order sensitivity that captures the curvature of the price response; ν (often denoted as Vega), which gauges the sensitivity to changes in volatility; Θ (theta), reflecting the rate of time decay; and ρ (rho), quantifying the sensitivity to interest rate fluctuations. In practical applications, dynamic hedging typically emphasizes adjustments based on Δ and Γ, as these factors play an important role in determining the necessary modifications to the hedging when the price of the underlying asset changes. Careful rebalancing of hedging positions based on these Greeks can effectively mitigate undesired risk exposures that may arise from nonlinear effects or market volatility. However, achieving such precision comes at a cost: the hedging strategy requires frequent trading, which inherently increases transaction fees and operational expenses, in addition to frequent attention given to the hedging portfolio.

The Black-Scholes model provides much of the theoretical foundation for dynamic hedging by offering a rigorous mathematical framework derived from no-arbitrage principles and continuous-time stochastic processes. Central to this framework is the Black-Scholes partial differential equation (PDE):

$$\frac{\partial V}{\partial t} + \frac{1}{2}\sigma^2 S^2 \frac{\partial^2 V}{\partial S^2} + rS\frac{\partial V}{\partial S} - rV = 0,$$

where V denotes the option price, σ represents the volatility of the underlying asset, S is the asset's current price, and r is the risk-free interest rate. This PDE encapsulates the dynamic interplay between the stochastic evolution of the underlying asset and the deterministic drift provided by the risk-free rate under the risk-neutral measure, and its solution yields closed-form formulas for European call and put options. These explicit pricing formulas not only facilitate the valuation of options but also provide the basis for calculating the Greeks, which represent the sensitivities of the option price to changes in various parameters such as the underlying asset's price (Δ), its curvature (Γ), volatility (ν or Vega), time decay (Θ), and interest rates (ρ). Consequently, these sensitivities are instrumental in informing dynamic hedging strategies, as they determine how the hedging portfolio should be continuously rebalanced in response to market movements, volatility shifts, and the passage of time.

The following section investigates deeper the details of the dynamic delta hedging strategy.

6.1.1 Dynamic Delta Hedging Strategy

As introduced in Chapter 5, the Black-Scholes model establishes a rigorous framework for option pricing by providing closed-form formulas for European options, where the call option price is given by

$$C = S_0 N(d_1) - Ke^{-rT} N(d_2)$$

and the put option price by

$$P = Ke^{-rT} N(-d_2) - S_0 N(-d_1),$$

with the variables d_1 and d_2 defined as

$$d_1 = \frac{\ln(S_0/K) + \left(r + \frac{\sigma^2}{2}\right)T}{\sigma\sqrt{T}}, \quad d_2 = d_1 - \sigma\sqrt{T},$$

where S_0 is the current underlying price, K the strike price, r the risk-free interest rate, T the time to maturity, and σ the volatility. To further elaborate on these concepts, consider an example where $S_0 = 100$, $K = 100$, $T = 1$ year, $r = 5\%$ (or 0.05), and $\sigma = 25\%$ (or 0.25), and assume that one standard option contract corresponds to 100 shares. Here, since $\ln(S_0/K) = \ln(1) = 0$, the numerator in the expression for d_1 simplifies to $0 + \left(0.05 + \frac{0.25^2}{2}\right)T = 0.05 + 0.03125 = 0.08125$; dividing by $\sigma\sqrt{T} = 0.25 \times 1$ yields $d_1 \approx \frac{0.08125}{0.25} = 0.325$, and hence $d_2 \approx 0.325 - 0.25 = 0.075$. Using standard normal tables or numerical routines, one obtains $N(d_1) \approx 0.628$ and $N(d_2) \approx 0.53$; furthermore, calculating $e^{-rT} \approx e^{-0.05} \approx 0.9512$ enables us to determine the first term of the call price as $S_0 N(d_1) = 100 \times 0.628 = 62.8$ and the second term as $Ke^{-rT} N(d_2) = 100 \times 0.9512 \times 0.53 \approx 50.31$, thereby resulting in a per-share call price of approximately $C \approx 62.8 - 50.31 = 12.49$; when scaled to a standard contract of 100 shares, the call option is priced at roughly $12.49 \times 100 = 1249$.

Furthermore, the Black-Scholes delta for a call option, defined as $\Delta_{\text{call}} = N(d_1)$, is approximately 0.628 per share; therefore, for a contract representing 100 shares, the total delta is approximately 62.8, indicating that to achieve a delta neutral hedge, one would need to short close to 63 shares per call contract, thus offsetting the sensitivity of the call option value to small changes in the price of the underlying asset. This means that the current movement in the hedging portfolio is to short 63 shares of stock for each call option contract. When we move to the next period, another rebalancing is often required due to changes in the asset price.

6.1.2 Continuous Rebalancing and Gamma Hedging

Suppose that shortly after the initial setup, the underlying stock price increases to 102 in the next period, while the time to maturity T remains effectively one year due to negligible elapsed time. Recomputing the Black-Scholes parameters with $S = 102$, we recalculate d_1 as

$$d_1 = \frac{\ln(102/100) + \left(0.05 + \frac{0.25^2}{2}\right) \times 1}{0.25} = \frac{\ln(1.02) + 0.08125}{0.25} \approx 0.4042,$$

where the term $\ln(1.02)$ captures the logarithmic return from the price increase and the additive term 0.08125 incorporates the effects of both the risk-free rate and the half-variance adjustment. Consequently, d_2 is updated as

$$d_2 = d_1 - 0.25 \approx 0.1542.$$

Using a standard normal cumulative distribution function, we find $N(0.4042) \approx 0.6577$, which implies that the call option's per-share delta, defined as $\Delta_{\text{call}} = N(d_1)$, is approximately 0.6577. Since each contract corresponds to 100 shares, the contract delta becomes 65.77. Recall that prior to the price change, the portfolio was hedged by shorting 63 shares, which was designed to effectively offset an earlier call delta of 62.8 per contract. Now, the updated net delta of the portfolio can be calculated as

$$\Delta_{\text{net}} = \Delta_{\text{call,new}} \times 100 - 63 = 65.77 - 63 = 2.77,$$

indicating a slight net long exposure to the underlying asset. Therefore, to re-establish a delta-neutral position, one would need to short an additional 2.77 shares. However, given that trading is carried out in whole shares, this is typically approximated by selling 3 shares, which adjusts the total delta to

$$65.77 - 66 \approx -0.23,$$

a value that is effectively zero for the most practical hedging purposes.

In this dynamic delta hedging process, we continuously update the hedge by buying or selling small increments of the underlying asset as its price changes, ensuring that the overall portfolio delta remains near zero. Specifically, if we denote the option's current delta by $\Delta_{\text{option}} = \frac{\partial V}{\partial S}$ and the delta contribution from the short position in the underlying by $\Delta_{\text{underlying}}$ (with a negative sign when short), the goal

6.1 Dynamic Hedging

is to maintain $\Delta_{net} = \Delta_{option} + \Delta_{underlying} \approx 0$. Because the option's delta is a function of the underlying asset price S, it changes as S fluctuates, thus necessitating periodic adjustments. The sensitivity of delta to changes in S is quantified by gamma, defined as

$$\Gamma = \frac{\partial^2 V}{\partial S^2},$$

which indicates how rapidly Δ_{option} changes with S. A high gamma implies that even a small change in S can lead to a significant shift in delta, thus increasing the frequency and magnitude of the required rebalancing. For example, if the delta of the option increases from Δ_{old} to Δ_{new} after a price change, the adjustment needed in the underlying position is approximately $\Delta_{new} - \Delta_{old}$ per share, scaled by the number of shares in the contract.

To further optimize hedging efficiency, we may also introduce a gamma hedging position by incorporating an additional derivative whose gamma, Γ_{hedge}, takes an opposite sign to that of the primary option, so that the net gamma $\Gamma_{net} = \Gamma_{option} + \Gamma_{hedge}$ is minimized. This reduction in gamma sensitivity can substantially lower the number of delta rebalancing trades required.

However, in practice, the theoretical benefits of such continuous rebalancing or gamma hedging must be balanced against transaction costs, market liquidity constraints, and the practicalities of trading in discrete units (often whole shares). Table 6-1 provides a detailed numerical illustration of these concepts by summarizing how positions, delta, and gamma adjust when the stock price changes from $100 to $102, including the additional trades required to restore delta neutrality. In summary, updating the hedge requires recalculating the delta of the option with each significant price movement and executing an offsetting trade in the underlying to maintain $\Delta_{net} \approx 0$. In addition, the greater the gamma, the faster Δ changes with S, and consequently, the more frequent the rebalancing becomes, highlighting the intricate interaction between delta and gamma in dynamic hedging strategies.

Table 6-1 Delta and gamma hedge after the stock rises to $102, starting from an initial delta hedge of 63 short shares at $100

Scenario	Position	Delta/Gamma
Initial hedge at $100	Long 1 call option	$\Delta_{option} \approx 62.8$, Γ_{option}
	Short 63 shares	$\Delta_{shares} = -63$, $\Gamma_{shares} = 0$
	Net position	$\Delta_{net} \approx -0.2$, $\Gamma_{net} = \Gamma_{option}$
Price increases to $102	Long 1 call option	$\Delta_{option,new} \approx 65.77$, Γ_{option}
	Additional short 3 shares	$\Delta_{new\ shares} = -3$, $\Gamma_{shares} = 0$
	Net position after adjustment	$\Delta_{net,new} \approx -0.23$, $\Gamma_{net} = \Gamma_{option}$
Gamma hedge	Add opposing gamma position	$\Gamma_{hedge} = -\Gamma_{option}$
	Net position with gamma hedge	$\Delta_{net} \approx 0$, $\Gamma_{net} = 0$

6.1.3 Dynamic Hedging in Action

In this section, we implement a dynamic hedging strategy using historical price data from Tesla (TSLA) and Walmart (WMT) that span January 1, 2024, to December 1, 2024, and we begin by applying the Black-Scholes model to compute the main option parameters such as volatility (σ), strike price (K), and time to maturity (T). Specifically, we estimate σ from the historical logarithmic returns of the underlying asset, and then, using these inputs, we calculate the option price V via the Black-Scholes formula, which in turn enables us to compute the delta $\Delta = \frac{\partial V}{\partial S}$ of the option. Recall that for a European call option, this delta is given by $\Delta = N(d_1)$, where $d_1 = \frac{\ln(S_0/K)+\left(r+\frac{\sigma^2}{2}\right)T}{\sigma\sqrt{T}}$ and $N(\cdot)$ denotes the standard normal cumulative distribution function.

Based on the calculated delta, if holding a call option, we short approximately $\Delta \times$ (contract size) shares (or purchase shares in the case of a put option) to initiate a delta-neutral position. As the underlying price evolves throughout the year, the computed delta adjusts accordingly, necessitating periodic recalibration of the hedge at discrete time intervals rather than continuous monitoring. Thus, this dynamic delta hedging process can mathematically ensure that the net portfolio sensitivity, given by $\Delta_{net} = \Delta_{option} + \Delta_{underlying}$, remains close to zero, thus mitigating the risk associated with small fluctuations in S. However, it is important to note that such continuous updating, while theoretically sound, must also account for practical considerations such as transaction costs and market liquidity constraints, which may impact the frequency and feasibility of rebalancing in a real-world trading environment.

Figure 6-1 shows the cumulative wealth curve for both stocks, suggesting that TSLA is much more volatile than WMT for this period and therefore requires more frequent hedging actions.

Recall that the dynamic nature of the hedge becomes particularly evident as the underlying stock price evolves over time, requiring a systematic and continuous recalibration of the hedging position at each discrete trading interval. Specifically, on each trading day t, we calculate the delta of the option $\Delta_t = \frac{\partial V(S_t,t)}{\partial S}$, where

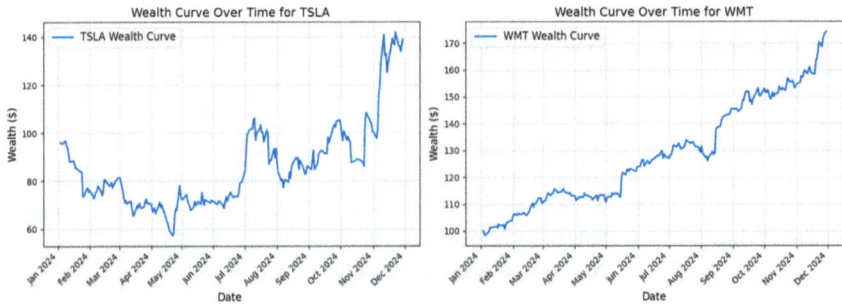

Figure 6-1 Cumulative wealth curve of both stocks

6.1 Dynamic Hedging

$V(S_t, t)$ represents the value of the option based on the current stock price S_t and the remaining time to maturity $T - t$. If this recalculated delta differs from the previous delta value Δ_{t-1}, the underlying position is adjusted by trading incremental $\Delta_t - \Delta_{t-1}$ shares, thus ensuring that the net portfolio delta, given by $\Delta_{\text{net}} = \Delta_t + \phi_t$ (with ϕ_t representing the current position in the underlying, typically negative for call options), remains approximately zero. This adjustment process can be formulated as maintaining $\Delta_t + \phi_t \approx 0$ at each rebalancing step. Importantly, transaction costs are incorporated into the model by associating a cost proportional to the absolute change in the underlying position, for example, $c \cdot |\Delta_t - \Delta_{t-1}|$, where c denotes the per-share transaction cost, thereby reflecting the financial impact of frequent rebalancing.

After each adjustment, the total portfolio value is updated to account for the current option price V_t, the market value of the underlying position $\phi_t S_t$, and the cash balance B_t, so that the overall portfolio value is given by $\Pi_t = V_t + \phi_t S_t + B_t$. The evolution of this portfolio value is then plotted to visually demonstrate how the dynamic hedge mitigates risk by stabilizing the portfolio's performance amid market fluctuations.

To further clarify the benefits of this strategy, we compare the performance of the dynamically hedged portfolio against that of an unhedged portfolio, which simply holds the option position without adjusting the underlying position. Performance metrics such as cumulative returns, computed as $R_{\text{cum}} = \prod_{t=1}^{T}(1+r_t) - 1$, volatility σ measured by the standard deviation of returns, and the Sharpe ratio $SR = \frac{E[R - r_f]}{\sigma}$ (with r_f representing the risk-free rate) are calculated for both scenarios.

As shown in Figure 6-2, we can see how dynamic hedging often reduces volatility and improves risk-adjusted performance, even if it sometimes lowers absolute returns. This trade-off illustrates the essence of risk management: Although hedging may forgo some upside potential, it also protects against severe downside outcomes. This trade-off can also be formally expressed as a decrease in the tail risk, where the probability of extreme losses, measured by metrics such as Value at Risk (VaR) or Conditional Value at Risk (CVaR), is substantially lowered. Specifically, although such hedging may sacrifice some upside potential, since positive convexity benefits are partly dampened, it is a deliberate choice to mitigate severe downside outcomes.

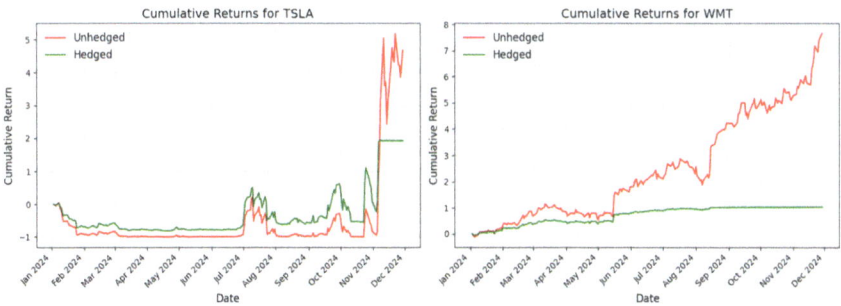

Figure 6-2 Comparing cumulative returns of both hedged and unhedged portfolios

Listing 6-1 implements this entire process step by step, performing a discrete approximation of continuously adjusting the hedge to keep the portfolio delta near zero. Note that for each ticker, we create a list *S* to store the cumulative return for each period to present the wealth curve, assuming a buy-and-hold strategy.

```
import numpy as np
import pandas as pd
import yfinance as yf
from scipy.stats import norm
import matplotlib.pyplot as plt
import warnings
import matplotlib.dates as mdates

warnings.filterwarnings('ignore')

# Parameters for the option
S0 = 100       # Initial stock price
K = 105        # Strike price
r = 0.05       # Risk-free interest rate
sigma = 0.2    # Volatility
T = 1          # Time to expiration in years

# Define tickers and date range
tickers = ['TSLA', 'WMT']
start_date = "2024-01-01"
end_date = "2024-12-01"

# Black-Scholes functions
def d1(S, K, r, sigma, T):
    with np.errstate(divide='ignore', invalid='ignore'):
        return (np.log(S / K) + (r + 0.5 * sigma ** 2) * T) / (sigma * np.sqrt(T))

def delta_call(S, K, r, sigma, T):
    d1_val = d1(S, K, r, sigma, T)
    return norm.cdf(d1_val)

# Download and prepare data
stock_data = {}
stock_returns = {}
stock_S = {}

for ticker in tickers:
    data = yf.download(ticker, start=start_date, end=end_date, interval='1d')
    if data.empty:
        raise ValueError(f"No data fetched for {ticker}. Check the symbol or date range.")
    close_prices = data['Close'].dropna()
    returns = close_prices.pct_change().dropna()
    S = [S0]
    for ret in returns:
        S.append(S[-1] * (1 + ret))
```

6.1 Dynamic Hedging

```python
    S = np.array(S)
    stock_data[ticker] = close_prices
    stock_returns[ticker] = returns
    stock_S[ticker] = S

# Initialize portfolio metrics
portfolio_value = {ticker: [] for ticker in tickers}
deltas = {ticker: [] for ticker in tickers}
shares_held = {ticker: [] for ticker in tickers}
cash_position = {ticker: [] for ticker in tickers}

transaction_cost = 0.01

for ticker in tickers:
    S_current = stock_S[ticker]
    N = len(S_current)
    dt = T / (N - 1)
    t_min = 1 / 252

    initial_delta = delta_call(S0, K, r, sigma, T)
    initial_shares = initial_delta * 100
    shares_held[ticker].append(-initial_shares)
    cash = initial_delta * S0 * 100
    cash_position[ticker].append(cash)
    portfolio = initial_delta * S0 * 100 - cash
    portfolio_value[ticker].append(portfolio)
    deltas[ticker].append(initial_delta)

    for i in range(1, N):
        t = max(T - i * dt, t_min)
        current_S = S_current[i]
        current_delta = delta_call(current_S, K, r, sigma, t)
        deltas[ticker].append(current_delta)

        delta_change = (current_delta - deltas[ticker][i - 1]) * 100
        shares_adjustment = np.round(delta_change)
        shares_held[ticker].append(shares_held[ticker][-1] - shares_adjustment)

        cash_change = shares_adjustment * current_S * (1 + transaction_cost)
        cash_position[ticker].append(cash_position[ticker][-1] + cash_change)

        option_value = current_delta * current_S * 100
        stock_position = shares_held[ticker][-1] * current_S
        portfolio = option_value + stock_position + cash_position[ticker][-1]
        portfolio_value[ticker].append(portfolio)

# Plot wealth curves side by side
fig, axes = plt.subplots(1, 2, figsize=(14, 5))
```

```python
for ax, ticker in zip(axes, tickers):
    S = stock_S[ticker]
    ax.plot(stock_data[ticker].index[1:], S[1:], label=f'{ticker}
        Wealth Curve', linewidth=2)
    ax.set_title(f'Wealth Curve Over Time for {ticker}', fontsize
        =14)
    ax.set_xlabel('Date', fontsize=12)
    ax.set_ylabel('Wealth ($)', fontsize=12)
    ax.grid(True, linestyle='--', alpha=0.7)
    ax.legend(fontsize=12)

    # Format the x-axis dates
    import matplotlib.dates as mdates
    ax.xaxis.set_major_locator(mdates.MonthLocator())  # Set
        major ticks to monthly intervals
    ax.xaxis.set_major_formatter(mdates.DateFormatter('%b %Y'))
    # Format as 'Jan 2024', etc.
    plt.setp(ax.get_xticklabels(), rotation=45, ha='right')

plt.tight_layout()
plt.show()

# Compare hedged vs unhedged portfolios
fig, axes = plt.subplots(1, 2, figsize=(14, 5))

for i, ticker in enumerate(tickers):
    S = stock_S[ticker]
    N = len(S)
    dt = T / (N - 1)
    t_min = 1 / 252
    unhedged_portfolio = []
    for j in range(1, N):
        t = max(T - j * dt, t_min)
        current_S = S[j]
        d1_val = d1(current_S, K, r, sigma, t)
        d2_val = d1_val - sigma * np.sqrt(t)
        if np.isnan(d1_val) or np.isnan(d2_val) or np.isinf(
    d1_val) or np.isinf(d2_val):
            option_price = max(0, current_S - K) * 100
        else:
            option_price = (current_S * norm.cdf(d1_val) -
                            K * np.exp(-r * t) * norm.cdf(d2_val)
    ) * 100
        unhedged_portfolio.append(option_price)

    hedged_port = np.array(portfolio_value[ticker][1:])
    unhedged_port = np.array(unhedged_portfolio)

    unhedged_returns = (unhedged_port - unhedged_port[0]) /
    unhedged_port[0]
    hedged_returns = (hedged_port - hedged_port[0]) / hedged_port
        [0]

```

6.1 Dynamic Hedging

```python
    axes[i].plot(stock_data[ticker].index[1:], unhedged_returns,
    label='Unhedged', color='red')
    axes[i].plot(stock_data[ticker].index[1:], hedged_returns,
    label='Hedged', color='green')
    axes[i].set_title(f'Cumulative Returns for {ticker}',
    fontsize=14)
    axes[i].set_xlabel('Date', fontsize=12)
    axes[i].set_ylabel('Cumulative Return', fontsize=12)
    axes[i].grid(True, linestyle='--', alpha=0.7)
    axes[i].legend(fontsize=12)

    axes[i].xaxis.set_major_locator(mdates.MonthLocator())
    axes[i].xaxis.set_major_formatter(mdates.DateFormatter('%b %Y
    '))
    plt.setp(axes[i].get_xticklabels(), rotation=45, ha='right')

plt.tight_layout()
plt.show()

for ticker in tickers:
    hedged_port = np.array(portfolio_value[ticker][1:])
    S = stock_S[ticker]
    N = len(S)
    dt = T / (N - 1)
    t_min = 1 / 252
    unhedged_portfolio = []
    for j in range(1, N):
        t = max(T - j * dt, t_min)
        current_S = S[j]
        d1_val = d1(current_S, K, r, sigma, t)
        d2_val = d1_val - sigma*np.sqrt(t)
        if np.isnan(d1_val) or np.isnan(d2_val) or np.isinf(
    d1_val) or np.isinf(d2_val):
            option_price = max(0, current_S - K)*100
        else:
            option_price = (current_S*norm.cdf(d1_val) - K*np.exp
    (-r*t)*norm.cdf(d2_val))*100
        unhedged_portfolio.append(option_price)

    unhedged_port = np.array(unhedged_portfolio)
    unhedged_daily_returns = np.diff(unhedged_port) /
    unhedged_port[:-1]
    hedged_daily_returns = np.diff(hedged_port) / hedged_port
    [:-1]

    def calculate_metrics(daily_returns):
        cumulative_return = np.prod(1 + daily_returns) - 1
        volatility = np.std(daily_returns)*np.sqrt(252)
        sharpe_ratio = (np.mean(daily_returns) / np.std(
    daily_returns))*np.sqrt(252)
        return cumulative_return, volatility, sharpe_ratio
```

```
unhedged_cum_ret, unhedged_vol, unhedged_sharpe = 
  calculate_metrics(unhedged_daily_returns)
hedged_cum_ret, hedged_vol, hedged_sharpe = calculate_metrics
  (hedged_daily_returns)

print(f"Risk Metrics for {ticker}:")
print("Unhedged: Cumulative Return = {:.4f}, Volatility = 
  {:.4f}, Sharpe Ratio = {:.4f}".format(unhedged_cum_ret, 
  unhedged_vol, unhedged_sharpe))
print("Hedged:   Cumulative Return = {:.4f}, Volatility = 
  {:.4f}, Sharpe Ratio = {:.4f}".format(hedged_cum_ret, 
  hedged_vol, hedged_sharpe))
print()
```

Listing 6-1 Dynamic delta hedging for call option contract

The summary in Table 6-2 displays the overall performance outcomes achieved through dynamic hedging and quantitatively demonstrates how such strategies can modify a portfolio's risk and return profile. As illustrated in the table, while a hedged strategy may sometimes lead to lower absolute returns—implying that the expected growth rate $E[R]$ is reduced—the corresponding decrease in volatility σ tends to enhance the Sharpe ratio. For example, in the case of TSLA, the hedged portfolio exhibits a higher SR, indicating that despite sacrificing some of the upside potential, the reduction in risk more than compensates in terms of risk-adjusted returns. Conversely, for WMT, which shows a consistent upward trend during the analyzed period, the hedging mechanism dampens the opportunity for higher growth to some extent, as reflected in its lower Sharpe ratio. This trade-off, which is characterized by the interplay between expected return and volatility, highlights a central theme of risk management: accepting a modest reduction in $E[R]$ can lead to a significantly lower σ and thereby a more stable portfolio, ultimately improving the risk-adjusted return even if the absolute returns are somewhat diminished.

Now let us turn to the case of static hedging that involves a forward contract.

Table 6-2 Overall metrics for TSLA and WMT

Stock	Strategy	Cumulative return	Volatility	Sharpe ratio
TSLA	Unhedged	4.6767	851.1622	1.1297
TSLA	Hedged	1.9256	4.2331	1.5846
WMT	Unhedged	7.6567	0.9249	2.9973
WMT	Hedged	1.0247	0.3227	2.5643

6.2 Static Hedging

For certain derivatives, one can devise a hedge that requires minimal or no rebalancing over time—a technique referred to as static hedging. Mathematically, suppose the derivative has a payoff function $f(S_T)$ at expiration T, where S_T is the underlying asset's price at maturity. The objective of static hedging is to construct, at inception, a replicating portfolio comprising positions in readily available instruments with payoff functions $g_i(S_T)$ and weights ϕ_i such that

$$\sum_{i=1}^{n} \phi_i \, g_i(S_T) \approx f(S_T)$$

for all possible values of S_T. This equation, derived from no-arbitrage principles, is either solved analytically for simpler instruments or numerically for more complex structures. By establishing such a portfolio at the beginning, the hedge is constructed once and for all, remaining largely unchanged until maturity, thereby eliminating the need for continuous adjustments that are needed in dynamic hedging. In contrast, dynamic hedging involves the continuous recalibration of the hedge to maintain a risk-neutral stance, typically by adjusting the underlying asset position according to the option's delta $\Delta = \frac{\partial V}{\partial S}$ and monitoring higher-order sensitivities such as gamma $\Gamma = \frac{\partial^2 V}{\partial S^2}$ as the underlying price S_t evolves.

Static hedging, while more straightforward and often more cost-effective due to a lack of repeated transaction costs, may not be as responsive to unanticipated price movements. Nonetheless, when the replicating instruments are liquid and the derivative's payoff is amenable to such a precise static replication, this approach can efficiently approximate the target payoff and offer a robust risk management strategy without the cumulative errors and costs associated with continuous rebalancing.

Let us start by looking at statically hedging a forward contract.

6.2.1 Static Hedging for a Forward Contract

Determining the fair value of a forward contract involves setting a forward price K that precludes any arbitrage opportunities and aligns the contract's value with the cost of replicating its eventual payoff. By definition, a forward contract is an agreement made at inception (time $t = 0$) to transact an underlying asset at a predetermined price K at a future maturity date T. This means that, if priced correctly, the contract's initial value should be zero, thus ensuring fairness for both parties and eliminating the possibility of risk-free profits. To see this, consider an asset currently priced at $S_0 = 120$ with a proposed forward price $K = 125$, a continuously compounded risk-free rate $r = 0.03$ per annum, and a time to maturity $T = 2$ years. The underlying asset's dynamics under the real-world measure P can be modeled by the stochastic differential equation (SDE):

$$dS_t = \mu S_t\, dt + \sigma S_t\, dW_t^P,$$

where μ is the drift and σ the volatility. However, in order to enforce no-arbitrage, we transition to the risk-neutral measure Q where the drift is replaced by the risk-free rate r, yielding

$$dS_t = r S_t\, dt + \sigma S_t\, dW_t^Q,$$

with W_t^Q representing a Brownian motion under Q. This change of measure guarantees that the discounted asset price $e^{-rt} S_t$ behaves as a martingale. Solving this SDE from time t to T results in

$$S_T = S_t \exp\!\left((r - \tfrac{1}{2}\sigma^2)(T-t) + \sigma(W_T^Q - W_t^Q)\right).$$

Taking the expectation under Q and applying the moment generating function of the normal distribution, $\mathbb{E}^Q\!\left[e^{\sigma(W_T^Q - W_t^Q)}\right] = e^{\frac{1}{2}\sigma^2(T-t)}$, we obtain

$$\mathbb{E}^Q[S_T \mid S_t] = S_t e^{r(T-t)}.$$

Thus, the time t value of the forward contract, which pays $S_T - K$ at maturity, is given by

$$F(S_t, t; K) = e^{-r(T-t)} \mathbb{E}^Q[S_T - K \mid \mathcal{F}_t] = e^{-r(T-t)}\left(S_t e^{r(T-t)} - K\right)$$

$$= S_t - K e^{-r(T-t)}.$$

This formula establishes a clear relationship between the current asset price S_t, the forward price K (appropriately discounted to present value), and the contract's fair value. Notably, by choosing K such that $S_t = K e^{-r(T-t)}$, the forward contract is initially priced at zero, thereby preventing any immediate arbitrage opportunities. This static hedging approach, which replicates the derivative's payoff using a cost-of-carry argument, underscores the interplay between replication strategies and risk-neutral pricing in ensuring that forward contracts are fairly valued and that the market remains arbitrage-free.

To replicate the payoff of a forward contract using a static hedge, we begin by constructing a replicating portfolio at time $t = 0$ that requires no further adjustments until maturity. The strategy involves purchasing the underlying asset at its spot price S_0 and financing part of this acquisition by borrowing funds at the risk-free rate r. Specifically, suppose $S_0 = 120$ and we have a forward contract with a designated forward price K. At $t = 0$, you buy the asset for S_0 and simultaneously borrow an amount equal to the present value of K, which is calculated as $K e^{-rT}$ for a contract

6.2 Static Hedging

with maturity T. For example, if $K = 125$, $r = 0.03$ per annum, and $T = 2$ years, then the amount borrowed is

$$Ke^{-rT} = 125e^{-0.03 \times 2} = 125e^{-0.06}.$$

Since $e^{-0.06} \approx 0.9418$, we have

$$125 \times 0.9418 \approx 117.72.$$

Thus, the net initial investment required to set up the hedge is

$$\text{Net Initial Investment} = S_0 - Ke^{-rT} = 120 - 117.72 = 2.28.$$

This net investment of 2.28 represents the initial value of the forward contract with the given parameters.

If our goal is to have a forward contract with zero initial cost—thereby eliminating any arbitrage opportunities—we set the forward contract's initial value to zero. Specifically, this is achieved by solving the equation

$$S_0 - Ke^{-rT} = 0,$$

which implies that

$$K = S_0 e^{rT}.$$

Substituting $S_0 = 120$, $r = 0.03$, and $T = 2$ yields

$$K = 120e^{0.06} \approx 120 \times 1.0618 \approx 127.42.$$

With $K \approx 127.42$, the forward contract is fairly priced with a zero initial net investment.

As time progresses toward maturity, the borrowed sum accrues interest deterministically at the rate r. Thus, by time T, the borrowed amount grows to

$$Ke^{-rT} e^{rT} = K.$$

At maturity, the asset is sold at the prevailing market price S_T, and the debt K is repaid. The net payoff from this replicating portfolio is then

$$\text{Net Payoff} = S_T - K,$$

which exactly mirrors the payoff of a long forward contract. For instance, if at maturity $S_T = 130$, the net payoff becomes $130 - 125 = 5$ (assuming the forward strike price is 125); alternatively, if $S_T = 115$, the net payoff is $115 - 125 = -10$.

This static replication is particularly efficient because it requires no rebalancing between $t = 0$ and $t = T$; the interest accrual is fully deterministic, and the asset does not generate intermediate cash flows (such as dividends) that might necessitate adjustments. Moreover, any deviation from the no-arbitrage condition (i.e., if the initial value of the replicating portfolio does not match the forward contract's value) would create an arbitrage opportunity, prompting market participants to exploit and thereby correct the mispricing.

To summarize the replication process, we have

- At $t = 0$: Purchase the underlying asset for S_0 and borrow Ke^{-rT}. The net cash outflow is

$$S_0 - Ke^{-rT}.$$

- Between $t = 0$ and $t = T$: Hold the asset without further adjustments while the borrowed amount accrues interest at the risk-free rate r, growing to K by time T.
- At $t = T$: Sell the asset for S_T and repay the debt of K. The net payoff is

$$S_T - K.$$

This one-time setup perfectly replicates the forward contract's payoff function, demonstrating that the forward's initial value must be consistent with the cost of establishing this static hedge.

Listing 6-2 illustrates this idea by plotting the net payoff $S_T - K$ for a range of possible maturity prices S_T. We set the initial parameters as above, simulate a range of values of S_T, and observe the linear relationship between S_T and the net payoff.

```python
import numpy as np
import matplotlib.pyplot as plt

# Parameters
S0 = 120        # Initial asset price
K = 125         # Forward price
r = 0.03        # Risk-free interest rate (continuously compounded)
T = 2           # Time to expiration in years

# Present value of the forward price
PV_K = K * np.exp(-r * T)

# Initial net investment to replicate the forward
cost_asset = S0
borrow_amount = PV_K
net_investment = cost_asset - borrow_amount

print(f"Initial Investment to replicate forward: ${net_investment:.2f}")

# Range of possible asset prices at maturity
```

6.2 Static Hedging

```
S_T_values = np.linspace(80, 160, 500)

# Net payoff of the replication at maturity
net_payoff = S_T_values - K

# Plot the relationship
plt.figure(figsize=(10, 6))
plt.plot(S_T_values, net_payoff, color='blue')
plt.axhline(0, color='black', linewidth=0.5)
plt.title('Net Payoff of Static Hedge for a Forward Contract at
     Maturity')
plt.xlabel('Asset Price at Maturity ($)')
plt.ylabel('Net Payoff ($)')
plt.grid(True)
plt.show()

# Output
Initial Investment to replicate forward: $2.28
```

Listing 6-2 Static hedging for forward contract

As shown in Figure 6-3, the linearity visually confirms that the static hedge perfectly replicates the forward payoff and that the forward value is consistent with the non-arbitrage principles.

Therefore, by linking the forward contract to a straightforward buy-and-borrow strategy, we demonstrate mathematically that the no-arbitrage forward price must reflect both the time value of money and the carrying costs associated with holding the underlying asset. In this replication approach, an investor purchases the asset

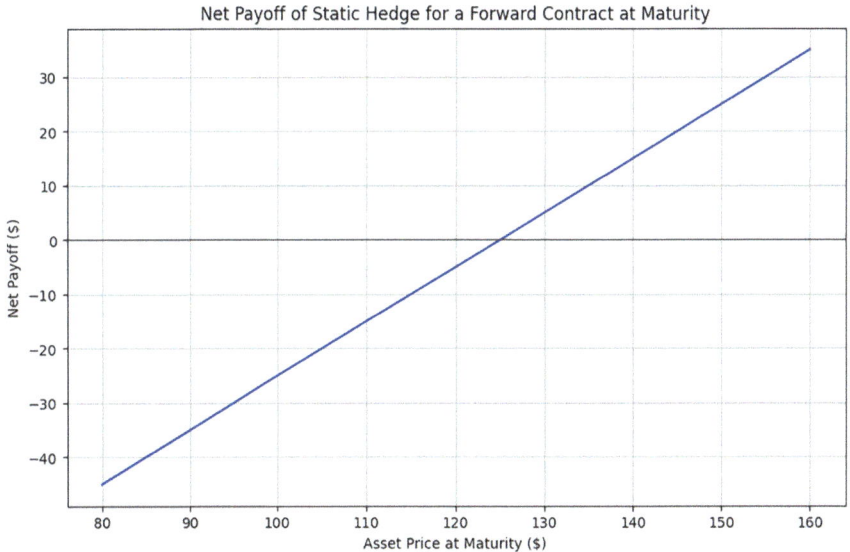

Figure 6-3 Net payoff curve of static hedge for a forward contract at maturity

at the current spot price S_0 and simultaneously borrows an amount equal to the present value of the forward price K, namely Ke^{-rT}, where r is the continuously compounded risk-free rate and T is the time to maturity. The net initial investment is thus

$$S_0 - Ke^{-rT}.$$

For the forward contract to be fairly priced—that is, to have zero initial value—this net investment must vanish, which requires that

$$S_0 - Ke^{-rT} = 0 \implies K = S_0 e^{rT}.$$

This formula encapsulates the principle that the forward price grows at the risk-free rate, capturing the time value of money. In more general terms, if the underlying asset incurs additional carrying costs or provides a convenience yield, the forward price can be adjusted to

$$K = S_0 e^{(r+u-c)T},$$

where u represents storage or other holding costs and c denotes any benefits such as a convenience yield. Any deviation from this fair pricing would yield a discrepancy between the cost of constructing the static replication portfolio and the contractual payoff $S_T - K$ at maturity, thereby opening arbitrage opportunities. Arbitrageurs would exploit such mispricing by, for instance, buying the asset and simultaneously selling the overpriced forward contract, or vice versa, until the no-arbitrage condition is restored. Thus, by ensuring that the initial value of the forward contract aligns precisely with the static replication cost, the forward price is set to prevent arbitrage and maintain market efficiency.

Next, we introduce static hedging for a European option.

6.2.2 Static Hedging for a European Put Option

To understand how to statically hedge a European put option, consider a put option with strike price K and maturity T, whose payoff at expiration is given by

$$(K - S_T)^+ = \max\{K - S_T, 0\},$$

where S_T is the price of the underlying asset at time T. This thresholding function implies that if $S_T < K$, the option pays $K - S_T$, and if $S_T \geq K$, the payoff is zero. The objective of a static hedge is thus to establish a replicating portfolio at the initial time t_0 that remains unchanged until maturity T and whose final payoff exactly matches that of the put option without requiring any rebalancing. To achieve this replication, we construct a portfolio comprising three components: first, a short position in one unit of the underlying asset, which yields a payoff of $-S_T$ at time

6.2 Static Hedging

T; second, a long position in K units of a zero-coupon bond maturing at T, each paying \$1, so that the bonds collectively yield K at maturity (with a present value of $Ke^{-r(T-t)}$ at time t_0 when r is the continuously compounded risk-free rate); and third, a long position in a European call option on the same underlying asset with the same strike K and maturity T, which at expiration pays $(S_T - K)^+$. Thus, the total payoff of the replicating portfolio at time T is given by

$$V_T = -S_T + K + (S_T - K)^+.$$

To verify that this portfolio indeed replicates the put payoff, we consider two cases. If $S_T \leq K$, the call option expires worthless so that $(S_T - K)^+ = 0$, and the portfolio payoff simplifies to

$$V_T = -S_T + K = K - S_T,$$

which is exactly the payoff $(K - S_T)^+$ since $K - S_T \geq 0$ in this region. Conversely, if $S_T > K$, the call option is in the money and pays $(S_T - K)^+ = S_T - K$, yielding

$$V_T = -S_T + K + (S_T - K) = 0.$$

In this scenario, the put option would also pay $(K - S_T)^+ = 0$ because $K - S_T < 0$, thereby ensuring that the portfolio payoff matches the put payoff in all cases.

This construction is intimately related to the concept of put-call parity, which for European options on non-dividend-paying stocks states that

$$C - P = S_0 - Ke^{-rT},$$

where C and P are the call and put prices, respectively, and S_0 is the current spot price of the underlying asset. Rearranging gives

$$P = C - S_0 + Ke^{-rT},$$

which is consistent with our replicating strategy: by taking a long call, shorting the underlying asset, and holding Ke^{-rT} in risk-free bonds, one can synthetically construct the payoff of a put option.

By strategically selecting these initial positions at t_0, we create a portfolio that yields exactly

$$V_T = (K - S_T)^+$$

at maturity, without any subsequent rebalancing. The absence of rebalancing is a direct consequence of the deterministic nature of the bond's accrual and the fact that the underlying asset and call option positions do not require interim adjustments when their payoffs are already fixed by expiration. This static hedging approach not only provides a clear illustration of the relationship between put and call options, the underlying asset, and the time value of money through discounting, but it also reinforces the fundamental principles of derivative pricing and risk management by demonstrating how arbitrage-free conditions can be maintained through perfect replication.

6.2.2.1 Put-Call Parity

The static hedging strategy for a European put option is fundamentally rooted in the put-call parity theorem, a cornerstone of options pricing for European options on non-dividend-paying assets. This theorem establishes that the sum of the put option price $P(S_t, t)$ and the current underlying asset price S_t is exactly equal to the sum of the call option price $C(S_t, t)$ and the present value of the strike price K, discounted over the time to maturity $T - t$ at the continuously compounded risk-free rate r. Mathematically, this relationship is expressed as

$$P(S_t, t) + S_t = C(S_t, t) + Ke^{-r(T-t)}.$$

Rearranging the equation to solve for the put price yields

$$P(S_t, t) = C(S_t, t) + Ke^{-r(T-t)} - S_t.$$

This expression shows that the price of a European put option can be replicated by constructing a portfolio comprising three elements:

1. A long position in one European call option with strike K and maturity T, which grants the right to purchase the underlying asset at K
2. A long position in a portfolio of zero-coupon bonds with a combined face value of K, whose present cost is $Ke^{-r(T-t)}$ (reflecting the time value of money)
3. A short position in one unit of the underlying asset, incurring a payoff of $-S_T$ at maturity

At expiration, the European call option pays $(S_T - K)^+$, the zero-coupon bonds mature to pay K, and the short asset position delivers $-S_T$, so that the total payoff of the replicating portfolio is

$$V_T = (S_T - K)^+ + K - S_T.$$

We can then consider the two cases (i.e., $S_T \leq K$ and $S_T > K$) to confirm that this portfolio replicates the put payoff $(K - S_T)^+$. Thus, by carefully selecting these initial positions, the replicating portfolio produces a payoff identical to that of the put option without requiring any dynamic rebalancing. This static hedge not only underscores the elegance of the put-call parity but also reinforces the consistency of option pricing. If market prices were to deviate from this parity, arbitrageurs could construct risk-free profit strategies by buying the underpriced instrument and selling the overpriced one until the equilibrium is restored.

6.2 Static Hedging

Moreover, the put-call parity relationship can be extended to more complex scenarios. For instance, if the underlying asset pays a continuous dividend yield q, the modified put-call parity becomes

$$P(S_t, t) + S_t e^{-q(T-t)} = C(S_t, t) + K e^{-r(T-t)},$$

ensuring that even with dividend payments, the replicating portfolio remains aligned with no-arbitrage principles.

In summary, by linking the static hedging strategy for a European put option to the mathematical framework provided by put-call parity, we see that the correct pricing of options inherently accounts for both the time value of money and the cost (or benefit) of carrying the underlying asset. This framework guarantees that the cost of establishing the replicating portfolio, comprised of a call option, zero-coupon bonds, and a short position in the asset, exactly equals the price of the put option, thereby ensuring consistent, arbitrage-free pricing in efficient markets.

6.2.2.2 Derivation Using Risk-Neutral Valuation

To derive the relationship between the prices of European put and call options, we begin within the risk-neutral valuation framework. Under the risk-neutral measure Q, the present value at time t of a European put option with strike K and maturity T that pays $(K - S_T)^+$ is given by

$$P(S_t, t) = e^{-r(T-t)} \mathbb{E}^Q\left[(K - S_T)^+ \mid \mathcal{F}_t\right],$$

where r is the continuously compounded risk-free rate, and $\mathcal{F}_t$ represents the information available at time t. Similarly, the price of a European call option with the same strike and maturity, which pays $(S_T - K)^+$ at expiration, is expressed as

$$C(S_t, t) = e^{-r(T-t)} \mathbb{E}^Q\left[(S_T - K)^+ \mid \mathcal{F}_t\right].$$

A key step in establishing put-call parity is to consider the linear combination

$$P(S_t, t) + S_t - K e^{-r(T-t)}.$$

Substituting the risk-neutral valuation of the put option, we have

$$P(S_t, t) + S_t - K e^{-r(T-t)} = e^{-r(T-t)} \mathbb{E}^Q\left[(K - S_T)^+ \mid \mathcal{F}_t\right] + S_t - K e^{-r(T-t)}.$$

Notice that we can rewrite the current price S_t in its forward form by recalling that under the risk-neutral measure

$$\mathbb{E}^Q[S_T \mid \mathcal{F}_t] = S_t e^{r(T-t)}.$$

Thus, expressing S_t as $e^{-r(T-t)} \cdot S_t e^{r(T-t)}$, the equation becomes

$$P(S_t, t) + S_t - Ke^{-r(T-t)} = e^{-r(T-t)} \left(\mathbb{E}^Q[(K - S_T)^+ | \mathcal{F}_t] + S_t e^{r(T-t)} - K \right).$$

Recognize that the term $S_t e^{r(T-t)} - K$ is equivalent to $\mathbb{E}^Q[S_T - K | \mathcal{F}_t]$. To combine the two components inside the expectation, consider the random variable

$$X = (K - S_T)^+ + (S_T - K).$$

We examine X under two cases. When $S_T \leq K$, we have $(K - S_T)^+ = K - S_T$ and $(S_T - K) = -(K - S_T)$, so that

$$X = (K - S_T) + (S_T - K) = 0.$$

When $S_T > K$, we have $(K - S_T)^+ = 0$ and $(S_T - K) = S_T - K$, yielding

$$X = 0 + (S_T - K) = S_T - K.$$

Thus, in all cases, we have

$$(K - S_T)^+ + (S_T - K) = (S_T - K)^+.$$

Substituting back, we obtain

$$P(S_t, t) + S_t - Ke^{-r(T-t)} = e^{-r(T-t)} \mathbb{E}^Q[(S_T - K)^+ | \mathcal{F}_t] = C(S_t, t).$$

Rearranging the expression leads to the celebrated put-call parity formula:

$$P(S_t, t) = C(S_t, t) + Ke^{-r(T-t)} - S_t.$$

This relationship shows that the price of a European put option can be directly determined from the price of a European call option, the current spot price S_t, and the present value of the strike price K. The derivation underscores how risk-neutral valuation and the no-arbitrage principle work together: if the put-call parity did not hold, market participants could construct arbitrage strategies to exploit the mispricing, thereby restoring equilibrium. This fundamental connection not only ensures consistency in option pricing but also serves as a critical tool for detecting mispricings and maintaining efficient market conditions.

6.2.2.3 Static Hedging of European Put Option in Action

To demonstrate the practical implementation of a static hedge for a European put option, we leverage put-call parity that specifies the mathematical link between the prices of European put and call options on the same underlying asset with identical

6.2 Static Hedging

strike K and maturity T. Specifically, recall that we can write the put option price as

$$P(S_t, t) = C(S_t, t) + Ke^{-r(T-t)} - S_t.$$

This equation implies that by knowing the price of a call option, the current price S_t, and the discounted strike $Ke^{-r(T-t)}$, we can construct a replicating portfolio that perfectly mimics the payoff of the put option at expiration. In practical terms, to replicate the put payoff $(K - S_T)^+$ at maturity, one can establish a portfolio at $t = 0$ comprising three components: a long position in one European call option, a long position in zero-coupon bonds with a face value of K (which cost Ke^{-rT} at inception), and a short position in one unit of the underlying asset. At maturity, the call option yields $(S_T - K)^+$, the bonds mature to pay K, and the short asset position results in a payoff of $-S_T$; together, these deliver a total payoff of

$$(S_T - K)^+ + K - S_T,$$

which simplifies to $(K - S_T)^+$ when considering the two cases $S_T \leq K$ and $S_T > K$.

In the code provided below, we first calculate the price of the European call option using the Black-Scholes formula, which requires as inputs the current asset price S_0, strike K, time to maturity T, risk-free rate r, and volatility σ. For our demonstration, we set the parameters as follows: $S_0 = 120$, $K = 110$, $r = 0.03$ (3% per annum), $T = 2$ years, and $\sigma = 0.25$ (25% annual volatility). With these inputs, the Black-Scholes model computes the call price $C(S_0, 0)$; then, using the put-call parity relation, we derive the corresponding put price via

$$P(S_0, 0) = C(S_0, 0) + Ke^{-rT} - S_0.$$

Subsequently, we simulate a range of possible terminal asset prices S_T and calculate the final payoffs for both the replicating portfolio and the European put option. These simulations serve to validate that the static hedge, established at inception without any need for rebalancing, indeed produces a terminal payoff identical to $(K - S_T)^+$. As illustrated in Listing 6-3 and Figure 6-4, the payoff profiles of the replicating portfolio and the put option are virtually indistinguishable, confirming the effectiveness of the static hedging strategy. This exercise not only provides a practical demonstration of put-call parity in action but also reinforces the theoretical underpinnings of static hedging and no-arbitrage pricing in the options market.

```python
import numpy as np
import matplotlib.pyplot as plt
from scipy.stats import norm

def black_scholes_call(S, K, T, r, sigma):
    """
    Compute the Black-Scholes price for a European call option.
    S: current asset price
    K: strike price
    T: time to maturity in years
    r: risk-free interest rate (annual, continuously compounded)
    sigma: volatility (annual)
    """
    d1 = (np.log(S / K) + (r + 0.5 * sigma**2) * T) / (sigma * np
        .sqrt(T))
    d2 = d1 - sigma * np.sqrt(T)
    call = S * norm.cdf(d1) - K * np.exp(-r * T) * norm.cdf(d2)
    return call

# Parameters
S0 = 120        # Current underlying asset price
K = 110         # Strike price
r = 0.03        # Risk-free rate (3%)
T = 2           # Time to maturity (2 years)
sigma = 0.25    # Volatility (25%)

# Compute the call option price using Black-Scholes
call_price = black_scholes_call(S0, K, T, r, sigma)

# Compute the present value of the strike price
PV_K = K * np.exp(-r * T)

# Put-call parity: P = C + PV(K) - S0
put_price_implied = call_price + PV_K - S0

print(f"European Call Option Price: ${call_price:.2f}")
print(f"Present Value of Strike: ${PV_K:.2f}")
print(f"Put Price from Put-Call Parity: ${put_price_implied:.2f}"
    )

# Simulate possible asset prices at maturity
S_T_values = np.linspace(60, 180, 500)

# Compute the payoff of the replicating portfolio
# Replicating portfolio = short underlying + K zero-coupon bonds
    + long call
payoff_short_asset = -S_T_values
payoff_bonds = K
payoff_call = np.maximum(S_T_values - K, 0)
portfolio_payoff = payoff_short_asset + payoff_bonds +
    payoff_call

# Compute the actual put payoff for comparison
```

6.2 Static Hedging

```python
put_payoff = np.maximum(K - S_T_values, 0)

# Plot the payoffs to compare
plt.figure(figsize=(10, 6))
plt.plot(S_T_values, portfolio_payoff, label='Replicating
    Portfolio Payoff', color='blue')
plt.plot(S_T_values, put_payoff, label='European Put Option
    Payoff', color='red', linestyle='--')
plt.axhline(0, color='black', linewidth=0.5)
plt.title('Static Hedge Replicating European Put Option Payoff')
plt.xlabel('Asset Price at Maturity ($)')
plt.ylabel('Payoff ($)')
plt.legend()
plt.grid(True)
plt.show()

# Outputs of interest
print(f"With these parameters, the static hedge set up at time 0
    costs: ${put_price_implied:.2f}")

# Ouptput
European Call Option Price: $25.21
Present Value of Strike: $103.59
Put Price from Put-Call Parity: $8.80
With these parameters, the static hedge set up at time 0 costs: \
    $8.80
```

Listing 6-3 Static hedging for replicating European put option payoff function

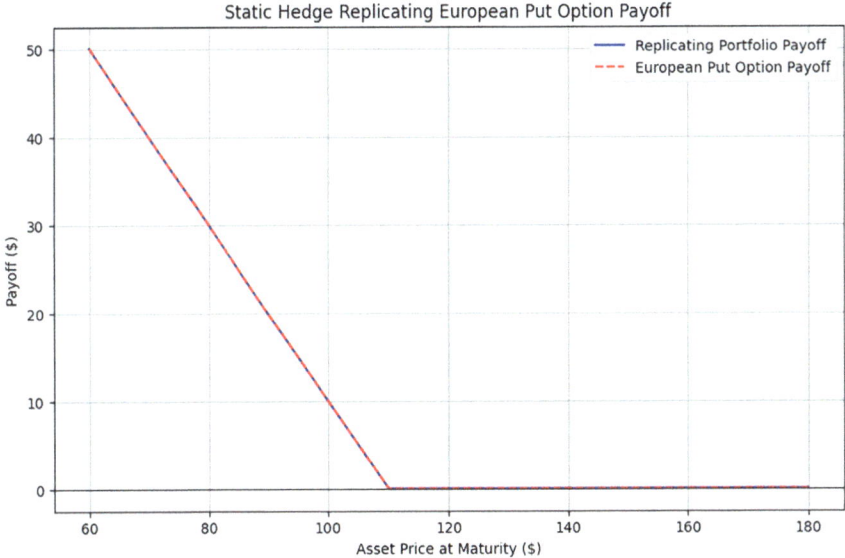

Figure 6-4 Replicating European put option via put-call parity

6.2.3 Static Hedging for Digital Option

A digital option, often referred to as a binary or all-or-nothing option, is a financial derivative that provides a fixed payout if the underlying asset's price satisfies a predetermined condition at maturity. In particular, a digital call option pays a specified amount, typically normalized to 1 if the asset's price S_T at expiration exceeds a strike price K; otherwise, it expires without value. The payoff of such an option can be succinctly represented by the indicator function

$$\Phi(S_T) = \mathbb{1}_{\{S_T \geq K\}},$$

which, in payoff form, is expressed as

$$\text{Payoff} = \begin{cases} 1, & \text{if } S_T \geq K, \\ 0, & \text{if } S_T < K. \end{cases}$$

To determine the fair price of a digital call option, we employ the risk-neutral valuation framework. Under this approach, the price at time t is the discounted expectation of its payoff under the risk-neutral measure Q:

$$DC(S; K) = e^{-r(T-t)} \mathbb{E}^Q\big[\mathbb{1}_{\{S_T \geq K\}} \mid \mathcal{F}_t\big] = e^{-r(T-t)} P^Q(S_T \geq K),$$

where r is the continuously compounded risk-free rate, T is the time to maturity, and $\mathcal{F}_t$ denotes the information available at time t. Here, $P^Q(S_T \geq K)$ is the risk-neutral probability that the asset's price will be at least K at expiration.

Within the Black-Scholes model, this probability is calculated using the cumulative distribution function (CDF) of the standard normal distribution, denoted by $N(\cdot)$. Consequently, the price of the digital call option is given by

$$DC(S; K) = e^{-r(T-t)} N(d_2),$$

with

$$d_2 = \frac{\ln\left(\frac{S}{K}\right) + \left(r - q - \frac{\sigma^2}{2}\right)(T-t)}{\sigma\sqrt{T-t}},$$

where S is the current price of the underlying asset, K is the strike price, q is the continuous dividend yield (which may be set to zero for non-dividend-paying assets), σ is the volatility of the asset, and $T - t$ is the time remaining to maturity. The term $\ln(S/K)$ captures the logarithmic distance between the asset price and the strike, while $\sigma\sqrt{T-t}$ normalizes this distance by the product of volatility and the square root of time, reflecting the uncertainty in the future price of the asset. The cumulative function $N(d_2)$ then represents the risk-neutral probability that S_T exceeds K.

6.2 Static Hedging

In a static hedging context, digital options can be replicated without continuous rebalancing. One common approach is to approximate the digital payoff using a portfolio of vanilla options. Recall that the derivative of a call option price with respect to its strike yields the negative of the discounted risk-neutral probability:

$$\frac{\partial C}{\partial K} = -e^{-r(T-t)} N(d_2).$$

Thus, by constructing a tight call spread—buying a call at strike K and selling a call at a slightly higher strike $K+\epsilon$—and taking the limit as $\epsilon \to 0$, one can replicate the payoff of a digital option. Mathematically, this finite-difference approximation is expressed as

$$\frac{C(K) - C(K+\epsilon)}{\epsilon} \approx -\frac{\partial C}{\partial K} = e^{-r(T-t)} N(d_2).$$

This approach illustrates the static hedge: once the replicating portfolio is constructed at inception, it will yield a terminal payoff that closely approximates $\mathbb{1}_{\{S_T \geq K\}}$ without the need for further adjustments, provided market conditions remain consistent with the Black-Scholes assumptions.

In summary, the fair price of a digital call option is determined by discounting the risk-neutral probability of a favorable outcome. The final pricing formula,

$$DC(S; K) = e^{-r(T-t)} N(d_2),$$

is derived from the risk-neutral expectation and is central to both theoretical and practical applications in option pricing. This method not only upholds the no-arbitrage principle but also serves as the foundation for constructing static hedges that replicate digital payoffs. Such replication techniques are particularly valuable in practice, as they allow for the creation of portfolios that mimic the behavior of digital options, thereby ensuring consistent pricing and effective risk management in financial markets.

6.2.4 Static Hedging with Constant Volatility

In the previous section, we assumed that the volatility remains constant. Here, we discuss an alternative method for replicating, or hedging, a digital call option under the same assumption. Our objective is to replicate the binary payoff of a digital call option, which pays 1 if the price of the underlying asset at maturity S_T satisfies or exceeds a predetermined strike K, and 0 otherwise. An effective method to achieve this replication is through a call spread strategy.

A call spread strategy involves two main actions: (i) purchasing a call option with a strike slightly below K, specifically at $K - h$, and (ii) selling a call option with a strike slightly above K, at $K + h$, where h is a small positive number. To ensure that

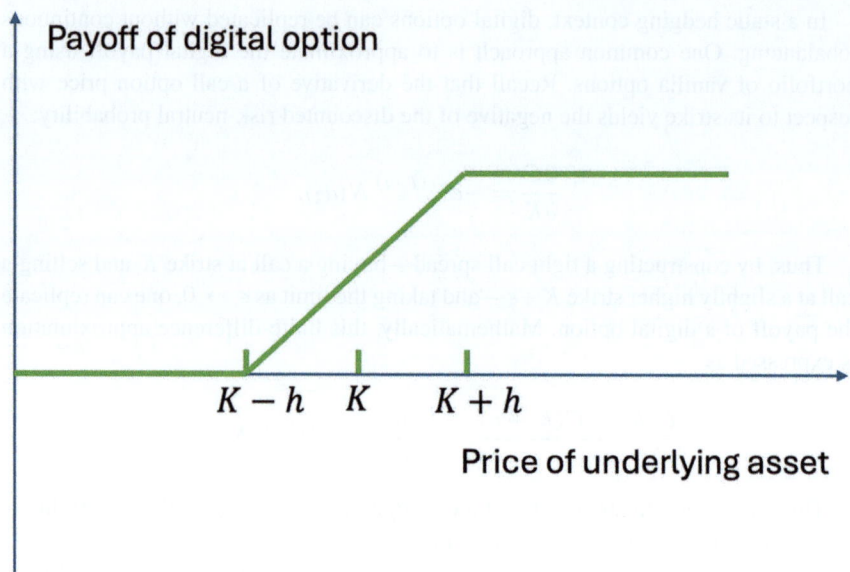

Figure 6-5 Call spread payoff to approximate digital option

the resulting payoff approximates that of a digital option as h becomes very small, each option is scaled by a factor of $\frac{1}{2h}$. This scaling is necessary because it adjusts the magnitude of the payoff difference so that, in the limit as $h \to 0$, the spread converges to a step function. Figure 6-5 illustrates this call spread strategy and its convergence to the digital payoff.

Now let $C(K - h, \sigma)$ and $C(K + h, \sigma)$ denote the Black-Scholes prices of call options with strikes $K - h$ and $K + h$, respectively, where the volatility σ is assumed constant. The value of the scaled call spread at any time t before maturity T is given by

$$\text{Call Spread Value} = \frac{C(K - h, \sigma) - C(K + h, \sigma)}{2h}.$$

To understand why this call spread replicates the digital call option, consider its payoff at maturity. There are three distinct cases:

1. If $S_T \geq K + h$: Both calls are in the money. The payoff from the call with strike $K - h$ is $S_T - (K - h)$, and from the call with strike $K + h$ it is $S_T - (K + h)$. The net payoff is

$$\frac{(S_T - (K - h)) - (S_T - (K + h))}{2h} = \frac{2h}{2h} = 1,$$

which exactly matches the digital option's payoff of 1.

6.2 Static Hedging

2. If $S_T \leq K - h$: Both call options expire worthless, so their payoffs are zero. Thus, the call spread payoff is

$$\frac{0-0}{2h} = 0,$$

matching the digital option's payoff of 0.

3. If S_T lies between $K-h$ and $K+h$: The call with strike $K-h$ is in the money, while the call with strike $K+h$ is either at the money or out of the money. In this interval, the net payoff of the spread increases linearly from 0 to 1 as S_T moves from $K-h$ to $K+h$. As h approaches zero, the width of this linear region diminishes, and the spread's payoff converges to a discontinuous jump from 0 to 1 at $S_T = K$.

To formalize this replication, we examine the limit as $h \to 0$. Using a Taylor series expansion of the call price about K, we have

$$C(K - h, \sigma) = C(K, \sigma) - h\frac{\partial C}{\partial K} + \frac{h^2}{2}\frac{\partial^2 C}{\partial K^2} + O(h^3),$$

$$C(K + h, \sigma) = C(K, \sigma) + h\frac{\partial C}{\partial K} + \frac{h^2}{2}\frac{\partial^2 C}{\partial K^2} + O(h^3).$$

Subtracting these two expansions yields the following result:

$$C(K - h, \sigma) - C(K + h, \sigma) = -2h\frac{\partial C}{\partial K} + O(h^3).$$

Dividing both sides by $2h$ gives

$$\frac{C(K - h, \sigma) - C(K + h, \sigma)}{2h} = -\frac{\partial C}{\partial K} + O(h^2).$$

Taking the limit as $h \to 0$ leads to

$$DC(S; K) = \lim_{h \to 0} \frac{C(K - h, \sigma) - C(K + h, \sigma)}{2h} = -\frac{\partial C(K, \sigma)}{\partial K}.$$

Within the Black-Scholes framework, the price of a European call option is given by

$$C(S, K, T - t, r, \sigma, q) = Se^{-q(T-t)}N(d_1) - Ke^{-r(T-t)}N(d_2),$$

where

$$d_2 = \frac{\ln(S/K) + (r - q - \frac{\sigma^2}{2})(T - t)}{\sigma\sqrt{T - t}}.$$

Differentiating $C(S, K, T - t, r, \sigma, q)$ with respect to K and noting that the derivative $-\frac{\partial C}{\partial K}$ recovers the discounted risk-neutral probability $e^{-r(T-t)}N(d_2)$, we obtain

$$DC(S; K) = -\frac{\partial C(K, \sigma)}{\partial K} = e^{-r(T-t)}N(d_2).$$

This derivation confirms that the digital call option's price can be derived from the call option pricing formula through differentiation. By constructing a call spread with strikes $K-h$ and $K+h$ and letting the spread width $2h$ tend to zero, we achieve a static hedge for the digital option. This hedge is static because, once the spread is established at inception, it requires no further rebalancing until maturity.

In summary, by utilizing a call spread strategy with appropriately scaled positions and taking the limit as $h \to 0$, we replicate the binary payoff of a digital call option. The mathematical derivation demonstrates that

$$\lim_{h \to 0} \frac{C(K-h, \sigma) - C(K+h, \sigma)}{2h} = e^{-r(T-t)}N(d_2),$$

thus validating the effectiveness of this replication method. This approach is advantageous in practice because it creates a robust static hedge that does not require continuous adjustments, thereby simplifying the management of digital options in various financial contexts.

Now let us turn to the case with a changing volatility.

6.2.5 Static Hedging with Changing Volatility

When volatility σ is not constant but instead varies with the strike price, a common phenomenon observed in practice as the volatility skew or smile, the static hedging strategy for replicating a digital call option becomes more intricate. In such cases, the volatility is modeled as a function of the strike, $\sigma = \sigma(K)$, which introduces an additional layer of dependency into the option pricing and hedging process.

Recall that, under constant volatility, one can replicate a digital call option by constructing a narrow call spread. Specifically, by purchasing a call option with a strike slightly below K (i.e., at $K-h$) and selling a call option with a strike slightly above K (i.e., at $K+h$), and by scaling the difference in prices by $\frac{1}{2h}$, the resulting spread converges to the digital payoff as $h \to 0$. In mathematical terms, the price of the digital call option $DC(S; K)$ in the constant volatility scenario is given by

$$DC(S; K) = \lim_{h \to 0} \frac{C(K-h, \sigma) - C(K+h, \sigma)}{2h} = -\frac{\partial C}{\partial K}(K, \sigma),$$

where $C(K, \sigma)$ denotes the price of a call option with strike K and constant volatility σ.

6.2 Static Hedging

However, when volatility is strike dependent, the call price becomes a function of both K and $\sigma(K)$, denoted as $C(K, \sigma(K))$. In order to replicate the digital option in this more general setting, we again construct a call spread, but now we must account for the variability of σ with respect to K. For a small $h > 0$, consider the Taylor series expansion of the call option price around the strike K:

$$C(K - h, \sigma(K - h)) = C(K, \sigma(K)) - h\frac{\partial C}{\partial K}(K, \sigma(K)) - h\frac{\partial C}{\partial \sigma}(K, \sigma(K))\frac{\partial \sigma(K)}{\partial K}$$
$$+ O(h^2),$$

$$C(K + h, \sigma(K + h)) = C(K, \sigma(K)) + h\frac{\partial C}{\partial K}(K, \sigma(K)) + h\frac{\partial C}{\partial \sigma}(K, \sigma(K))\frac{\partial \sigma(K)}{\partial K}$$
$$+ O(h^2).$$

Subtracting these two expansions gives

$$C(K - h, \sigma(K - h)) - C(K + h, \sigma(K + h))$$
$$= -2h\frac{\partial C}{\partial K}(K, \sigma(K)) - 2h\frac{\partial C}{\partial \sigma}(K, \sigma(K))\frac{\partial \sigma(K)}{\partial K} + O(h^2).$$

Dividing the result by $2h$ and taking the limit as $h \to 0$ yields the digital call option price under nonconstant volatility:

$$DC_\sigma(S; K) = \lim_{h \to 0} \frac{C(K - h, \sigma(K - h)) - C(K + h, \sigma(K + h))}{2h}$$
$$= -\frac{\partial C}{\partial K}(K, \sigma(K)) - \frac{\partial C}{\partial \sigma}(K, \sigma(K))\frac{\partial \sigma(K)}{\partial K}.$$

The first term, $-\frac{\partial C}{\partial K}(K, \sigma(K))$, is the familiar derivative of the call price with respect to the strike and corresponds to the digital call price in the constant volatility framework. The second term, $-\frac{\partial C}{\partial \sigma}(K, \sigma(K))\frac{\partial \sigma(K)}{\partial K}$, captures the additional cost incurred due to the strike dependence of volatility. Here, the sensitivity $\frac{\partial C}{\partial \sigma}(K, \sigma(K))$ is known as vega, which measures how the call option price changes with respect to volatility, and $\frac{\partial \sigma(K)}{\partial K}$ represents the slope of the volatility skew.

In the Black-Scholes model, vega is given by

$$\frac{\partial C}{\partial \sigma}(K, \sigma(K)) = e^{-q(T-t)} S\sqrt{T - t}\,\phi(d_1),$$

where $\phi(d_1)$ is the standard normal probability density function evaluated at d_1, and q is the continuous dividend yield. Since $\phi(d_1) \geq 0$ for all d_1, the product

$$-\frac{\partial C}{\partial \sigma}(K, \sigma(K))\frac{\partial \sigma(K)}{\partial K}$$

is nonnegative when the volatility skew is negative (i.e., when $\frac{\partial \sigma(K)}{\partial K} < 0$), which is typically observed in equity markets. This observation implies that

$$DC_\sigma(S; K) \geq -\frac{\partial C}{\partial K}(K, \sigma(K)) = DC(S; K),$$

meaning that the digital call option is more expensive under nonconstant volatility than it would be under constant volatility. The additional term accounts for the increased likelihood of extreme moves implied by the skew, and it ensures that the static hedging strategy remains accurate and reflective of actual market conditions.

In conclusion, when volatility varies with the strike price, the static hedging approach for a digital call option must be adjusted to include the extra term

$$-\frac{\partial C}{\partial \sigma}(K, \sigma(K))\frac{\partial \sigma(K)}{\partial K},$$

which captures the impact of the volatility skew on the option price. This results in a digital call option price

$$DC_\sigma(S; K) = -\frac{\partial C}{\partial K}(K, \sigma(K)) - \frac{\partial C}{\partial \sigma}(K, \sigma(K))\frac{\partial \sigma(K)}{\partial K},$$

that is generally higher than the price computed under the assumption of constant volatility. This enhanced pricing formula not only improves the accuracy of the static hedge in a realistic setting but also provides a more robust framework for managing the risk associated with digital options in markets where volatility exhibits a skew or smile.

6.2.6 Static Hedging of Digital Call Option in Action

In this section, we illustrate the implementation of a static hedging strategy specifically designed for a digital call option by constructing a call spread that replicates its distinctive binary payoff. The method involves determining the prices of two European call options whose strike prices are positioned symmetrically around the digital option's strike: one with a strike of $K - h$ and the other with a strike of $K + h$, where h is a small positive number. The interval between these strikes, $2h$, essentially controls the granularity of the approximation, thereby influencing both the sensitivity and precision of the call spread in closely mimicking the digital option's payoff structure.

6.2 Static Hedging

As shown in Listing 6-4, to approximate the digital call option's price, we calculate the difference between the prices of the two call options and then scale this difference by the factor $\frac{1}{2h}$. This scaling is critical, as it normalizes the payoff difference, ensuring that as h decreases, the call spread's payoff converges more accurately to the binary outcome—1 if the underlying asset's price at maturity exceeds K, and 0 otherwise. To further substantiate this approximation, we compute the exact price of the digital call option using the Black-Scholes formula, which integrates the cumulative distribution function of the standard normal distribution to evaluate the risk-neutral probability of the asset finishing above the strike. This Black-Scholes-derived price serves as a benchmark, allowing us to gauge the fidelity of the call spread approximation in replicating the digital option's intended payoff.

```python
# Parameters
S0 = 120            # Current stock price
K = 100             # Strike price
r = 0.03            # Risk-free interest rate (3%)
T = 0.5             # Time to maturity (6 months)
sigma = 0.25        # Volatility (25%)
h = 0.25            # Small increment for strikes

# Calculate call option prices at K - h and K + h
call_price_lower = black_scholes_call(S0, K - h, T, r, sigma)
call_price_upper = black_scholes_call(S0, K + h, T, r, sigma)

# Calculate the approximate digital call option price using the
    call spread
digital_call_price_approx = (call_price_lower - call_price_upper)
    / (2 * h)

# Calculate the exact digital call option price in Black-Scholes
d2 = (np.log(S0 / K) + (r - 0.5 * sigma ** 2) * T) / (sigma * np.
    sqrt(T))
digital_call_price_exact = np.exp(-r * T) * norm.cdf(d2)

print(f"Approximate Digital Call Option Price using Call Spread:
    {digital_call_price_approx:.6f}")
print(f"Exact Digital Call Option Price from Black-Scholes: {
    digital_call_price_exact:.6f}")

# Simulate asset prices at maturity
S_T = np.linspace(90, 110, 1000)

# Payoff of the digital call option
digital_payoff = np.where(S_T >= K, 1, 0)

# Payoff of the call spread
call_payoff_lower = np.maximum(S_T - (K - h), 0)
call_payoff_upper = np.maximum(S_T - (K + h), 0)
call_spread_payoff = (call_payoff_lower - call_payoff_upper) / (2
    * h)
```

```
35
36  # Plot the payoffs
37  plt.figure(figsize=(10, 6))
38  plt.plot(S_T, digital_payoff, label='Digital Call Option Payoff',
        color='green')
39  plt.plot(S_T, call_spread_payoff, label='Call Spread Payoff (h
        ={})'.format(h), color='orange', linestyle='--')
40  plt.title('Digital Call Option vs. Call Spread Replication')
41  plt.xlabel('Asset Price at Maturity $S_T$')
42  plt.ylabel('Payoff')
43  plt.legend()
44  plt.grid(True)
45  plt.show()
46
47  # Output
48  Approximate Digital Call Option Price using Call Spread: 0.828816
49  Exact Digital Call Option Price from Black-Scholes: 0.835360
```

Listing 6-4 Static hedge for digital call option

To evaluate the effectiveness of replication, we simulate a range of potential underlying asset prices at maturity and calculate the corresponding payoffs for both the digital call option and the call spread. The payoff of the digital option is a step function that shifts from zero to one at the strike price. In contrast, the call spread's payoff transitions smoothly between these two values, demonstrating the approximation process. As the interval h decreases, the call spread's payoff curve increasingly resembles the binary payoff of the digital option. Figure 6-6 illustrates

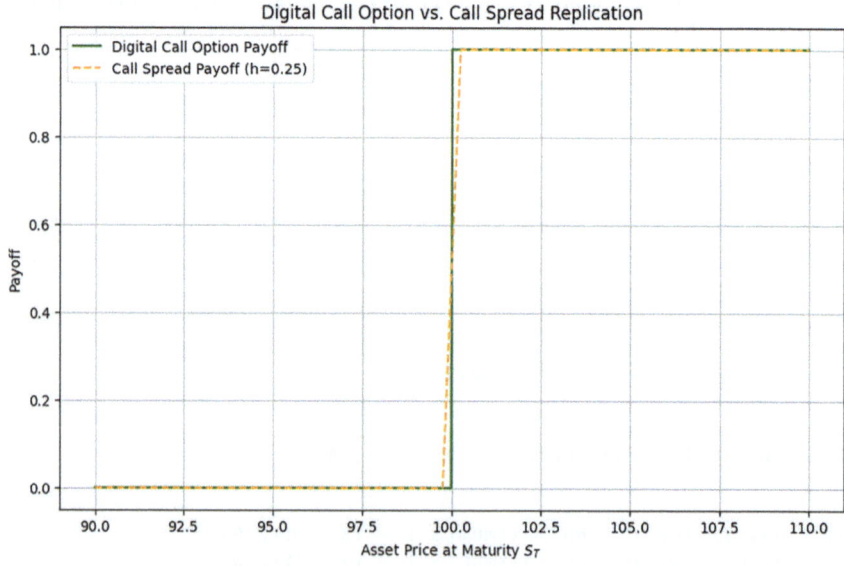

Figure 6-6 Replicating digital call option via call spread

how the call spread effectively captures the payoff of the digital option, especially as h approaches zero.

This implementation demonstrates the practicality of static hedging in financial markets. By constructing a simple portfolio of call options, we can replicate the payoff of a digital option without the need for continuous adjustments. Furthermore, by experimenting with different values of the h interval, we can observe how the accuracy of the replication improves as the interval decreases, thus enhancing the precision of the hedging strategy.

6.3 Summary

In this chapter, we examined two fundamental approaches to hedging, dynamic and static, and their roles in mitigating financial risk. We began by discussing derivative hedging in general, emphasizing the use of instruments such as options, futures, forwards, and swaps to transfer and manage risk. These instruments enable market participants to protect portfolios from adverse price movements, thereby contributing to the stability and predictability of financial outcomes.

Dynamic hedging, as illustrated by the Black-Scholes framework, involves continuous or frequent rebalancing of positions to maintain a delta-neutral portfolio. By calculating sensitivities, most notably delta and gamma, traders can adjust their positions in real time, thus counteracting the impact of small fluctuations in the underlying asset's price. Although this approach offers a high degree of precision and adaptability, it comes at the cost of increased transaction expenses and operational complexity, particularly when factoring in practical issues such as discrete trading and market liquidity constraints.

In contrast, static hedging is based on the construction of a replicating portfolio at inception that remains fixed until maturity. We demonstrated this concept through the static hedging of forward contracts and European put options. In these cases, replicating portfolios are derived by matching the yield of the derivative, using combinations of the underlying asset, zero-coupon bonds, and options, so that the yield of the portfolio's terminal is exactly that of the target instrument. Although static hedging reduces the frequency of transactions and associated costs, it does not adjust to unexpected market movements, potentially leaving residual risk.

We further extended the analysis to digital options, illustrating how a call spread can be used to approximate the binary payoff characteristic of a digital call option. The methodology involves computing the prices of call options with strikes $K - h$ and $K + h$ and scaling their difference by $\frac{1}{2h}$, thus demonstrating that the finite-difference approximation converges to the derivative $-\frac{\partial C}{\partial K}$ as h tends to zero. This derivation not only corroborates the theoretical pricing formula obtained from the Black-Scholes model but also provides a practical framework for constructing static hedges under idealized market conditions.

Additionally, the chapter addressed the impact of non-constant volatility on static hedging. When volatility exhibits a skew or smile, that is, when it varies with the strike, the replication strategy must incorporate an extra term involving vega and the derivative of the volatility function with respect to the strike. This adjustment ensures that the price of the digital call option is accurately captured under a non-constant volatility regime, reflecting a more realistic market environment.

In general, this chapter highlighted that both dynamic and static hedging strategies have distinct advantages and trade-offs. Dynamic hedging offers the flexibility to respond instantaneously to market changes and manage multiple sensitivities, making it well-suited for managing complex derivatives. In contrast, static hedging provides a more cost-effective and operationally simpler alternative, particularly when the derivative's payoff can be perfectly replicated at inception. By understanding the underlying mathematical principles and practical implications of these strategies, investors and institutions can select and implement hedging techniques more effectively that align with their risk profiles, operational capabilities, and prevailing market conditions.

7. Managing Model Risk in Finance

In the fast-changing world of financial markets, the use of quantitative models has become essential for decision-making, risk management, and strategic planning. These models range from traditional frameworks, such as the Black-Scholes option pricing model, to advanced machine learning (ML) algorithms. Their purpose is to capture the complexities of financial instruments and market behavior. However, using these models carries risks. Model risk—the possibility of negative consequences resulting from decisions based on inaccurate or flawed models—has become a significant concern for financial institutions, regulators, and stakeholders.

Model risk can take various forms, primarily stemming from differences between a model's assumptions and the actual conditions of the financial environment it aims to represent. These discrepancies can arise from model specification errors, where the selected mathematical framework does not adequately capture the essential dynamics of the underlying assets or markets. For example, assuming constant volatility in option pricing overlooks the observed volatility smile, which can result in mispriced derivatives.

Even if the model specification is correct, another source of model risk is linked to parameter estimation. Financial models often use historical data to estimate parameters such as mean returns, variances, and correlations. Although statistical estimation techniques can be powerful, they are vulnerable to issues like sampling errors, overfitting, and multicollinearity. These problems can distort the parameter values and, in turn, affect the model's outputs. For instance, if a model is overfitted to historical price data, it may show excellent performance on past data (in-sample) but perform poorly on new, unseen data (out-of-sample), diminishing its usefulness in real-world situations.

Numerical implementation issues also play an important role in model risk. Many complex financial models rely on numerical methods for solutions, such as Monte Carlo simulations or finite difference methods. These techniques introduce approximation errors and computational uncertainties. The choice of discretization steps, convergence criteria, and algorithmic stability can greatly affect the accuracy and reliability of the model results. Inaccurate numerical solutions can result in incorrect pricing, ineffective hedging strategies, and flawed risk assessments.

Model risk tends to increase in situations where models are regarded as black boxes, especially with the rise of machine learning and artificial intelligence in finance. The lack of transparency in these models makes it difficult to understand and trust their outputs. This opacity can prevent the identification of model limitations and vulnerabilities, raising the likelihood of unexpected and significant financial losses. To effectively manage model risk, a comprehensive approach is essential. This includes thorough validation processes to evaluate model assumptions, sensitivity analyses to comprehend the impact of various parameters, and ongoing monitoring to identify any decline in model performance over time. Furthermore, implementing strong governance frameworks ensures that models are developed, implemented, and used responsibly, with clear accountability and oversight mechanisms in place.

In summary, model risk poses a significant challenge in the financial sector, closely linked to the mathematical foundations and execution of quantitative models. As financial institutions increasingly adopt complex modeling techniques, especially those that utilize advanced computational power and machine learning, the need to understand and manage model risk thoroughly becomes paramount. Addressing model risk is vital for preserving financial stability, ensuring accurate risk assessments, and maintaining trust in the quantitative tools that support modern finance.

In the following sections, we will explore the four essential components of training a modern machine learning model: data, model class, cost function, and optimization algorithm. We will also discuss the risks associated with each component and provide strategies for managing and alleviating these risks, building on previous work by Cohen et al. (2023).

7.1 Model Risk Due to Data

Data serves as the foundation for machine learning models, especially in the financial sector, where accuracy and reliability are crucial. In financial applications, data are the key input that enables models to identify patterns, make predictions, and guide strategic decision-making processes. The quality, quantity, and relevance of this data are vital factors that determine a model's performance, its ability to adapt to new situations, and, ultimately, the reliability of its results.

Mathematically, a machine learning model can be represented as a function $f_\mathbf{w}$ parameterized by a set of weights $\mathbf{w}$, which maps the input features $\mathbf{X}$ to the predicted outputs $\hat{\mathbf{y}}$:

$$\hat{\mathbf{y}} = f_\mathbf{w}(\mathbf{X})$$

The training process involves adjusting the parameters $\mathbf{w}$ to minimize a cost function $Q(\mathbf{w})$, which quantifies the discrepancy between the model predictions $\hat{\mathbf{y}}$

7.1 Model Risk Due to Data

and the true target values **y**:

$$Q(\mathbf{w}) = \frac{1}{N}\sum_{i=1}^{N} l\left(y_i, \hat{y}_i\right)$$

Here, $l(\cdot,\cdot)$ denotes a loss function, such as the mean squared error (MSE) for regression tasks:

$$l\left(y_i, \hat{y}_i\right) = \frac{1}{2}(y_i - \hat{y}_i)^2$$

The effectiveness of the optimization process is highly dependent on the quality of the data used during training. Poor-quality data, characterized by noise, biases, or insufficient representation of the underlying phenomena, can result in inaccurate parameter estimates, leading to models that not only perform poorly on the training data but also, more importantly, fail to generalize to new, unseen data. This inability to generalize is a major source of model risk, where decisions based on the model's predictions could result in adverse financial outcomes.

Generalization is a model's capacity to perform well on unseen data, effectively capturing the underlying data-generating process instead of just memorizing the training data. This concept can be mathematically defined through the relationship between expected risk and empirical risk. The expected risk $R(f_\mathbf{w})$ is defined as the expected loss in the true data distribution $P_{\text{true}}(X, y)$:

$$R(f_\mathbf{w}) = \mathbb{E}_{(X,y)\sim P_{\text{true}}}\left[l(y, f_\mathbf{w}(X))\right]$$

In contrast, the empirical risk $Q(\mathbf{w})$ is the average loss in the training dataset. A model that generalizes well has a low expected risk by effectively minimizing empirical risk while avoiding overfitting the training data. Overfitting occurs when a model captures noise or irrelevant patterns in the training data, which leads to poor performance on new, unseen data. On the other hand, underfitting happens when the model is too simplistic to capture the underlying structure of the data, resulting in high errors on both the training data and the new data.

Data is generally divided into three separate subsets—training, validation, and test sets—to effectively assess and improve a model's generalization abilities. This division helps reduce overfitting and provides unbiased evaluations of model performance.

The training set is the primary dataset used to train and adjust the model parameters $\mathbf{w}$. During training, the model learns to optimize (often in a minimization setting) the empirical risk $Q(\mathbf{w})$ by iteratively updating $\mathbf{w}$ based on the loss computed on the training data. The following update rule is an instance of the gradient descent algorithm, commonly used in training modern neural networks.

$$\mathbf{w}_{t+1} = \mathbf{w}_t - \eta\nabla_\mathbf{w} Q(\mathbf{w}_t)$$

where η is the learning rate, and $\nabla_{\mathbf{w}} Q(\mathbf{w}_t)$ is the gradient of the cost function with respect to the weights at iteration t.

The validation set is an important evaluation dataset used to fine-tune hyperparameters and select the best model configuration. Unlike the training set, the validation set is not used to update the model's parameters directly. Instead, it offers insight into how modifications to the model architecture, learning rate, regularization parameters, and other hyperparameters impact performance. By assessing the empirical risk $R_{\text{val}}(f_{\mathbf{w}})$ on the validation set, we can make informed decisions about the model's optimal hyperparameter configuration that could potentially lead to a low true risk.

$$R_{\text{val}}(f_{\mathbf{w}}) = \frac{1}{N_{\text{val}}} \sum_{i=1}^{N_{\text{val}}} l\left(y_i^{\text{val}}, \hat{y}_i^{\text{val}}\right)$$

Using a representative validation set can help us select generalizable models and prevent overfitting by ensuring that the model performs well on unseen data.

The test set is an independent dataset reserved explicitly for evaluating the final model's generalization performance. Once the model has been trained and the hyperparameters have been optimized using the training and validation sets, the test set offers an unbiased estimate of the expected risk.

$$R_{\text{test}}(f_{\mathbf{w}}) = \frac{1}{N_{\text{test}}} \sum_{i=1}^{N_{\text{test}}} l\left(y_i^{\text{test}}, \hat{y}_i^{\text{test}}\right)$$

This final evaluation ensures that the model's performance metrics accurately reflect its ability to generalize to new, unseen data, providing a realistic assessment of its utility in practical financial applications.

The integrity of the train-validation-test split, along with the quality of the data in each subset, significantly affects a model's ability to generalize. If the training data fail to represent the diverse scenarios that the model will encounter in production, it may struggle to generalize effectively. For example, in financial markets, structural changes such as regulatory shifts or economic crises can make historical data less relevant to predict future behavior.

Insufficient data can lead to models that do not accurately capture the underlying distribution, resulting in high variance and poor generalization. On the other hand, overly complex models trained on limited data may overfit, picking up noise instead of meaningful patterns. Furthermore, financial data often display temporal dependencies and non-stationarities. Therefore, it is crucial to ensure that the train-validation-test split maintains the temporal order of the data to prevent information leakage and to accurately evaluate the model's performance in real-world, time-sensitive situations.

In cases where certain events, such as financial crises, occur infrequently, the training set may not have enough examples to identify these critical patterns. As

7.1 Model Risk Due to Data

a result, models may struggle to predict or respond effectively to such events. To address these imbalances, techniques such as resampling, synthetic data generation, or cost-sensitive learning may be required. Furthermore, improper separation of datasets can lead to data leakage, where information from the test set unintentionally influences the training process. This contamination can artificially inflate performance metrics, misleading stakeholders about the model's actual ability to generalize.

To enhance a model's ability to generalize and reduce associated risks, several data management strategies can be utilized. An effective approach is k-fold cross-validation, which provides a more reliable estimate of a model's generalization performance by ensuring that each data point participates in both the training and validation sets across different iterations.

Additionally, incorporating regularization methods, such as L1 or L2 penalties, can help limit model complexity, encouraging the development of simpler models that generalize more effectively. Careful selection and transformation of features based on domain knowledge can improve the model's capacity to identify relevant patterns while avoiding overfitting to noise.

Implementing thorough data cleaning, normalization, and transformation procedures also ensures that the data used for training is consistent, accurate, and compliant with necessary economic constraints.

Data is essential for training and ensuring the effectiveness of machine learning models, particularly in the financial sector, where the stakes are high. The relationship between data quality, model complexity, and training methods directly influences a model's ability to apply historical observations to future situations. By carefully managing the train-validation-test split, addressing biases and errors in the data, and using strategies to improve generalization, we can significantly reduce model risk. Crucially, ensuring that the data $(\mathbf{X}, \mathbf{y})$ accurately represents the true underlying distribution $P_{\text{true}}(X, y)$ is essential for the model $f_{\mathbf{w}}$ to effectively approximate the true mapping f_{true}:

$$f_{\mathbf{w}} \approx f_{\text{true}} \quad \text{when} \quad (\mathbf{X}, \mathbf{y}) \sim P_{\text{true}}(X, y)$$

By diligently managing data and understanding generalization risks, financial ML models can deliver reliable and robust performance, aiding sound decision-making and reducing potential financial losses.

7.1.1 Data Risks in Financial Machine Learning

In the realm of financial machine learning, data-related risks are a significant concern because they can adversely affect the performance and reliability of models. These risks stem from various issues, including biases, errors, and deficiencies in the datasets used for training and evaluation. It is crucial to comprehend and address these risks to develop robust models that can effectively generalize to new unseen data.

Biases in data can introduce systematic errors into model predictions, undermining their validity and usefulness. Several forms of bias are particularly pertinent in financial datasets:

7.1.1.1 Sampling Bias (Backward-Looking Data)

Sampling bias occurs when the training data do not accurately represent the wider population or the conditions in which the model will be used. For example, a model trained on data from a specific regional market may not perform well in a different market due to differences in market structure, participant behavior, or regulatory conditions. This shift in data distribution can result in significant increases in prediction errors when the model is applied to the target population. Therefore, it is crucial to use representative training data.

Such a distributional shift may also occur in terms of the time dimension. Financial datasets are inherently historical, reflecting past market behaviors and asset performances. Relying solely on these data assumes that future market dynamics will follow historical patterns. However, financial markets are vulnerable to structural changes, regulatory changes, and unforeseen events that can significantly alter these underlying dynamics. Mathematically, this issue arises when there is a discrepancy between the training data distribution $P_{\text{train}}(X, y)$ and the future data distribution $P_{\text{future}}(X, y)$:

$$P_{\text{train}}(X, y) \neq P_{\text{future}}(X, y)$$

This divergence, or distributional bias, can lead to models that perform well on historical data but poorly on future data, increasing the model risk due to poor generalization.

7.1.1.2 Spurious Correlations

In high-dimensional financial datasets, it is common to observe correlations that are statistically significant but lack any causal or meaningful economic basis. For example, a predictive model might identify a strong relationship between the price of a particular stock and an unrelated index by chance. Such correlations, which arise without a genuine underlying connection, are referred to as spurious correlations.

Incorporating spurious correlations into a model can lead to overfitting, which occurs when the model learns to capture random noise in the training data instead of true, generalizable patterns. Specifically, a model may achieve a low in-sample error by optimizing the empirical risk on the observed data, but this success does not necessarily mean it will have a low expected risk. In other words, while the model may perform well on the training dataset, it might struggle to generalize to unseen data.

The difference between in-sample performance and out-of-sample reliability emphasizes the importance of carefully selecting features that have both theoretical and economic justification. By incorporating domain expertise and human judgment into the feature selection process, we can avoid relying on arbitrary or irrelevant relationships. This approach ultimately enhances the model's ability to generalize. By prioritizing features grounded in sound financial principles, we can reduce the risk of overfitting, ensuring that the model captures meaningful and robust patterns rather than just noise.

7.1.1.3 Class Imbalance (Imbalanced Inputs)

Critical financial events, such as defaults, fraud, or market crashes, are relatively rare. This leads to imbalanced datasets where the minority class (e.g., instances of default) is underrepresented compared to the majority class (e.g., non-default instances). Training models on imbalanced data can bias the model toward the majority class, which reduces its ability to detect and predict events in the minority class. The extent of this imbalance can be quantified using the imbalance ratio:

$$\text{Imbalance Ratio} = \frac{N_{\text{majority}}}{N_{\text{minority}}}$$

where N_{majority} and N_{minority} are the numbers of samples in the majority and minority classes, respectively. Addressing class imbalance is crucial for models where accurate prediction of minority events has significant implications.

7.1.1.4 Data Errors and Preprocessing Challenges

In the field of financial machine learning, the accuracy and integrity of data preprocessing are crucial to ensuring the reliability of model predictions. Mistakes and shortcomings in data handling can pose significant risks, undermining the training process and hindering the model's ability to generalize effectively. Among these challenges, data leakage is a particularly concerning issue, but other preprocessing errors also require careful attention.

Data leakage occurs when information from outside the training dataset unintentionally affects the model training process. This contamination can result in overly optimistic performance estimates during evaluation, which can obscure the model's true predictive abilities. An example of data leakage is the inclusion of features in training data that depend on future information. Suppose that we have input features X and target variables y. Ideally, training data X_{train} should contain only information available up to the prediction point. However, if future information X_{future} is erroneously included, the training data becomes

$$X_{\text{train}} = \{X_{\text{past}}, X_{\text{future}}\}$$

In this scenario, the model $f_{\mathbf{w}}$ learns to associate future-dependent features with the target variable:

$$\hat{y} = f_{\mathbf{w}}(X_{\text{train}}) = f_{\mathbf{w}}(X_{\text{past}}, X_{\text{future}})$$

Including such future data violates the principle of temporal causality that should guide financial predictions. As a result, models may perform impressively on training data but struggle when applied to real-world, forward-looking situations. This issue occurs because the model uses information that would not have been accessible at the time of prediction, which artificially inflates the performance metrics.

Preventing data leakage requires strict data management practices. A key approach is to clearly separate the training, validation, and test datasets, ensuring that the preprocessing steps are limited to each subset independently. For example, when scaling feature, parameters such as mean (μ) and standard deviation (σ) should be calculated exclusively from the training data:

$$\mu_{\text{train}} = \frac{1}{N_{\text{train}}} \sum_{i=1}^{N_{\text{train}}} X_i^{\text{train}}$$

$$\sigma_{\text{train}} = \sqrt{\frac{1}{N_{\text{train}}} \sum_{i=1}^{N_{\text{train}}} (X_i^{\text{train}} - \mu_{\text{train}})^2}$$

These computed parameters are then applied to normalize both the training, validation, and test datasets:

$$X_i^{\text{train\_norm}} = \frac{X_i^{\text{train}} - \mu_{\text{train}}}{\sigma_{\text{train}}}$$

$$X_i^{\text{validation\_norm}} = \frac{X_i^{\text{validation}} - \mu_{\text{train}}}{\sigma_{\text{train}}}$$

$$X_i^{\text{test\_norm}} = \frac{X_i^{\text{test}} - \mu_{\text{train}}}{\sigma_{\text{train}}}$$

This method ensures test data remains untouched during training, preserving evaluation integrity.

In addition to data leakage, preprocessing challenges also include managing missing data, detecting outliers, and ensuring feature consistency. Poorly addressing missing values can introduce biases that skew the model's learning process. For example, imputing missing values using global statistics, such as the mean or median, without considering temporal dependencies can obscure important underlying patterns that are essential for accurate predictions. In other words, if X_{missing} denotes the missing entries in X, improper imputation might replace these with

$$X_{\text{imputed}} = \mu_{\text{global}}$$

where μ_{global} does not account for temporal or contextual variations, leading to biased estimations. This means that μ_{global} may be calculated using test data in the future, while it should only be based on the information available in the training set.

7.1 Model Risk Due to Data

Outlier detection is a crucial step in data preprocessing. Financial data often includes extreme values that can significantly impact model training. If outliers are not managed properly, the model may overfit to these anomalies, which can decrease its ability to generalize well to new data. Outliers can be identified using measures such as the z-score.

$$z_i = \frac{X_i - \mu}{\sigma}$$

where $|z_i| > 3$ might indicate an outlier. Carefully deciding whether to remove, transform, or retain outliers is crucial for maintaining the model's robustness. Such a decision may also lead to drastically different ML models developed downstream.

Standardizing the representation of input variables is essential for ensuring feature consistency and preventing discrepancies that may confuse the model. For instance, categorical variables should be uniformly encoded across all datasets to maintain this consistency.

$$\text{One-Hot Encoding}: \quad X_{\text{categorical}} = \text{OneHot}(X_{\text{categorical}})$$

Differences in encoding schemes between training and test sets can cause misaligned feature spaces, which adversely affect model performance.

To represent the cumulative impact of these preprocessing challenges, consider the overall transformation function T applied to the raw data X:

$$X_{\text{processed}} = T(X) = T_{\text{scaling}}(T_{\text{imputation}}(T_{\text{outlier\_handling}}(X)))$$

Each transformation T_i must be carefully designed to avoid introducing biases or leaking information. The integrity of the processed data directly influences the empirical risk $Q(\mathbf{w})$ minimized during training.

$$Q(\mathbf{w}) = \frac{1}{N} \sum_{i=1}^{N} l\left(y_i, f_{\mathbf{w}}(X_i^{\text{processed}})\right)$$

If T introduces bias or leaks information, the minimization of $Q(\mathbf{w})$ does not accurately reflect the true risk $R(f_{\mathbf{w}})$:

$$R(f_{\mathbf{w}}) = \mathbb{E}_{(X,y) \sim P_{\text{true}}} [l(y, f_{\mathbf{w}}(X))]$$

This discrepancy is represented by

$$\Delta R = R(f_{\mathbf{w}}) - Q(\mathbf{w})$$

which indicates a misalignment between training objectives and real-world performance, thereby raising model risk.

To address preprocessing challenges, it is essential to implement strict data-handling protocols. One effective technique is pipeline encapsulation, which involves confining each preprocessing step within a defined sequence that is consistently applied during both the training and evaluation phases. This approach helps prevent unintentional data leakage. Additionally, employing time-series cross-validation methods ensures that temporal dependencies are maintained, further protecting against leakage and improving the model's ability to generalize.

7.1.1.5 Violation of Economic Principles

In financial machine learning, it is essential that the data used comply with fundamental economic principles to ensure the development of reliable and effective models. Key economic concepts, such as the absence of arbitrage opportunities and the law of one price, are crucial for maintaining market efficiency. When financial data violates these principles, it can lead models to detect and exploit patterns that are not economically viable. This can result in strategies that are unprofitable or excessively risky in real-world trading environments.

In emerging markets, historical options price data for both listed and over-the-counter (OTC) contracts can sometimes be inconsistent with no-arbitrage constraints. For example, Cohen et al. (2020) have highlighted the reasons for these inconsistencies, revealing that price data can misleadingly indicate the presence of arbitrage opportunities. These anomalies can arise from various factors, including stale quotes that were incorrectly recorded as current in historical datasets.

When a machine learning model is trained on flawed data, it may mistakenly identify certain discrepancies as genuine arbitrage opportunities and assume they offer risk-free profit. However, in a well-functioning market, these discrepancies would be quickly corrected by arbitrageurs. As a result, the model's strategies could become ineffective, potentially leading to significant financial losses.

The law of one price states that identical goods should have the same price in efficient markets, taking into account transaction costs and other frictions. If historical data indicate that two identical assets are priced differently without a justifiable reason, a model might see this as an opportunity to buy the cheaper asset and sell the more expensive one, anticipating a risk-free profit. However, in reality, such price differences are usually short-lived and quickly corrected by market participants, which means that the model's strategy is unlikely to generate the expected returns.

Violations of these economic principles can arise from various sources. One primary source is data record errors, where mistakes in data entry, such as logging outdated or incorrect prices, introduce false signals of arbitrage opportunities. For example, if stale quotes are mistakenly recorded as live prices in historical datasets, the resulting data may falsely indicate that certain assets are underpriced or overpriced, misleading the model into developing trading strategies based on these inaccuracies.

Another significant source of economic principle violations is market microstructure noise, which is particularly prevalent in high-frequency trading environments. Rapid and often erratic price movements can create temporary price discrepancies that do not reflect true market inefficiencies. These fleeting anomalies can confuse models, causing them to interpret random fluctuations as meaningful patterns, which undermines their ability to make accurate predictions.

Regulatory and structural changes within financial markets also contribute to violations of economic principles. Sudden changes in market regulations or structural frameworks can disrupt historical price relationships, making past data less relevant or even misleading for future predictions. For example, the introduction of new trading rules or the emergence of new financial instruments can alter market dynamics in ways that historical data do not account for, leading models to base their strategies on outdated or incorrect assumptions.

Illiquid markets present another challenge, as they are more susceptible to price discrepancies that can persist longer than in more liquid markets. In markets with low trading volumes, the lack of sufficient trading activity can result in prolonged price imbalances, which can mislead models trained on such data into believing that these discrepancies represent exploitable opportunities. This misinterpretation can lead to the development of strategies that are ineffective or even harmful when applied in practice.

When machine learning models are exposed to data that violate these economic principles, several adverse outcomes can ensue. One major consequence is overfitting to anomalies. Models may become overly specialized in recognizing and exploiting these false patterns, which reduces their ability to generalize to actual market conditions. This overfitting means that while the model may perform exceptionally well on historical data, its performance deteriorates when faced with new, real-world data that do not contain the same artificial discrepancies.

Unreliable predictions are another significant risk. Strategies based on flawed data can lead to inconsistent and unpredictable performance, reducing trust in the utility of the model. For example, a model trained on data that inaccurately suggests persistent arbitrage opportunities might generate trading signals that fail to yield the expected profits when deployed, as the supposed opportunities do not exist in the live market.

7.1.2 Mitigation Strategies

To effectively address data risks in financial machine learning, it is essential to adopt a comprehensive approach that improves both the quality and representativeness of the data used. By implementing robust strategies, we can mitigate the adverse effects of data-related issues and strengthen models against potential pitfalls, leading to more reliable and accurate predictions. The following strategies are crucial for managing data risks.

7.1.2.1 Synthetic Data Generation and Resampling Techniques

Synthetic data generation seeks to enhance existing datasets by creating artificial data points that replicate the statistical characteristics of real data. Techniques such as Generative Adversarial Networks (GANs) and Variational Autoencoders (VAEs) are employed to learn the underlying distribution $P(X, y)$ and generate new samples $\tilde{X}, \tilde{y}$:

$$\tilde{X}, \tilde{y} \sim P_{\text{synthetic}}(X, y)$$

These methods help tackle the issue of data scarcity, particularly for rare events, and they also assist in balancing datasets to reduce class imbalance. In financial datasets, critical events such as defaults or market crashes occur much less frequently than in normal trading periods, resulting in imbalanced datasets. This imbalance can lead models to favor the majority class, causing them to overlook the minority class, which often has significant financial implications.

Resampling techniques can be utilized to address this issue. Methods such as oversampling the minority class, undersampling the majority class, or generating synthetic samples using techniques such as the Synthetic Minority Oversampling Technique (SMOTE) can help create a more balanced dataset. Additionally, using generative models like GANs or VAEs allows for the creation of new, realistic samples that enhance the minority class. As a result, the model becomes more attuned to patterns in the minority class, improving its predictive capabilities in critical situations.

7.1.2.2 Market Simulation Engines

Market simulation engines, especially those utilizing Agent-Based Modeling (ABM), create a controlled environment to produce data that mirror complex market interactions. In ABM, individual agents with defined behaviors interact within a simulated market, resulting in emergent phenomena that can be studied and analyzed.

$$\text{Simulated Market Dynamics} = \text{ABM}(\text{Agent Behaviors, Market Rules})$$

These simulations can create scenarios that have not occurred historically, but are plausible under specific conditions. They enable the stress testing of models against extreme events and allow for the exploration of the impacts of various market structures or regulations. However, the accuracy of the simulation depends largely on the realism of the agent behaviors and the validity of the market rules incorporated into the model. Careful calibration and validation are essential to ensure that the simulated data is realistic and relevant for training purposes.

7.1.2.3 Standardized Data Cleaning and Preprocessing Methodologies

Implementing rigorous and standardized data cleaning and preprocessing protocols can help ensure data integrity and consistency. This includes

- **Enforcing Economic Constraints:** Adjusting data to align with fundamental economic principles, such as the absence of arbitrage, ensures that models are trained on realistic data. For example, prices can be modified to eliminate negative spreads, or interest rate curves can be adjusted to remain arbitrage-free. This

7.1 Model Risk Due to Data

practice helps prevent models from learning patterns that are not economically viable.
- **Data Normalization and Standardization:** Scaling features to have consistent ranges or distributions is vital for model training, especially for algorithms sensitive to feature scales. Techniques such as min-max scaling or z-score normalization help ensure that no single feature disproportionately influences the model due to its scale.
- **Handling Missing Data:** Employing appropriate imputation methods that consider temporal dependencies while avoiding the introduction of future information is crucial. Techniques like forward filling or interpolation, when applied carefully, can mitigate the risks associated with missing values without violating temporal causality.
- **Outlier Detection and Treatment:** Identifying and appropriately addressing outliers can prevent them from unduly influencing model training. Statistical methods or robust estimation techniques can help detect anomalies. Decisions regarding whether to remove, transform, or retain outliers should be made carefully to maintain the model's robustness.

Following standardized methodologies reduces the chances of errors during preprocessing and improves the reproducibility of model development. Furthermore, we emphasize additional best practices in data processing and monitoring to enhance model performance and reliability:

- **Feature Selection and Engineering:** Using domain knowledge to identify and create relevant features can help capture meaningful patterns in the data while eliminating irrelevant or misleading variables. In particular, financial expertise in market dynamics, economic indicators, and asset behaviors can be leveraged to select meaningful features. For example, rather than relying solely on raw price data, engineered features such as moving averages, volatility indices, or macroeconomic factors can provide deeper insight into market trends. This careful selection and transformation of features not only enhances the model's ability to identify genuine patterns but also reduces the risk of overfitting to noise or false correlations that do not reflect real-world scenarios.
- **Continuous Data Monitoring:** Implementing ongoing monitoring mechanisms helps ensure that the data pipeline remains robust and that incoming data maintain its quality over time. This includes tracking data distributions, detecting drift, and setting up alerts for anomalies. Continuous monitoring facilitates the timely identification and resolution of issues such as data degradation, changes in underlying patterns, or the introduction of new types of errors, thus maintaining the model's effectiveness and reliability.
- **Data Validation Procedures:** Beyond initial cleaning, establishing comprehensive validation steps is vital to maintaining data integrity. This involves cross-referencing datasets with reliable external sources, performing statistical checks to ensure consistency, and verifying that the data align with expected business rules and constraints. Robust validation procedures help in the early

detection of discrepancies and ensure that the data entering the models accurately represent real-world conditions.

7.2 Model Risk Due to Model Selection

The model risk associated with a specific model selection procedure is particularly pronounced. Since ML methods often aim to develop models from flexible, non-parametric families, this process effectively merges the classical tasks of model selection and calibration into a single step. This approach differs from traditional handcrafted models, which are typically lower-dimensional and designed to capture specific known relationships within the data. Although machine learning models provide greater flexibility and the potential to identify complex patterns, they also introduce structural risks due to their sensitivity to training data and the choices made in the algorithms.

For example, replacing the classical paradigm of selecting a martingale model calibrated to market data with fitting large non-parametric models on historical data introduces significant sensitivity to the training dataset and the algorithms used. If the hypothesis space does not align well with the underlying data-generating process, the model may suffer from a high approximation error (to be introduced later) and fails to capture essential market dynamics. This misalignment can result from neglecting economic principles or the inherent constraints in financial data, leading to models that do not accurately reflect real-world conditions. In applications like end-to-end deep reinforcement learning for hedging strategies, large hypothesis spaces associated with complex architectures can also result in models that perform exceptionally well on simulated or historical data but struggle to generalize to real market conditions.

To better understand some essential concepts, let's explore model architecture, model class, hypothesis space, hyperparameters, bias in model selection, and approximation error. Model architecture refers to the structural design of a neural network. It includes elements such as depth (the number of layers), width (the number of neurons in each layer), and the types of activation functions used. These architectural choices influence how data flows through the network and how features are transformed at each stage.

The model class consists of all models that share the same architecture but differ in their parameter values, such as weights and biases. Essentially, the model class represents the variety of models that can be created by adjusting these parameters within a fixed architectural framework.

The hypothesis space refers to the set of all possible functions that a specific model class can represent. This is determined by the model architecture and the configurations of its parameters. For neural networks, the hypothesis space is influenced by several factors, including the number of layers in the network, the number of neurons in each layer, and the types of activation functions used, all of which are hyperparameters that need to be determined before training a neural

7.2 Model Risk Due to Model Selection

network. For example, a neural network can be expressed as

$$f_{\mathbf{w}}(\mathbf{X}) = \text{NeuralNetwork}(\mathbf{X}; \mathbf{w})$$

where $f_{\mathbf{w}}$ denotes the function mapping input features $\mathbf{X}$ to outputs, parameterized by the weight vector $\mathbf{w}$. The network architecture defines the structure and flow of the data through the model (focusing on model selection), while the parameters $\mathbf{w}$ (comprising weights and biases) are the adjustable components optimized during the training process (focusing on model estimation). Modifying the architecture, such as adjusting the number of layers or the type of activation functions, fundamentally changes the hypothesis space, thereby altering the functions the model can potentially represent.

As a result, the hypothesis space is the set of all possible functions that can be generated by varying the parameters within a specific model class. Selecting an appropriate hypothesis space is crucial because it directly impacts the model's ability to learn from data and generalize to new, unseen situations. A well-chosen hypothesis space ensures that the model is neither too simplistic to capture the underlying data patterns nor too complex, which could lead to overfitting of the training data. Formally, for a given architecture, the hypothesis space $\mathcal{H}$ can be expressed as

$$\mathcal{H} = \{f_{\mathbf{w}}(\mathbf{X}) = \text{NeuralNetwork}(\mathbf{X}; \mathbf{w}) \mid \mathbf{w} \in \mathbb{R}^d\}$$

where $\mathbf{w}$ represents the weight vector comprising all parameters of the network, and d is the dimensionality of the parameter space.

Hyperparameters are key configurations that dictate both the training process and the structure of a model, but are not derived from the data itself. These high-level, predefined parameters include learning rates, regularization coefficients, batch sizes, and architectural choices, such as the number of layers and neurons. Selecting a model involves identifying the optimal set of hyperparameters and architectural configurations that strike a balance between model complexity and the ability to generalize to new data.

7.2.1 Model Bias and Approximation Error

The approximation error measures the discrepancy between the true underlying function $f^*(\mathbf{X})$ that generates the data and the best possible function $\hat{f}(\mathbf{X})$ within the chosen hypothesis space $\mathcal{H}$. It quantifies how well the hypothesis space can, at best, approximate the true function. The approximation error is defined as

$$\text{Approximation Error} = \inf_{\hat{f} \in \mathcal{H}} \mathbb{E}_{\mathbf{X}}\left[\left(f^*(\mathbf{X}) - \hat{f}(\mathbf{X})\right)^2\right]$$

This error occurs when the hypothesis space is too limited to capture the complexity of $f^*(\mathbf{X})$, leading to systematic discrepancies regardless of the training data used.

Bias in statistical learning theory is closely related to approximation error. It measures the error introduced when we simplify a complex real-world problem by using a simpler model from the hypothesis space. A model with high bias makes strong assumptions about the data, which can result in missing important patterns. The bias at a specific input $\mathbf{X}$ is given by

$$\text{Bias}(\mathbf{X}) = \mathbb{E}_{\mathcal{D}}\left[\hat{f}_{\mathcal{D}}(\mathbf{X})\right] - f^*(\mathbf{X})$$

where $\hat{f}_{\mathcal{D}}(\mathbf{X})$ is the prediction made by the model trained on the dataset $\mathcal{D}$, and the expectation is on all possible training datasets.

Model risk occurs when the selected hypothesis space results in significant approximation errors due to excessive bias. If the hypothesis space does not include functions that are close to the true function, the model will consistently produce inaccurate predictions, regardless of how well the parameters are estimated from the data. This systematic error can have serious consequences, particularly in fields like finance, where accurately modeling complex relationships is essential.

In financial modeling, selecting an overly simplistic hypothesis space, such as using linear models for relationships that are inherently nonlinear, can lead to high bias and significant approximation errors. This situation, known as underfitting, prevents the model from capturing essential market dynamics, resulting in poor predictive performance and increased model risk. On the other hand, choosing a highly complex hypothesis space may reduce approximation errors but can introduce high variance, leading to overfitting and another form of model risk.

The bias-variance trade-off encapsulates this balance between approximation error (bias) and estimation error (variance). The total expected prediction error (EPE) can be decomposed as

$$\text{EPE} = \mathbb{E}_{\mathbf{X}}\left[(\text{Bias}(\mathbf{X}))^2 + \text{Variance}(\mathbf{X}) + \sigma^2\right]$$

where the bias term reflects the approximation error due to the limitations of the hypothesis space, the variance term represents the estimation error from the model's sensitivity to fluctuations in the training data (more on this later), and the irreducible error (σ^2) denotes the inherent noise in the data that no model can capture. A model with high bias (high approximation error) will have a large systematic error because it cannot adequately represent the true function. This contributes significantly to the model risk, as predictions will consistently deviate from reality.

7.2.2 Mitigation Strategies

To reduce model risk related to bias and approximation errors, proper design and selection of the hypothesis space are needed. Expanding the hypothesis space by using more flexible models can better capture the complexity of the true function. For example, increasing the number of layers or neurons in a neural network enables it to approximate more complex functions, thereby minimizing approximation errors. However, this flexibility must be balanced with the risk of overfitting, which can lead to high variance and diminish the model's ability to generalize effectively.

Regularization techniques, such as L1 and L2 regularization, are essential for managing the complexity of the hypothesis space. By adding penalties for large weights, these techniques help constrain the model, preventing it from becoming overly complex and reducing the risk of overfitting. This balance between expanding the hypothesis space and applying regularization plays an important role in addressing the bias-variance trade-off. It ensures that the model is flexible enough to capture important patterns while remaining robust against noise in the training data.

Cross-validation and model selection criteria are common techniques used to control the approximation error. By using cross-validation, practitioners can assess how changes in the hypothesis space affect the model's performance on unseen data. This process helps to select a model that minimizes the total expected prediction error by striking an optimal balance between bias and variance. Additionally, model selection criteria, such as the Akaike Information Criterion (AIC) and the Bayesian Information Criterion (BIC), provide quantitative metrics for evaluating the trade-off between model fit and complexity. These metrics aid in choosing an appropriate hypothesis space.

Incorporating domain knowledge, also termed inductive bias, into model design can significantly reduce approximation errors. By embedding financial theories and constraints, we ensure that the hypothesis space includes functions that are realistic and relevant to the specific application. This alignment between the model's assumptions and the known properties of the data helps minimize bias, enhancing the model's ability to accurately capture true underlying relationships without being misled by irrelevant patterns.

Finally, continuous monitoring and adjustment of the model are also essential in managing approximation error and overall model risk. As more data become available, or as the underlying data-generating processes evolve, it may be necessary to adjust the hypothesis space to maintain the model's effectiveness. This dynamic approach ensures that the model remains aligned with the current state of the data, thereby minimizing the approximation error and sustaining predictive performance over time.

Figure 7-1 illustrates two different scenarios of approximation error. The left panel represents a model class that corresponds to a smaller hypothesis space (thus a smaller circle) and a bigger approximation error, identified by the distance between the star (optimal model with minimal true risk) and the point within the circle that is closest to the star. The right panel represents a larger hypothesis class that gives a

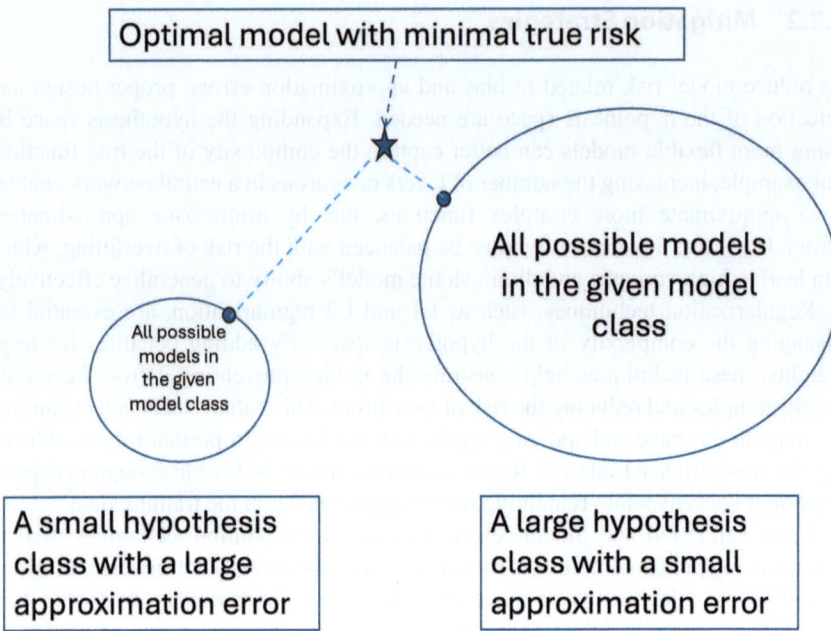

Figure 7-1 Illustrating the approximation error for different hypothesis space

lower approximation error. However, it is also more difficult to estimate and identify the corresponding point that is closest to the star.

7.3 Model Risk Due to Cost Function

The cost function, also known as the loss function, is fundamental to the training process of models. It measures the difference between the predicted outputs $\hat{\mathbf{y}}$ and the actual target values $\mathbf{y}$, serving as an objective metric that the optimization algorithm aims to minimize. In financial applications, selecting the appropriate cost function is especially crucial, as it directly impacts the model's behavior, its sensitivity to different types of errors, and the decisions made based on its predictions. Using an unsuitable or misaligned cost function can introduce significant model risk, leading to suboptimal performance, biased predictions, or unintended consequences.

Recall that the cost function $Q(\mathbf{w})$ for a model parameterized by $\mathbf{w}$ can be defined as a summation of individual loss over the entire training dataset:

$$Q(\mathbf{w}) = \frac{1}{N} \sum_{i=1}^{N} l\left(y_i, f_{\mathbf{w}}(\mathbf{X}_i)\right)$$

7.3 Model Risk Due to Cost Function

where $l(y_i, \hat{y}_i)$ is the loss incurred for a single prediction $\hat{y}_i = f_\mathbf{w}(\mathbf{X}_i)$. The form of the loss function $l(\cdot, \cdot)$ determines how prediction errors are penalized. A common choice for evaluating regression tasks is the mean squared error (MSE):

$$l_{\text{MSE}}(y_i, \hat{y}_i) = \frac{1}{2}(y_i - \hat{y}_i)^2$$

and the cross-entropy loss for (binary) classification tasks:

$$l_{\text{CE}}(y_i, \hat{y}_i) = -y_i \log(\hat{y}_i) - (1 - y_i) \log(1 - \hat{y}_i)$$

The choice of cost function affects how sensitive a model is to various types of errors and shapes the optimization landscape. In finance, where the implications of predictions can differ greatly based on the context, using an unsuitable cost function can even increase model risk. If the cost function does not accurately represent the financial consequences of prediction errors, the model can be optimized for an incorrect objective. For example, using MSE in a context where large errors are significantly more costly than small ones can lead to poor risk management decisions. Although MSE penalizes errors quadratically and gives more weight to larger mistakes, this approach may not align with the actual financial losses associated with those prediction errors.

Some cost functions are more sensitive to outliers than others. MSE, for example, is particularly affected due to its quadratic nature, which heavily penalizes large deviations. This characteristic can be problematic when dealing with financial data that often contain extreme values or anomalies, thus necessitating proper feature standardization to alleviate this impact. This sensitivity may cause the model to focus too much on fitting outliers, resulting in overfitting and poor generalization to new data.

In addition, a cost function that does not include mechanisms to penalize model complexity can potentially lead to overfitting. Overfitting occurs when the model captures the noise and specific details of the training data, which reduces its ability to generalize to new, unseen data. As a result, the risk associated with the model increases because its predictions can become unreliable in real-world situations. The costs associated with overestimating and underestimating a target variable can also be significantly different. A symmetric cost function, such as MSE, does not consider this asymmetry and may lead to suboptimal decisions. For example, underestimating risk can result in more severe consequences than overestimating it. However, a symmetric cost function treats both types of errors as equal.

The mathematical characteristics of the cost function also play an important role in the optimization process. Nonconvex or nondifferentiable cost functions can complicate training, leading to convergence problems or suboptimal solutions. This can result in models that fail to accurately capture the underlying patterns in the data, which in turn increases the approximation error and model risk. In contrast, convex cost functions, such as MSE, are often easier to optimize and often have closed-form solutions in simple models such as linear regression.

7.3.1 Mitigation Strategies

To manage model risk associated with the choice of cost function, several mitigation strategies can be utilized. One effective approach is to incorporate regularization terms. Regularization adds a penalty term to the cost function, which discourages overly complex models by penalizing large parameter values. This technique helps prevent overfitting and enhances the model's ability to generalize to new data. The regularized cost function $Q_{\text{reg}}(\mathbf{w})$ can be written as

$$Q_{\text{reg}}(\mathbf{w}) = Q(\mathbf{w}) + \lambda \Omega(\mathbf{w})$$

where λ is the regularization coefficient that controls the trade-off between fitting the data well and keeping the model parameters small, and $\Omega(\mathbf{w})$ is the regularization term that measures the size or magnitude of the model parameters. Common choices for $\Omega(\mathbf{w})$ include L1 regularization (Lasso) and L2 regularization (Ridge). L1 regularization is given by

$$\Omega_{L1}(\mathbf{w}) = \|\mathbf{w}\|_1 = \sum_{j=1}^{d} |w_j|$$

It promotes sparsity in model parameters, effectively selecting features by driving less significant weights to zero. L2 regularization is expressed as

$$\Omega_{L2}(\mathbf{w}) = \frac{1}{2}\|\mathbf{w}\|_2^2 = \frac{1}{2}\sum_{j=1}^{d} w_j^2$$

It discourages the use of large weights but does not enforce sparsity, allowing the impact to be distributed across all parameters. This approach leads to more stable solutions. By incorporating regularization, the model becomes less sensitive to fluctuations in the training data, which reduces variance and improves robustness. This directly mitigates the risk of overfitting and enhances the model's ability to generalize effectively.

An effective strategy is to customize the cost function to align with business objectives. Designing a cost function that properly reflects the specific financial context could potentially reduce model risk. This approach involves using asymmetric loss functions that penalize overestimations and underestimations differently, taking into account the actual costs associated with prediction errors. For instance, the Quantile Loss function is particularly useful when the costs are not symmetric.

$$l_\tau(y_i, \hat{y}_i) = \begin{cases} \tau(y_i - \hat{y}_i) & \text{if } y_i \geq \hat{y}_i \\ (1-\tau)(\hat{y}_i - y_i) & \text{if } y_i < \hat{y}_i \end{cases}$$

where $\tau \in (0, 1)$ controls the degree of asymmetry. Creating custom loss functions that accurately reflect the financial impact of errors can be advantageous. For instance, in portfolio optimization, it can be helpful to include metrics like Value at Risk (VaR) or Conditional Value at Risk (CVaR) in the loss function to address tail risks. By customizing the cost function to align with the specific risks and costs associated with a financial application, the model can be guided to produce predictions that are not only statistically sound but also economically meaningful.

Using robust loss functions is another effective way to reduce the impact of outliers and anomalies in data. Robust loss functions are designed to be less sensitive to extreme values. A notable example is the Huber loss, which merges the benefits of MSE and Mean Absolute Error (MAE). It behaves quadratically for small errors and linearly for large errors.

$$l_\delta(y_i, \hat{y}_i) = \begin{cases} \frac{1}{2}(y_i - \hat{y}_i)^2 & \text{if } |y_i - \hat{y}_i| \leq \delta \\ \delta|y_i - \hat{y}_i| - \frac{1}{2}\delta^2 & \text{if } |y_i - \hat{y}_i| > \delta \end{cases}$$

where δ is a threshold parameter. This loss is a robust loss function that minimizes the impact of outliers by assigning zero weight to errors that surpass a certain threshold. Utilizing robust loss functions decreases the model's susceptibility to anomalies, thereby enhancing its stability and reliability.

As for the choice of λ, one often employs cross-validation and hyperparameter tuning techniques to assess how different values affect the model's performance on unseen data. These techniques include grid search, random search, or more sample-efficient Bayesian optimization designed to find the optimal values that balance the trade-off between bias and variance.

In addition, ensuring that the cost function is both convex and smooth can significantly enhance the optimization process, leading to more reliable convergence toward either a global minimum or a good local minimum. By selecting cost functions that are convex and differentiable, we can address the challenges posed by nonconvex or nondifferentiable functions, which can lead to suboptimal models. For instance, using cross-entropy loss for classification tasks guarantees convexity in linear models, making the optimization process more manageable. In the case of neural networks, even though the overall optimization landscape may still be nonconvex, opting for smooth activation functions and loss functions can contribute to achieving better optimization results.

7.4 Model Risk Due to Optimization Procedure

The optimization procedure is a crucial part of the training procedure of machine learning models, particularly in finance, where accurate predictions and robustness are essential. It plays a key role in how effectively a model minimizes its cost function and identifies the optimal parameters within the hypothesis space. If an optimization algorithm is poorly chosen or not tuned properly, it can lead to significant model risk. This may result in suboptimal convergence, getting stuck in poor local minima, excessive sensitivity to training data, or overfitting, all of which can harm model performance and increase the risk of negative outcomes.

Complex machine learning models, such as deep neural networks, involve solving nonconvex optimization problems due to the intricate nature of their cost functions and hypothesis spaces. The cost function $Q(\mathbf{w})$, parameterized by the model weights $\mathbf{w}$, is minimized during training:

$$\mathbf{w}^* = \arg\min_{\mathbf{w}} Q(\mathbf{w})$$

Nonconvexity means that $Q(\mathbf{w})$ may have multiple local minima, saddle points, and flat regions. This complexity makes it difficult to locate the global minimum or to find a solution that generalizes well. The choice of optimization algorithm affects the path taken through the parameter space, ultimately determining which local minimum is identified.

For instance, stochastic gradient descent (SGD) and its variants are commonly used optimization algorithms for training neural networks. SGD updates the model parameters iteratively using mini-batches of data, which introduces randomness into the optimization process.

$$\mathbf{w}_{t+1} = \mathbf{w}_t - \eta_t \nabla_{\mathbf{w}} Q_{\mathcal{B}_t}(\mathbf{w}_t)$$

where η_t is the learning rate at iteration t, $\mathcal{B}_t$ is the mini-batch of data sampled at iteration t, and $\nabla_{\mathbf{w}} Q_{\mathcal{B}_t}(\mathbf{w}_t)$ is the gradient of the cost function computed over the mini-batch. The noise inherent in sampling different mini-batches aids SGD in escaping shallow local minima and saddle points, potentially directing it toward flatter minima that are linked to better generalization.

7.4.1 Estimation Error

In statistical learning theory, the total error of a model is decomposed into two primary components: the approximation error and the estimation error. As introduced earlier, the approximation error arises from the inherent limitations of the chosen hypothesis space $\mathcal{H}$ in representing the true underlying function $f^*(\mathbf{X})$. It quantifies the smallest discrepancy between $f^*(\mathbf{X})$ and any function within $\mathcal{H}$. This indicates that a smaller hypothesis space may result in a higher approximation error because of its limited ability to capture complex patterns in the data.

The estimation error arises from determining the optimal parameters within the hypothesis space using a limited set of training data. It measures the difference between the best possible model $\hat{f}$ in $\mathcal{H}$ (in terms of the true risk) and the model $f_{\mathbf{w}}$ learned from the data.

$$\text{Estimation Error} = \mathbb{E}_{\mathbf{X}}\left[\left(\hat{f}(\mathbf{X}) - f_{\mathbf{w}}(\mathbf{X})\right)^2\right]$$

7.4 Model Risk Due to Optimization Procedure

Estimation error reflects sample variability and the optimization algorithm's efficiency in identifying the optimal parameters within $\mathcal{H}$. The optimization process has a direct impact on the estimation error. A well-designed and well-tuned optimization algorithm can significantly reduce the estimation error by identifying parameters that closely approximate the optimal solution. In contrast, a poorly designed or suboptimal algorithm may struggle to find the appropriate parameters within the hypothesis space, leading to higher estimation errors.

The optimization process in machine learning models used in finance carries several risks. One significant concern is structural risk, which arises from the flexibility and high-dimensional parameter spaces of models, such as deep neural networks. This means that a more flexible model is more difficult to train. Additionally, as introduced earlier, the nonconvex nature of the optimization landscape can result in nonunique solutions. Depending on the initial conditions and stochastic factors, the optimization algorithm may converge to different local minima.

The sensitivity of the model is another crucial issue to consider. When using high-dimensional inputs and complex models, even small changes in the inputs or parameters can cause significant variations in the model's outputs. Furthermore, randomness during training—due to factors such as variations in initialization, dropout, and the use of stochastic gradient descent—can contribute to the unpredictability of the resulting models, potentially increasing estimation errors.

Robustness and adversarial vulnerabilities present significant risks for financial ML models. Both intentional and unintentional adversarial attacks, such as data poisoning or the exploitation of inherent weaknesses, can target these models. If an optimization algorithm does not prioritize robustness, it may converge on solutions that perform poorly when exposed to minor perturbations, which can lead to increased estimation errors and model risk. Furthermore, financial markets are dynamic, and data distributions can change over time, resulting in model drift. Optimization algorithms that focus excessively on fitting historical data without mechanisms to adapt to new data may produce models that do not generalize well, leading to higher estimation errors when applied to current market conditions.

Another significant risk is overfitting due to excessive optimization, such as training a neural network for too long. When an optimization algorithm concentrates solely on minimizing the training cost function, it can end up capturing noise instead of the underlying patterns in the data. This can result in models that exhibit low training error but high estimation error when faced with unseen data.

Comparing handcrafted models with ML models also reveals certain optimization-related risks. Handcrafted models in finance are typically low-dimensional, producing smoother and more interpretable outputs. They often use convex optimization procedures, which result in unique and stable solutions with lower estimation errors due to simpler optimization processes. However, these models may experience high approximation errors if they fail to capture the complex dynamics of the market.

On the other hand, ML models offer greater flexibility and can reduce approximation errors by identifying intricate patterns in the data. However, their complex optimization landscapes and high-dimensional parameter spaces can lead to

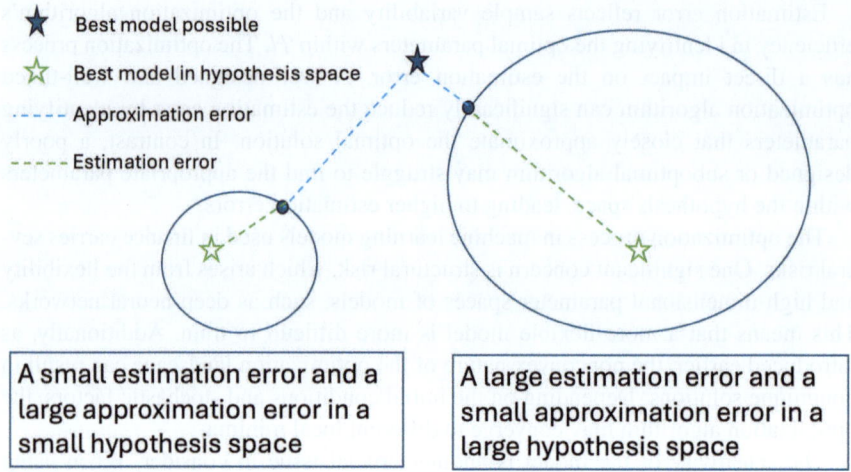

Figure 7-2 Comparing estimation error and approximation error of two different hypothesis spaces

increased estimation errors, primarily due to challenges in the optimization process. The nonconvex nature of these models and their sensitivity to training conditions can make the optimization process more likely to converge on suboptimal solutions.

Figure 7-2 compares the estimation error and the approximation error of two different hypothesis spaces (due to two different model classes). The left circle corresponds to a small hypothesis space, which tends to lead to a small estimation error (simpler models are easier to train) and a large approximation error (insufficient model complexity to capture the true underlying relationship). The right circle corresponds to a large hypothesis space, which likely leads to a large estimation error (since complex models are difficult to train) and a small approximation error (capable of capturing the underlying relationship).

7.4.2 Mitigation Strategies

To effectively manage the model risk associated with the optimization process and minimize estimation errors, several strategies can be used. First, it is essential to choose an appropriate optimization algorithm that fits the model architecture and the specific problem domain. For deep neural networks, popular algorithms include SGD with momentum, Adam, and RMSProp. These algorithms are preferred because they efficiently handle nonconvex landscapes and large datasets. Designed to navigate complex optimization landscapes, they tend to increase the likelihood of finding robust solutions that generalize well.

Tuning hyperparameters such as learning rates, batch sizes, and momentum coefficients is crucial to improving model convergence and generalization. Techniques like grid search, random search, and Bayesian optimization can be used to find the best configurations that improve performance. Moreover, the proper initialization of model parameters can significantly influence the optimization process. Using methods like Xavier or He initialization helps maintain the variance of activations across layers, leading to better convergence. This approach also reduces estimation errors by preventing problems such as vanishing or exploding gradients.

Incorporating regularization techniques, such as L1 or L2 regularization, dropout, and batch normalization, helps prevent overfitting during the optimization process. Regularization adds constraints that encourage the optimization algorithm to find solutions with better generalization properties by penalizing overly complex models. In addition, implementing early stop criteria is an effective strategy. This involves halting training when the model's performance on a validation set no longer improves (for several iterations in a row). By doing this, we can prevent the model from overfitting the training data, thereby reducing estimation error and ensuring that the model remains applicable to unseen data.

Ensemble methods, which involve combining multiple models that have been trained with different initializations or optimization algorithms, can potentially reduce the estimation error by averaging individual models. By doing so, it reduces the risk associated with relying on a single optimization outcome, resulting in more stable and reliable predictions. Furthermore, robust optimization techniques, such as adversarial training, which involves training models on perturbed data, can improve performance under challenging conditions. These methods help the optimization algorithm identify solutions that are less sensitive to variations in input, thereby improving the model's resilience and further reducing estimation error.

In addition, regular monitoring of optimization metrics, such as training and validation loss curves, gradient norms, and parameter distributions, offers valuable insights into the optimization process. These diagnostics help identify and address issues such as vanishing or exploding gradients, allowing for timely adjustments to the optimization procedure. In addition, incorporating expert knowledge into the model and optimization process can significantly improve regularization and stability. By adjusting model architectures to incorporate specific financial features, applying constraints, or adding penalties to the loss function, the optimization algorithm is guided toward more realistic and economically meaningful solutions.

Analyzing the geometry of the cost function could also help to understand the optimization landscape and inform the choice of optimization strategies. Recognizing potential challenges, such as flat regions or sharp minima, allows practitioners to adjust their optimization procedures accordingly, leading to more effective navigation through the parameter space.

7.5 Conclusion

In the complex and ever-changing landscape of financial markets, managing model risk is crucial for ensuring the reliability and effectiveness of quantitative models. In this chapter, we have explored the various aspects of model risk related to machine learning models in finance. We identified key areas, including data integrity, model selection, alignment of cost functions, and the optimization process. Each of these components is vital to the overall performance and robustness of financial models.

Data are the foundation of ML models, and the quality of these data greatly affects the model's ability to generalize and perform accurately in real-world situations. We examined the inherent risks associated with data, such as sampling bias, spurious correlations, class imbalance, and challenges in data preprocessing. These issues can result in models that either fail to capture important market dynamics or become overfit to noise, increasing the chances of making incorrect predictions. To improve data quality and ensure models are trained on robust and representative datasets, it is essential to implement mitigation strategies such as synthetic data generation, market simulation engines, and standardized data cleaning methodologies.

Model selection adds another layer of complexity and risk. Although more complex ML models tend to capture intricate patterns, it also makes them prone to high estimation errors and overfitting. We discussed the importance of balancing approximation and estimation errors through careful design of the hypothesis space, the use of regularization techniques, and the incorporation of domain knowledge. By choosing appropriate model architectures and employing rigorous validation practices, practitioners can achieve an optimal balance that minimizes both bias and variance, thus reducing model risk.

The selection of a cost function is crucial because it determines how models penalize various types of errors, ultimately influencing the optimization process. An inappropriate cost function can result in models that do not align with financial goals, either by placing too much emphasis on certain errors or by neglecting the asymmetric costs associated with underestimating and overestimating. We emphasized the importance of tailoring cost functions to reflect business objectives. This includes using robust loss functions to address outliers and ensuring that cost functions are both convex and smooth to enable effective optimization.

Optimization procedures can increase model risk by affecting how well models navigate complex, nonconvex landscapes to find optimal or near-optimal solutions. The effectiveness of the optimization algorithm has a direct impact on estimation error, which measures the difference between the learned model and the best possible model within the hypothesis space. Risks such as converging to poor local minima, sensitivity to hyperparameters, and overfitting due to excessive optimization highlight the need for robust optimization strategies. Techniques such as hyperparameter tuning, regularization, early stopping, ensemble methods, and adaptive optimization algorithms are essential to mitigate these risks and ensure that the models generalize well to unseen data.

Comparing ML models with traditional handcrafted models highlights the trade-offs involved. Handcrafted models are often simpler and more interpretable, and they tend to have a lower estimation error because of their straightforward optimization processes. However, they can struggle with higher approximation errors as they may not effectively capture complex market behaviors. On the other hand, ML models offer the flexibility to model intricate patterns and reduce approximation error. However, they can lead to an increase in the estimation error

7.5 Conclusion

and are more vulnerable to optimization-related risks. This comparison emphasizes the importance of adopting a balanced approach that takes advantage of the strengths of both methodologies while addressing their respective weaknesses.

In conclusion, effectively managing model risk in financial machine learning requires a comprehensive approach that addresses risks related to data quality, model selection, cost function alignment, and optimization procedures. By implementing thorough mitigation strategies—such as data preprocessing, regularization, robust optimization, and continuous monitoring—financial institutions can develop models that are not only accurate and reliable but also resilient to the ever-evolving market conditions. As the financial landscape continues to advance with the integration of sophisticated ML techniques, the importance of diligent model risk management cannot be overstated. It is essential to ensure that the models are built on a foundation of high-quality data, properly selected architectures, well-aligned cost functions, and robust optimization processes to protect against potential financial losses and maintain trust in quantitative decision-making tools.

References

Cohen, Samuel N., Christoph Reisinger, and Sheng Wang. 2020. Detecting and repairing arbitrage in traded option prices. *Applied Mathematical Finance*. To appear. arXiv:2008.09454v1.

Cohen, Samuel N., Derek Snow, and Lukasz Szpruch. 2023. Black-box model risk in finance. In *Machine Learning and Data Sciences for Financial Markets*, 633–654. Cambridge: Cambridge University Press.

Marani, Marco, Gabriel G. Katul, William K. Pan, and Anthony J. Parolari. 2021. Intensity and frequency of extreme novel epidemics. *Proceedings of the National Academy of Sciences* 118 (35): e2105482118. https://doi.org/10.1073/pnas.2105482118

Markowitz, Harry. 1952. Portfolio selection. *The Journal of Finance* 7 (1): 77–91. https://doi.org/10.1111/j.1540-6261.1952.tb01525.x

Sharpe, William F. 1966. Mutual fund performance. *The Journal of Business* 39 (1): 119–138.

Index

A
ABM, *see* Agent-Based Modeling (ABM)
ACF, *see* Autocorrelation function (ACF)
Absolute return, 32, 38, 176
Agent-Based Modeling (ABM), 212
AIC, *see* Akaike Information Criterion (AIC)
Akaike Information Criterion (AIC), 217
Annualized return, 32, 40–41, 46, 48
Approximation error, 215–218, 222
ARCH model, *see* Autoregressive Conditional Heteroskedasticity (ARCH) model
Asset liquidity risk, 17, 21
Assets, 22–26, 28, 125
Autocorrelation function (ACF), 105, 106
Autoregressive Conditional Heteroskedasticity (ARCH) model, 105

B
Basel regulatory framework, 19
Bayesian Information Criterion (BIC), 217
Bayesian optimization, 221, 224
BIC, *see* Bayesian Information Criterion (BIC)
Bitcoin, 25
Black-box model, 6, 18
Black-Scholes-Merton (BSM) model, 147, 148, 161
Black-Scholes model, 163, 164, 166, 167, 170, 187, 199
Borrower's creditworthiness, 15, 65, 66, 70
Brownian motion, 135, 157, 163

C
Capital Asset Pricing Model (CAPM), 47
CAPM, *see* Capital Asset Pricing Model (CAPM)
CCF, *see* Credit conversion factor (CCF)

CDF, *see* Cumulative distribution function (CDF)
Classification threshold, 90, 93
Commodity risk, 7, 21
Conditional Value at Risk (CVaR), 171, 221
Cost function
   cross-entropy loss, classification tasks, 219
   definition, 218
   financial applications, 218
   geometry, 225
   mathematical characteristics, 219
   mitigation strategies, 220–221
   MSE, 219
   nonconvex/nondifferentiable, 219
   outliers, 219
   overfitting, 219
   selection, 226
Coupons, 7, 16, 22, 23
Covered call strategy
   additional income, 161
   asset, 152
   asset price, 160
   Black-Scholes formula, 157
   Brownian motion, 157
   call contracts, 155
   call options, 157
   implementation, 152, 157–159
   initial outlay, 152, 156
   investors, 156, 161
   mean profit, 159
   payoff curves, 154–155
   payoffs, 153, 154, 156
   premium, 152, 156
   scenarios, 156, 160
   short call, 153, 154, 156
   trade-off, 152
   vs. unhedged position, 159
COVID-19, 1, 11, 69

Credit conversion factor (CCF), 76–78
Credit migration matrix, 16
Credit risk, 5, 21
    credit spread risk, 15–16
    default risk, 15
    downgrade risk, 16
    PD, 16
    transition probabilities, 16
Credit risk management, 66
    credit card lending, 65
    EAD (*see* Exposure at default (EAD))
    ECL (*see* Expected credit loss (ECL))
    full credit management life cycle, 66
    home ownership loans, 65
    LGD (*see* Loss given default (LGD))
    PD (*see* Probability of default (PD))
    subprime mortgage lending, 65
Credit spread, 15, 16
Cryptocurrencies, 25, 27, 28
Cumulative distribution function (CDF), 113, 190
CVaR, *see* Conditional Value at Risk (CVaR)

D
Daily volatility, 44–45, 100
Data monitoring, 213
Data normalization, 213
Data standardization, 213
Data validation, 213–214
Decision-making, 201
Deep neural networks, 18, 222–224
Delta hedging, 163, 164, 169
Delta neutral, 126, 164, 167, 170
Derivatives
    futures and forwards, 26–27
    options, 26
    swaps, 27
    traditional investments, 26
Diversification, 7–8, 125
Dividend-paying stocks, 24, 25, 27, 28
Dynamic hedging
    adjustment process, 171
    benefits, 171
    Black-Scholes model, 166
    call option contract, 172–176
    closed-form pricing formula, 135
    continuously adapting, 166
    cumulative wealth curve, TSLA & WMT, 170
    delta, 170, 171
    downside risk measures, 139–140
    dynamic delta hedging strategy, 167–168
    fine-tuned adaptability, 165
    gamma hedging, 168–169
    GBM, 134, 135, 138
    Greeks, 165, 166
    hedged *vs.* unhedged portfolios, 171
    hedging portfolio, 167
    libraries, 137
    metrics, TSLA & WMT, 176
    OLS, 136
    optional hedge ratio, 135, 138–139
    parameters, 137–138, 166, 170
    PDE, 166
    portfolio, 165
    portfolio value, 171
    price movements, 135
    profit & loss (P&L), 141–142
    rebalancing, 168–169
    risk metrics, 142
    rolling out, 139
    SDE, 135
    sensitivities, 166, 199
    spot price, 136
    vs. static hedging, 165, 199, 200
    stock price, 170
    techniques, 166
    trade-off, 176
    variance, 136
    Wiener process, 135

E
EAD, *see* Exposure at default (EAD)
Economic constraints, 212–213
Ensemble methods, 72, 225, 226
Environmental, social, and governance (ESG) risk, 20, 21
EPE, *see* Expected prediction error (EPE)
ES, *see* Expected Shortfall (ES)
ESG risk, *see* Environmental, social, and governance (ESG) risk
Ethereum, 25
Expected credit loss (ECL), 15, 67–70, 76, 78, 79, 93
    anticipated financial loss, 67
    calculation, 68–69
    Capital Adequacy Ratio (CAR), 80–81
    capital regulation using RWAs, 79–82
    EAD, 67–70, 76–81, 93
    in housing mortgage loan, 78–79
    LGD, 67, 69, 70, 73–79, 81, 93
    PD, 66–68, 70–73, 82, 83
    in regulatory compliance frameworks, 67
    stress loss (SL), 68–70
    unexpected loss (UL), 68, 69, 81
Expected prediction error (EPE), 216

Index

Expected Shortfall (ES), 112, 114, 123
Exposure at default (EAD), 67–70, 76–81, 93
   behavioral models, 77
   CCF, 76–78
   estimation, 76–77
   ML models, 77
   PD and LGD, 76
   standardized approach, 76–77

F

Feature engineering, 213
Feature selection, 206, 213
Finance, 31, 96, 125, 163, 202
Finance derivatives, 163
Financial crisis, 19, 65, 66, 106
Financial derivatives, 125, 126, 161
Financial events, 207
Financial institutions, 122, 202
Financial instruments, 125, 126, 165
   bonds, 22
   classification, 27, 28
   derivatives, 26–27
   high-risk assets, 25–26
   low-risk assets, 22–23
   moderate-risk assets, 23–24
   stocks, 22
Financial machine learning
   biases, 206
   class imbalance, 207
   data errors and preprocessing challenges
      accuracy and integrity, 207
      bias or leaks information, 209
      data-handling protocols, 210
      data leakage, 207, 208
      future data, 207
      missing values, 208
      One-Hot Encoding, 209
      outlier detection, 209
      parameters, 208
      pipeline encapsulation, 210
   data-related risks, 205
   economic principles, 210–211
   mitigation strategies
      data cleaning and preprocessing methodologies, 212–214
      market simulation engines, 212
      resampling techniques, 212
      synthetic data generation, 211–212
   spurious correlations, 206–207
Financial markets, 105, 106, 134, 201, 204, 223
Financial modeling, 135, 216
Financial models, 43, 45, 135, 201, 226

Financial risk, 1, 4, 21
   credit risk, 5, 15–16
   ESG risk, 20, 21
   legal risk, 5
   liquidity risk, 5, 17
   market risk, 5–15
   model risk, 5, 18
   operational risk, 5, 17–18
   systemic risk, 5, 19–20
Fixed-for-floating exchange models, 164
Foreign exchange (or forex) risk, 7
Funding liquidity risk, 17, 21
Futures contracts, hedging, 163
   advantages, 126
   basis risk, 133–134
   concept, 127
   dynamic hedging strategy (*see* Dynamic hedging strategy)
   exchanges, 127
   hedging mechanism
      basis risk, 127
      fluctuations, 127
      scenario, 127–128
      short hedge, 129
   optimal hedge ratio (*see* Optimal hedge ratio)
   scenario analysis, maturity, 132–133
   standardized agreements, 126, 127
   uses, 127
   versatile tool, 127

G

GANs, *see* Generative Adversarial Networks (GANs)
GARCH model, *see* Generalized Autoregressive Conditional Heteroskedasticity (GARCH) model
Generalized ARCH (GARCH), 105, 123
Generalized Autoregressive Conditional Heteroskedasticity (GARCH) model, 45, 105, 123
Generative Adversarial Networks (GANs), 12, 211
Geometric Brownian Motion (GBM), 134, 161
Government bonds, 23, 27, 28, 80, 81
Gradient boosting machines (GBMs), 73, 134–138, 147, 148

H

Handcrafted models, 214, 223, 226
Hedging, 125
   delta, 163, 164, 169

dynamic (*see* Dynamic hedging)
European put option, 165
exposure, 164
forward contracts, 164
futures contracts (*see* Futures contracts, hedging)
mechanism, 127–129
option contracts (*see* Option contracts, hedging)
options, 163
portfolio variance, 163
static (*see* Static hedging)
strategies, 161
techniques, 164
High-risk assets
commodities, 25
cryptocurrencies, 25
private equity and venture capital, 25–26
stocks (equities), 25
High-yield bonds, 24, 27, 28
Historical simulation approach, 114–115
Hyperparameters, 215, 224

I
Idiosyncratic risk, 95
International Financial Reporting Standard 9 (IFRS 9), 19
Investment-grade corporate bonds, 23, 27, 28
Investors, 13, 60, 104, 164, 200

J
Junk bonds, 23, 24

L
Legal and regulatory risks, 19, 21
LGD, *see* Loss given default (LGD)
Liquidity risk, 5, 17, 21
Logarithmic/log return, 39, 63, 168, 170
Long-Term Capital Management (LTCM), 19
Loss given default (LGD), 15, 67, 69, 70, 73–79, 81, 93
definition, 74
collateral valuation, 74–75
expert judgment and heuristics, 75
historical recovery, 74
machine learning models, 75
and PD, 73, 76
statistical models, 75
Low-risk assets
cash and cash equivalents, 22–23
government bonds, 23

LTCM, *see* Long-Term Capital Management (LTCM)

M
Machine learning (ML), 201, 202
Machine learning models, 210, 211, 214, 221–223, 226
MAE, *see* Mean Absolute Error (MAE)
Market conditions, 13, 25, 122, 126, 151, 211
Market-neutral strategy, 95
Market risk, 5, 21, 95
asset classes, 95
commodity risk, 7
currency exchange rates, 95
currency risk, 7
diversification, 7–8, 14
equity risk, 6–7
factors, 6
global minimum-variance (GMV), 14
hedging, 12
integration, 123
interest rate risk, 7
managing, 95
MDD (*see* Maximum drawdown (MDD))
metrics, 95, 96, 122
proactive risk management, 13
risk parity strategies, 13
stock prices, 95
stop-loss orders, 13
tactical asset allocation, 12–13
and transaction costs, 12
VaR (*see* Value at Risk (VaR))
variance (*see* Variance)
wealth curve, strategies, 8–11
weight for the bond index (AGG), 15
Maximum drawdown (MDD), 122, 123
calculation, 108, 110–111
cumulative returns and running maximum, 111, 112
daily drawdown, 112
and VaR/ES, 112
definition, 107
features, 108–110
non-parametric measure, 109
portfolio, 109
potential loss, 109
profiting strategy, 109
sequence of returns, 109
severity of losses, 108
time period, 110
time scale, 110
vs. variance, 108
portfolio's value, 107, 108

Index   235

potential severity of losses, 107
Mean Absolute Error (MAE), 221
Mean squared error (MSE), 203, 219
Mitigation strategies, 211, 217, 220, 226, 227
ML, *see* Machine learning (ML)
Model risk, 5, 18, 21, 201
   components, 202
   constant volatility, 201
   cost function (*see* Cost function)
   data, 226
      data leakage, 205
      financial crises, 204
      financial data, 204
      financial machine learning (*see* Financial machine learning)
      financial sector, 205
      generalization, 203
      implementation, 205
      insufficient data, 204
      k-fold cross-validation, 205
      machine learning model, 202, 205
      optimization process, 203
      overfitting/underfitting, 203
      regularization methods, 205
      subsets, 203
      test set, 204
      training process, 202–203
      training set, 203–204
      train-validation-test split, 204, 205
      validation set, 204
   financial sector, 201
   hypothesis space, 216
   managing, 227
   models, 201
   model selection (*see* Model selection)
   model specification, 201
   numerical implementation, 201
   optimization procedure (*see* Optimization procedure)
Model selection, 226
   approximation error, 215–218
   bias, 216
   classical paradigm, 214
   hyperparameters, 215
   hypothesis space, 214, 215
   mitigation strategies, 217–218
   model architecture, 214, 215
   model class, 214
   neural network, 215
Moderate-risk assets, 23–24
Monte Carlo simulation, 120–122, 201
Monthly volatility, 44–45
MSE, *see* Mean squared error (MSE)
Multi-period returns, 41–42

N
Neural networks, 18, 73, 75, 77, 203–204, 214, 215, 217, 221–224

O
Operational risk, 5, 17–18, 21
Optimal hedge ratio
   basis risk, 129
   calculation, 131
   determination, 129
   hedged position, 130
   idealized assumption, 129
   negative signs, 131
   number of futures con, 131
   variance, 130
Optimization procedures, 226
   estimation error, 222
      adversarial vulnerabilities, 223
      vs. approximation error, 224
      handcrafted models, 223
      model sensitivity, 223
      optimization process, 223
      overfitting, 223
      robustness, 223
      structural risk, 223
   hypothesis space, 221
   machine learning models, 222
   mitigation strategies, 224–225
   nonconvexity, 222
   SGD, 222
Option contracts, hedging
   covered call strategy (*see* Covered call strategy)
   vs. futures contracts, hedging, 126
   hedging strategies, 141, 142
   investors, 126
   options, 141
   protective put strategy (*see* Protective put strategy)
   underlying asset, 141
OTC, *see* Over-the-counter (OTC)
Over-the-counter (OTC), 210

P
Pandemics, 1, 3, 11
Partial differential equation (PDE), 166
PD, *see* Probability of default (PD)
PDE, *see* Partial differential equation (PDE)
Percentage return, 32, 38–39
Portfolio, 4, 44, 107, 125, 151, 221
Probability of default (PD), 16, 23, 66–68, 82, 83

borrower's creditworthiness, 70
build PD model
    application data, 82
    behavioral data, 82
    categorical data, 86–87
    data processing and exploration, 83–84
    logistic regression model, 88
    missing data, 86
    model evaluation, 88–90
    outliers, 84–86
    ROC curve, 90–93
    train-test split, 87
calculation, 71
decision trees and random forests, 72–73
GBMs, 73
logistic regression, 71–72
machine learning classifiers, 73
neural networks, 73
SVM, 73
Protective put strategy, 142
    asset, 142
    asset price paths, 148
    BSM model, 147, 148
    GBM, 147
    hedged *vs.* unhedged positions, 150–151
    implementation, 147
    initial outlay, 142
    insurance, 143
    maturity, 143
    parameters, 147–148
    payoff curves, 143, 145–147
    payoffs, 142, 144, 149–150
    P&L, 143
    plot, 144–145
    premium, 142, 144, 148
    put options, 143, 144, 148
    scenarios, 151
    strategies comparison, 150
    trade-off, 142

R

Real estate investment trusts (REITs), 24, 27, 28
Receiver Operating Characteristic (ROC) curve, 90–93
Regularization techniques, 217, 220, 225
REITs, *see* Real estate investment trusts (REITs)
Relative frequency, 3, 4
Resampling techniques, 212
Return
    absolute return, 38
    annualized return, 32, 40–41

capital appreciation, 32
description, 31–32
dividends, 32
interest payments, 32
logarithmic/log return, 39
measure, 38
percentage return, 38–39
risk-adjusted return, 33
single-*vs.* multi-period returns, 41–42
sources of return, 32
total *vs.* price return, 39–40
Risk
    annualization of riskmeasures, 43–44
    forms, 33
    and return, 33
    stable *vs.* volatile stocks
        PDF, 35, 36
        wealth curve, 33–35
    variance and standard deviation, 42, 43
    volatility of the asset, 42, 43
Risk-adjusted return
    portfolio selection strategies
        data preparation, 48–49
        define portfolios, 49–52
        optimization strategies, 52–63
    Sharpe ratio, 46
    Sortino ratio, 47
    Treynor ratio, 47–48
Risk management, 161, 163, 165, 201
    probability distribution, 3
    relative frequency, 3, 4
    S&P 500 price curve, 1–3
Risk mitigation, 76, 142, 164
Risk-return trade-off, 37–38
Risk-weighted assets (RWAs), 79–82
Robustness, 66, 73, 209, 220, 223
Robust optimization techniques, 225, 227
RWAs, *see* Risk-weighted assets (RWAs)

S

SDE, *see* Stochastic differential equation (SDE)
SGD, *see* Stochastic gradient descent (SGD)
Sharpe ratio, 46–48, 50, 51, 53, 54, 60, 63, 171, 176
Single-period returns, 33, 40–43
SMOTE, *see* Synthetic Minority Oversampling Technique (SMOTE)
Sortino ratio, 47, 48, 50, 51, 54, 60, 63
Spot/cash market, 127, 131–133
Static hedging
    changing volatility
        Black-Scholes model, 195–196

Index 237

call option price, 195
    digital call option, 194–196
    strike price, 194, 196
constant volatility
    call spread strategy, 191, 192, 194
    call spread value, 192, 193
    digital call option, 191, 192, 194
    replication, 193
derivatives, 177
digital call option, 197–198
    Black-Scholes formula, 197
    call spread, 196, 198
    European call options, 196
    payoff, 198, 199
    portfolio, 199
    prices, 197
    replication, 198
digital option, 190–191
establishing hedge, 165
European call option, 193
European put option
    Black-Scholes formula, 187
    implementation, 186–187
    payoff, 183, 187
    payoff function, 188–189
    portfolio, 182, 183
    price, 187
    put-call parity, 184–185, 187, 188
    put option, 182
    rebalancing, 183
    risk-neutral valuation framework, 185–186
    simulations, 187
    zero-coupon bonds, 187, 199
forward contract, 180–181
    Arbitrageurs, 182
    asset, 177
    current asset price & forward price, 178
    definition, 177
    forward price, 182
    investor, 181
    maturity, 179
    net initial investment, 179, 182
    net payoff curve, 181
    payoff, 178
    SDE, 178
    static replication, 179
    value determination, 177
no-arbitrage principles, 177
non-constant volatility, 199
objective, 177, 182
portfolio, 177, 199
transaction costs, 177
volatility function, 200

Statistical learning theory, 216, 222
Stochastic differential equation (SDE), 135, 178
Stochastic gradient descent (SGD), 222, 224
Stocks (equities), 25
Strategic planning, 69, 201
Stress loss (SL), 68–70, 93
Stress testing, 18, 69, 113, 212
Support vector machines (SVM), 73
SVM, *see* Support vector machines (SVM)
Synthetic Minority Oversampling Technique (SMOTE), 212
Systemic risk, 5, 19–20

T
Tesla (TSLA), 170, 176
Traditional frameworks, 201
Treynor ratio, 47–48, 50, 52, 55, 60, 63

U
UL, *see* Unexpected loss (UL)
Unexpected loss (UL), 68, 69, 81, 93

V
VAEs, *see* Variational Autoencoders (VAEs)
Value at Risk (VaR), 122, 123, 221
    calculation methods, 114
    daily returns, 116
    definition, 113
    ES, 114
    historical simulation approach, 114–115
    mathematical properties, 113–114
    Monte Carlo simulation, 120–122
    parameter approach (*see* Variance-covariance method)
    portfolio, 114
    quantile measure, 113
    regulatory bodies, 113
    uses, 113
    Variance-covariance method (*see* Variance-covariance method)
VaR, *see* Value at Risk (VaR)
Variance, 122, 123
    ACF and PACF plots, 106, 107
    Bessel's correction, 97, 99
    calculation, 97
    daily adjusted close price of Apple, 102
    dataset, 96
    definition, 96
    finance, 96
    high volatility, 96

limitations
   asset returns, 104
   autocorrelation, 105–106
   non-symmetric returns, 104
   normal distribution, 104
   outliers, 101–103
   volatility clustering, 105
sample variance, unbiasedness, 97–99
series of returns, 96–97
statistics, 96
stock data and calculating variance, 100–101
Variance-covariance method
   calculation, 117–118
   daily P&L and rolling, 119–120
   limitations, 118
   loss, 116
   portfolio, 117
   portfolio returns, 116
   return distribution, 118
   standard normal distribution, 117
   z-score, 116, 118
Variational Autoencoders (VAEs), 211, 212

W
Walmart (WMT), 170, 176
Wiener process, 135

Y
Yield-enhancement strategy, *see* Covered call strategy

MIX
Papier aus verantwortungsvollen Quellen
Paper from responsible sources
FSC® C105338

If you have any concerns about our products,
you can contact us on
ProductSafety@springernature.com

In case Publisher is established outside the EU,
the EU authorized representative is:
**Springer Nature Customer Service Center GmbH
Europaplatz 3, 69115 Heidelberg, Germany**

Printed by Libri Plureos GmbH
in Hamburg, Germany